A SHORT HISTORY OF
THE LIBERAL PARTY
1900–1984

Also by Chris Cook

THE AGE OF ALIGNMENT: ELECTORAL POLITICS IN BRITAIN, 1922–29
SOURCES IN BRITISH POLITICAL HISTORY, 1900–51 *(5 vols, with Philip Jones et al.)*
THE SLUMP *(with John Stevenson)*
BY-ELECTIONS IN BRITISH POLITICS *(ed. with John Ramsden)*
EUROPEAN POLITICAL FACTS, 1918–73 *(with John Paxton)*
BRITISH HISTORICAL FACTS, 1830–1900 *(with Brenda Keith)*
THE LONGMAN ATLAS OF MODERN BRITISH HISTORY, 1700–1970 *(with John Stevenson)*
THE POLITICS OF REAPPRAISAL, 1918–39 *(ed. with Gillian Peele)*
CRISIS AND CONTROVERSY: ESSAYS IN HONOUR OF A. J. P. TAYLOR *(ed. with Alan Sked)*
EUROPEAN POLITICAL FACTS, 1848–1918 *(with John Paxton)*
POST-WAR BRITAIN: A POLITICAL HISTORY (with Alan Sked)
THE LONGMAN HANDBOOK OF MODERN BRITISH HISTORY, 1714–1980 *(with John Stevenson)*
THE LABOUR PARTY *(ed. with Ian Taylor)*

A Short History of the Liberal Party 1900–1984

SECOND EDITION

Chris Cook

MACMILLAN

First Edition 1976
Second Edition 1984

Published by
THE MACMILLAN PRESS LTD
London and Basingstoke
Companies and representatives
throughout the world

Typeset by
Wessex Typesetters Ltd
Frome, Somerset

Printed in Hong Kong

British Library Cataloguing in Publication Data
Cook, Chris
A short history of the Liberal Party, 1900–1984.—
2nd ed.
1. Liberal Party—History   2. Great Britain—
Politics and government
I. Title
324.24106′09   JN129.L42
ISBN 0–333–37026–0
ISBN 0–333–37324–3 Pbk

Contents

Introduction and Acknowledgements

This volume attempts a relatively short survey of the fortunes of the Liberal Party during the present century. Since the history of the party after 1900 must be seen in the context of the Victorian era, the first two chapters of the book are devoted to a brief survey of the main events of that period.

No person writing on the history of the Liberal Party can fail to be indebted to the important studies produced by Roy Douglas and Trevor Wilson.[1] This book incorporates new material and more recent published studies, but its debt to both authors remains high.

In producing a short survey, many episodes have necessarily to be passed over briefly. In particular, the halcyon years of Liberalism from 1906 to 1914, together with the First World War, have been only briefly surveyed here, for they have both been extensively written about. For other periods (such as 1945 to 1956) the story is short because very little of lasting importance happened to the depleted Liberal ranks.

This book has been written in the hope that students both of history and of politics will find it of use. In addition, as the next general election comes closer, it is hoped that the facts and figures given here on the contemporary Liberal Party will be of relevance both to the specialist and to the general reader.

The author owes a considerable debt to the Warden and Fellows of Nuffield College, Oxford, whose hospitality and generosity made the planning and writing of this book possible. Much of the research for this book was done at the London School of Economics. A particular debt is owed to colleagues and friends there who helped at various stages in its production. For help on particular points I should like to thank Lord Beloff, David Butler, Roy Douglas, Ross McKibbin, Kenneth Morgan, Alan Butt Philip, Trevor Wilson and Philip Woods. For his great help with proof-reading I should like to thank Dr John Ramsden. The index was compiled by Mrs Beryl McKie. Much of the

---

[1] See R. Douglas, *The History of the Liberal Party, 1895–1970* (1971) and T. Wilson, *The Downfall of the Liberal Party* (1966). For the Victorian period, the brilliant study by John Vincent, *The Formation of the Liberal Party, 1857–1868* (1966). is indispensable.

typing for the first edition of this book was done with unfailing energy
and kindness by Eileen Pattison and Jean Ali. Finally, my thanks are due
to the publishers, The Macmillan Press, and in particular to Tim
Farmiloe.

Polytechnic of North London   CHRIS COOK

1 The Liberal Tradition

Almost eighty years have now passed since the Liberal electoral landslide of 1906. Nearly seventy years have gone by since Lloyd George supplanted Asquith as Prime Minister in December 1916. For sixty years, since the electoral débâcle of October 1924, the Liberal Party has been the Cinderella of British politics. During this period the party has endured repeated dissension and decline. At times, as in February 1957 when its parliamentary representation sank to a mere five, it seemed it might disappear altogether.

Yet despite the oft-repeated forecasts of politicians and historians, the party still remains. Its fighting spirit is still very much in evidence. In 1962, with a sensational by-election victory in suburban Orpington, the party achieved a major, if temporary, revival. Again, in 1973, a remarkable series of electoral victories brought the party into the forefront of British politics. In the subsequent General Election of February 1974 the party polled over 6 million votes. With the Alliance of Liberal and Social Democrats, in the June 1983 election the whole map of British politics began to be redrawn.

It is with the varying fortunes of the party since 1900 that this book is concerned. But the fate of the party this century can only be seen in perspective against the background of Victorian politics in which the Liberal Party grew up so successfully.

In the confused and changing period of British politics between the Reform Acts of 1832 and 1867 the Liberal Party of the Victorian era gradually took shape. However, there is no single satisfactory moment when the Liberal Party can be said to have been born. The nearest is, perhaps, June 1859. On this occasion, at the famous meeting in Willis's rooms, the Whig, Peelite and Radical leaders in Parliament combined together to oust the minority Government of Disraeli and Derby.

However, although 1859 marks an important stage in the evolution of the party, the new government of Palmerston, which included for the first time both Gladstone and Lord John Russell and which survived until Palmerston's death in October 1865, was less a 'Liberal' ministry than a reconstituted Whig Government. The decisive date at which the Victorian Liberal Party came of age was 1868. In the general election of that year, following the Second Reform Bill, a definite Liberal victory heralded the formation of Gladstone's first administration.

The Parliamentary Liberal Party which slowly took shape in the decade after 1859 was almost unrecognisable from the unified, disciplined parties of the twentieth century. It was less a party in the modern sense than a loose alliance of groups of many shades of political opinion and widely differing social background. From the beginning, the Liberal Party was an uneasy coalition. The most divergent shades of opinion within the Liberal ranks were represented by the Whigs and the Radicals. It was this division which constituted the most obvious potential split within the political coalition that made up mid-nineteenth-century Liberalism.

The division of Whigs and Radicals was one of both social background and political ideology. The great Whig family groupings – such names as Portland, Argyll and Devonshire – formed the traditional aristocratic core of the party. The Liberalism of these great landowners was much more the product of tradition, loyalty and history rather than of any very specific programme or set of principles. However, despite their innate conservatism, the Whig grandees played a crucial part in nineteenth-century Liberalism – even after successive Reform Acts in 1832 and 1867 had reduced their influence in the Commons. Their importance lay neither in their numbers (although they formed a large and important group in the House of Lords) nor in their immense wealth, but rather in their domination of the key posts in Liberal ministries. It was the Whigs much more than the Radicals who held the vital offices in Gladstone's Cabinet.

Their political programme was extremely limited. Such interest as they possessed in moderate reform rapidly waned in the field of parliamentary and electoral reform. Here, their own political vested interests were deeply affected, since any measure of reform would inevitably strike at Whig influence in the surviving small boroughs. Within the Liberal ranks the Whigs constituted an exclusive caste in the upper reaches of political society. Thus the leadership of Lord John Russell, despite his close association with parliamentary reform, was acceptable partly because he came from the same social stratum as the Grosvenors, Cavendishes and Fitzwilliams.

Gladstone, on the other hand, represented a break with the past. Socially, he always remained outside the powerful inner circle of Whig society which Palmerston had successfully manipulated. Politically, Gladstone was suspect both as a former Peelite and a known advocate of reform. In this respect, Gladstone was more in sympathy with the opposite end of the Liberal political spectrum, the Radicals.

Standing in marked contrast to the passivity of the Whigs, the Radicals provided the party with its main areas of growth and with its most advanced political ideas. The Radicals themselves were a diverse group. Whilst they included in their ranks such intellectuals as Henry Fawcett or John Stuart Mill, their most important element was the Nonconformist manufacturing interest. Such men as Samuel Morley, William Rathbone and John Bright were representative of this group. It was from constituencies in Lancashire, Yorkshire and the industrial Midland counties that these Radical dissenters and businessmen were chiefly returned. And it was from this group that there came the strongest demands for radical reform – for extension of the franchise, the secret ballot, the extension of state education and the abolition of church rates.

This Radical group was the one section of the party firmly committed to challenging the established order both in Church and State. Their great obstacle to reform was not the conservatism of the Whig hierarchy but the inertia of the mass of moderate Liberals who constituted the bulk of the parliamentary party. These moderate Liberals, often landowners, lawyers and army and naval officers, were distrustful of Radical enthusiasm. To this extent they tended to be a conservative force within the party, although usually willing to follow the lead of the Liberal Front Bench.

It was these three elements – Whigs, Radicals and the mass of moderates – which made up the Parliamentary Liberal Party. However, just as important as these developments within the party at Westminster was the evolution of the party at the grass-roots in the constituencies. The development of the Parliamentary party coincided with, and was indeed linked with, important new social forces at work in the country.

Three particular factors were at work which helped mould Liberalism. The first was the growth of the cheap daily provincial press. Helped by the repeal of the stamp and paper duties between 1855 and 1861, the numbers and circulation of the provincial press leaped forward. Many of these new papers were dominated by Liberal families – the Baines family with the *Leeds Mercury* or the Cowens' *Newcastle Chronicle*. This rapidly expanding provincial press helped build up an articulate, radical, self-conscious provincial Liberalism which became one of the pillars of the new Liberal Party.

A second source of Liberal strength lay in militant Nonconformity. Traditionally, the Nonconformists had always looked to the old Whig Party as their natural allies against the Anglican Tories. For the Nonconformists, the Liberal Party seemed the best instrument to realise the religious and educational reforms they so much desired. However, by 1868 the Nonconformists were no longer willing to act as the 'poor relation' of the Whigs, Mid-century militant Nonconformity now constituted a vocal force in its own right.

The rise of the new working-class voters in the mid-nineteenth-century was another phenomenon closely allied to the evolution of the Liberal Party. As with the Nonconformists, the working class looked to the Liberal Party, not merely for reform in such areas as trade union rights, wages and hours of work, franchise extension and social reform, but in a much more significant way. Their political emancipation was symbolised by supporting and voting for the Liberal Party.

In the ten years after 1859, by being able to harness both militant Nonconformity and a rising working-class political consciousness to their party, as well as having a prime voice in the new provincial press, the Liberal Party became of major political importance. It was a party which, because it had established links with new and dynamic forces at work in the country, stood to be the party of the future.

The person who turned this potential into reality was W. E. Gladstone. And the period which marked the heyday of political Liberalism was the years of the two great ministries he headed: 1868 to 1874, and 1880 to 1885. In 1867, Gladstone was 58. He had begun his political life as a reactionary Tory and High Churchman, having become M.P. for Newark in 1832. However, the great determinant in Gladstone's future political career was his religion. Gladstone was a fervent believer that politics must be a field for Christian action. A corollary of this was his concept of 'freedom'. For Gladstone, the struggle of a nation fighting to be free – whether Bulgaria in 1876 or Ireland a decade later – just as the freedom of people to pursue the ideal of self-fulfilment and moral development – was a moral cause which overruled all else. This passionate moralism, plus his dominating personality, his brilliant administrative gifts and his supreme oratory, were Gladstone's strength – and weakness – in politics. Indeed, Gladstone was often a bad party leader and manager, tactless and awkward with many of his colleagues, and neglecting vital issues both of policy and organisation in order to pursue, ruthlessly and relentlessly, his personal crusades.

In 1867, however, Gladstone's years as Premier lay ahead. A more immediate issue had arisen which showed the extent to which the Liberal Party could be divided even by an issue which had never lacked prominent Liberal advocates. The occasion was the struggles which preceded the passing of the Second Reform Bill. The most notable Liberal opponents of parliamentary reform were the Adullamite 'cave' of Whig politicians. Centring on Robert Lowe, Lord Grosvenor, Lord Clanricarde and Lord Elcho, they never numbered more than twelve in any organised form.[1] But they were able to attract the support of

[1] M. Cowling, *1867: Disraeli, Gladstone and Revolution* (Cambridge, 1967) p. 100.

dissident Radical industrialists and rural Liberals, as well as the inevitable Whigs. Thus, when the Russell Reform Bill was defeated in June 1866, 44 Liberals voted in the majority against the government. It was Disraeli's subsequent advocacy of household suffrage which made the 'cave' less dangerous by depriving it of a Conservative refuge. Indeed, Gladstone admitted that he and many Liberals were 'bowled over' by Disraeli's proposals since they were still thinking in terms of a limited borough franchise. As an attempt to control the Liberal leadership the 'cave' had its Radical counterpart in John Bright and his followers, who were dedicated to the removal of the reactionary Whigs from their political ascendancy and to the introduction of a wide measure of parliamentary reform – an endeavour where he, too, was 'trumped' by Disraeli.[2]

It was against this background that the Liberals fought the general election of December 1868. As Professor Hanham has correctly written, the outcome of the election did not involve great speculation. It was widely believed that the minority Conservative Government would, in fact, suffer defeat at the polls. However, though Gladstone and the Liberals achieved an important victory in 1868, the size of this Conservative defeat was in many ways less than had been expected. Partly, this was a consequence of Gladstone's declaration in favour of the disestablishment of the Irish Church.

Gladstone's proposals for a comprehensive programme for the disestablishment and disendowment of the Irish Church, together with the ending of the Maynooth grant, not only alarmed certain sections of public opinion, but also created unease within the Parliamentary Liberal Party. Two groups, in particular, were apprehensive about disestablishment. John Bright, together with other Radicals, would have preferred to give priority to the land question, disregarding the views of such people as Cardinal Manning who regarded the Irish establishment as the root of bitterness in Ireland. However, whilst Bright was hardly likely to desert Gladstone on this question, this was not the case with those Whig landowners in the counties who thoroughly disapproved of Gladstone and all his Irish works. Several influential Whigs either deliberately refused to play an active part in the election or positively encouraged their tenants to vote Conservative in order to teach the Liberals a sharp lesson.

The outcome, overall, was to return Gladstone to power with a majority of over 100, an increase of 40 over 1865. The counties, however, produced a different result. Maurice Cowling has calculated that, in the counties affected by the 1867 Reform Bill, there had been 32

[2] Ibid., p. 301.

Liberals and 34 Conservatives elected in 1865. In 1868 the figures were 30 Liberals and 57 Conservatives.[3] Much of this Liberal failure to advance in the counties can be attributed to opposition to disestablishment. Certainly, the inactivity of Whig patrons in such constituencies as South Shropshire and West Surrey cost the party dearly.[4]

At the same time, certain working-class areas in which the Liberals had previously done well came out as decisively as the Whigs against disestablishment. This was particularly noticeable in Lancashire, where traditional anti-Irish feeling had recently been reinforced by Fenian terrorism in Manchester. Not only Gladstone himself, but such other leading Liberals as Milner-Gibson and Hartington, were all defeated in Lancashire partly because of Protestant-Conservative revulsion over Ireland. Gladstone, after his defeat in South West Lancashire, was returned for Greenwich. As Sir Charles Dilke drily remarked, Gladstone was much more likely to become a democratic leader now he sat for a big town.

These defections from Liberalism in Lancashire, together with the Conservative advance in the counties, were easily offset by the Liberal gains in the large cities and by the substantial Liberal majorities in Wales, Scotland and Ireland. As Professor Vincent has observed, these Liberal majorities in Wales and Scotland, gained with very little overt electioneering, were often for causes for which the Liberal leadership was indifferent or even hostile.[5]

However, despite the various disturbing features of the election returns – most particularly, signs that the Radicals had reached their peak too soon in urban England – the outlook for the Liberal Party after December 1868 seemed set fair. More united and more popular than it was to be again, the Liberals seemed set for a constructive and full term in office.

With Gladstone's own personal ascendancy unchallenged, the Liberal leader set out to construct his Cabinet. Its personnel reflected the changed composition of the parliamentary party and the diverse supply of capable men now thought appropriate for the important ministerial posts. Unlike the almost wholly Whig Cabinets of Palmerston and Russell, it contained only five members who could definitely be classified as Whigs: de Grey, Clarendon, Granville, Hartington and Chichester Fortescue. Against this, there were seven 'new men', all of them commoners, with a varying degree of commitment to reform:

[3] Ibid., Appendix II, p. 344.

[4] D. Southgate. *The Passing of the Whigs* (1962) p. 333. See also A. F. Thompson. 'Gladstone's Whips and the General Election of 1868'. *English Historical Review*, LXIII. pp. 12-24. (1948).

[5] J. Vincent, *The Formation of the Liberal Party* (1966) p. 52.

Robert Lowe (Chancellor of the Exchequer), H. A. Bruce (Home Secretary), H. C. E. Childers (First Lord of the Admiralty), John Bright (President of the Board of Trade) and G. J. Goschen (President of the Poor Law Board). Two members of the Cabinet, apart from Gladstone, are best described as Peelites: the Duke of Argyll (Secretary for India) and Edward Cardwell (Secretary for War). The followers of Peel, long departed from the Tory fold, still retained a strong sense of their own identity as a separate group among the Liberals and, for this reason, were likely to act as a moderating and cohesive element among the Whigs and Radicals of this composite Cabinet.

The new ministry had lacked neither talent nor leadership. Yet within five years the reforming enthusiasm of the government was spent and the party was deeply divided and disarrayed. Indeed, much of Gladstone's energy was absorbed in dealing with the dissension and opposition from within the ranks of his own party.

The heart of the problem was not difficult to discover. The Liberals were still a party composed of so many differing factions and interest groups – social, political and religious – that it was almost impossible for the government to undertake the kind of reforms it envisaged without mortally offending one of its own constituent sections. Gladstone was himself unable to attract the constant confidence and unfailing support of any group: he was always distrusted by the Whigs; his views on Ireland already alarmed the moderates; his moderation in reforming measures was to disillusion the dissenters, Catholics and Radicals.

The issue above all others on which the party was to flounder was Ireland, the province which Gladstone had proclaimed it was his mission to pacify. The uneasiness of the Whigs over Ireland first manifested itself in 1869 over the Bill to disestablish and disendow the Irish Church. This was eventually carried in the form that Gladstone desired, with endowments being converted 'mainly for the relief of unavoidable calamity and suffering'.[6] But the Whigs in the Lords felt that this was too sweeping a move and one not necessarily guaranteed to bring religious or social peace. For some time they argued in vain for a scheme of concurrent endowment, giving both the Catholic and Protestant priests a house and land. The Irish Land Bill of the following year, surprisingly, earned the ideological disapproval of Bright and Lowe rather than the opposition of the Whigs. The Bill aimed to 'prevent the landlord from using the terrible weapon of undue and unjust eviction by so framing the handle that it shall cut his hands with the sharp edge of pecuniary damages'.[7] This was in fact an extension to the

[6] John Morley, *William Ewart Gladstone*, 3 vols (1903).
[7] Ibid., I, 928.

rest of Ireland of the Ulster system of 'tenant right'. It was opposed by
Bright on the grounds that what was needed in Ireland was a wholesale
transfer of land ownership from the present owners to the down-
trodden occupiers. It was attacked by Lowe as an invidious extension
of state intervention. But most of the Whig landowners concentrated
in the Lords seem to have agreed with Chichester Fortescue that
'this Bill will limit my power as a landlord but only when that power
is unjustly abused'.[8]

This increasing Whig disillusion with the Liberals was aggravated
by three other measures unconnected with Ireland. Each provided a
further milestone in the steady drift of the Whigs towards Conservatism. First, Cardwell initiated in 1871 the abolition by Royal War-
rant of the system of purchasing commissions in the Army. Secondly, in
1870 Lowe secured open competition for entry to the Civil Service –
where the Minister at the head of the department approved. (This was
accepted by all the Ministers except Clarendon at the Foreign Office.)
Thirdly, open voting was ended by the Ballot Act of 1872. The first two
reforms radically altered the long-established apparatus for advancement which had benefited Whig families. The third abolished a system
which many of the older Whigs still held to be an integral and worthy
part of the constitution.

Meanwhile, Gladstone's administration faced not only rumblings
from the right but a damaging and open split with the Nonconformists
over W. E. Forster's Education Bill in 1870. The Nonconformists were
'the largest, most active and most high-principled section of the party.
As such they seemed to be in a position to claim the redress of their
grievances.'[9] The Education Bill, however, failed to end sectarian education, as demanded by Joseph Chamberlain and Robert Dale, founders of the National Education League in 1869, and by Edward Miall, a
veteran champion of dissent. Instead it gave a privileged position to the
Church of England: denominational schools were to continue where
they were working efficiently; elsewhere they were to be supplemented
by school boards, who were given religious liberty. John Morley, later
to be Gladstone's biographer, pointed out the irony of the circumstances surrounding this measure: 'Mr Disraeli had the distinction of
dishing the Whigs, who were his enemies. Mr Gladstone on the other
hand dished the Dissenters, who were his friends. Unfortunately, he
omitted one element of prime importance in those rather nice transactions. He forgot to educate his party.'[10] Although Miall declared that

---

[8] Southgate, *The Passing of the Whigs*, p. 347.

[9] H. T. Hanham, *Elections and Party Management: Politics in the Time of Disraeli and Gladstone* (1959) p. 114.

[10] Morley, *Fortnightly Review*, Feb. 1874.

'it was a lover's quarrel, and nothing more need be said about it', the Act led to a long period of Nonconformist anti-government agitation and to the most virulent attacks on Forster, and finally shattered the illusion that the Liberal Party would become 'the mouth-piece of the Nonconformists'.[11]

This was not the only religious interest group that Gladstone offended. In 1871 the University Test Act abolished the need for entrants to Oxford and Cambridge to subscribe to the thirty-nine Articles and thus alarmed many Anglicans. In 1873 a misguided desire for compromise led to a plan for a new university in Ireland, which failed to gain the support of either Anglicans or Catholics. Gladstone had in fact proposed to set up a university insulated from Ireland's religious strife by an absence of teaching in theology, modern history or moral and mental philosophy. This idea was immediately attacked by disappointed Catholics as a proposal for a 'godless college', and when it was defeated in the Commons (by 287 to 284) 35 Irish Liberals voted against it.

The Irish University Bill was not the only Liberal measure to alienate two possible sources of support at one blow. Bruce's Liquor Licensing Bill of 1872 was strongly opposed by the Temperance Liberals of the United Kingdom Alliance who, like the members of the National Education League, had vainly hoped for better things from their own Government. It also started the flight of the drink trade, caught between the twin evils of Liberal Temperance societies and the new restraints of Liberal legislation, towards the Conservatives.

The Liberals could take comfort that dissenters at least could find no acceptable home outside the Liberal Party. But a number of minor measures, inept decisions and misfortunes combined to accelerate the progress of the Government down the precipice of its own unpopularity with the more uncommitted voters in the country. Lowe's proposal to tax matches brought out the match factory workers to rouse public opinion against the government. The final settlement of the *Alabama* claims at $15 million was seen as a humiliation for Britain that contrasted strongly with the results of Palmerston's policy in the previous decade; the same was felt over British acquiescence over the abrogation by Russia of the demilitarisation of the Black Sea. The Collier and Ewelme cases focused disproportionate public attention on the government's possible misuse of its right to certain judicial and ecclesiastical appointments.

Much more fundamental than these minor problems was the Trade Unionist agitation against the 1871 Trade Union Act, the Liberal legis-

---

[11] Hanham, *Elections and Party Management*, p. 119.

lation which followed the Royal Commission on Trade Unions set up in 1867. The 1871 Act, although giving the unions full legal recognition, took from them the right of 'peaceful picketing'. This was done by passing a separate Criminal Law Amendment Act which in fact reinforced the old 1825 Act making unions liable to prosecution. This legislation from the Liberal Government was bitterly resented by the unions – a resentment which grew in intensity by the way in which the law was applied.

The net result of all these factors was that the unity and purpose which had brought the party to power was split. By 1873 the party was deeply divided, its legislative zeal gone completely and its popularity faded. The whole process of loss of popularity was given added momentum by the vivid campaigning speeches of Disraeli, and by the fact that the government's inexorable decline was regularly made obvious in frequent by-elections. The culmination of this demoralisation came when Disraeli refused to form a minority government after Gladstone's defeat in 1873.

Against this political background, it was not surprising that by the beginning of 1874 Gladstone had decided to dissolve Parliament and go to the country on a campaign to repeal Income Tax. To Gladstone, this was the popular issue which would unite the party and ensure success at the polls. Gladstone's course of action was accelerated by the refusal of Cardwell and Goschen to accept the proposed reductions in their estimates. Accordingly, the dissolution was announced on 24 January 1874. The news caught not only such bodies as the National Education League unprepared, but took the country by surprise.

Gladstone's calculated plans, however, soon went astray. During the campaign Disraeli was able, in his famous phrase, to deride the Liberals as a 'range of exhausted volcanoes'. The outcome of the 1874 election was an overall majority of 50 for the Conservatives. Among the Liberal casualties was Joseph Chamberlain at Sheffield. In England the most noticeable loss of support occurred among the middle classes in the boroughs, where the Liberals lost 32 seats. This was partly due to the appeal of Disraelian Conservatism, and partly to the failure of Liberal organisers either to supply strong central support and direction, or to keep in touch with those local associations which had aided them in 1868. As a result, many such associations had either ceased to exist or had been alienated from giving whole-hearted support to the party through lack of understanding of Liberal policies. Though Gladstone declared that the party had been 'borne down in a torrent of gin and beer', loss of working-class support together with the reaction of the middle-class voter in suburban England, in response to the increasing manifestations of working-class power, had been more responsible for the defeat.

The only comfort that Liberals could derive from the election was that a spell in opposition would give the party a chance to reorganise itself in decent obscurity. Furthermore, many of those sections of the party which had caused trouble during the life of the government in fact rallied back to the Liberal flag at the election. This was particularly true of the dissenters, who probably accounted for the fact that the Liberals won back in 1874 ten of the seats that they had lost in recent by-elections. But this could not obscure the fact that many energetic party workers now preferred to work for a particular pressure group rather than for the party, and that Liberal support was now more than ever confined to a hard core in the boroughs, with declining support in the counties, Wales and Scotland. Even more ominous for the future of Liberalism were the results from Ireland. There 58 of the 105 members returned were Home Rulers, wiping out the semi-permanent Liberal majority in Ireland overnight, and reducing orthodox Liberal representation in Ireland to a mere 12 members.

The period immediately after the 1874 defeat was one of confusion among the Liberal leadership. Gladstone was anxious to retire. He wanted, as Morley wrote, 'an interval between Parliament and the grave'. He also felt himself out of sympathy with the tumultuous politics of the new generation of mainly Radical Liberals, particularly on the questions of education and religion. Perhaps more important, he could discern 'no great positive aim' in contemporary politics that might have given him personal satisfaction. Dispossessed of the initiative of office, the party itself also lacked a sense of direction or purpose, Both were to be supplied within the next few years – but not by the official leadership in Parliament.

When Gladstone finally announced his withdrawal from the leadership in January 1875, there was no very obvious successor. Forster, the man best qualified to succeed to the leadership in the Commons, was ruled out by the nonconformist campaign against him. The post eventually fell to the Marquis of Hartington, a Whig of rather more limited political ability, who was considered adequate for what promised to be a dull Parliament. His position was made somewhat easier by the departure of Disraeli to the Lords in 1876, leaving Sir Stafford Northcote to lead the Conservatives in the Commons. Hartington's task was, however, complicated in the first place by muffled rumblings of dissatisfaction from the Radicals – principally Chamberlain, Dilke and Morley – who had lost, in Gladstone, the most respected advocate of reform, and were now forced to exist under Whig leadership and to watch a growing series of mild Conservative reforming measures. Secondly, Hartington was easily overshadowed by

Gladstone whenever the latter chose to take part in a debate, and indeed was almost totally eclipsed by him, though still nominal leader, when Gladstone erupted back to prominence.

Although the Liberal Party was in opposition from 1874 to 1880, these six years were a period of great importance in the evolution of the party, most particularly in the creation and development of party organisation following the founding at Birmingham, in 1877, of the National Liberal Federation.

Prior to 1877, the structure of party organisation differed very little from that of the Conservatives at this date. At the centre, the work was divided between the Whips and the Liberal Registration Association, formed by the Whips and a small body of Liberal M.P.'s in 1861. The Whips looked after candidatures, party funds and political patronage, whilst the Liberal Registration Association attempted to supervise and co-ordinate the work of the constituency Liberal associations. These local associations looked after the task of local registration (a process at which the political parties had become more adept than the official overseers) and organised the election campaigns, often working with a local part-time paid agent.

In theory, the Liberal machine was adequate. In practice, however, it suffered a series of defects which rendered it less efficient that that of the Conservatives. After the retirement of the principal agent, Drake, in 1865, the party lacked a replacement for twenty years, despite the obvious importance of the post. The work was divided between the Whips (already over-worked and under-staffed), the Liberal Registration Association and the party's local agents.[12] At the same time, the officials of the Liberal Registration Association were frequently able to make little impression upon those urban areas where very efficient local Liberal organisations were in control, and where such local managers as Edward Baines in Leeds were extremely unlikely to admit any outside interference. The problem was not confined to the boroughs. In the counties the party was equally incapable of inducing the Whigs, who controlled these county associations, into greater activity. Thus, until the coming of the National Liberal Federation in 1877, and with it a more influential and efficient central party organisation, the Liberals in the constituencies were often allowed to rest in Whig-induced lethargy or to waste their efforts and votes on duplicating candidatures.

Prior to the Reform Bills of 1867 and 1868 these deficiencies of organisation, though important, were not vital. However, the remodelling of the franchise (adding approximately 938,000 new electors to an

---

[12] Hanham, *Elections and Party Management*, pp. 349 ff.

existing electorate of 1,057,000 in England and Wales, with corresponding increases in Scotland and Ireland) and the Redistribution Bill
brought about vast changes, not only in the structure of parliamentary
representation but also, over the longer term, in the whole response of
both political parties to the possibilities of more democratic participation in the choice of governments and in their policies.

The overall effect of the 1867 Reform Act was to introduce household
franchise in the towns and the £12 occupancy franchise in the counties.
The fact that Disraeli had been manoeuvred into accepting the Hodg-
kinson amendment which abolished compounding (i.e. the payment of
rates by tenants through their landlords) enabled large numbers of
tenants to become enfranchised as rate-paying occupiers. The accompanying Redistribution Bill for England and Wales took away 45 seats
from boroughs with a population of under 10,000. Sometimes (as in the
case of Thetford) the borough was disfranchised completely. Elsewhere
(as in the case of Devizes) representation was reduced from two members to one. Whig acquiescence in these changes was partly explained
because 25 additional seats were given to the counties.

An interesting experiment introduced by the Act affected the
double-member constituencies of Manchester, Leeds, Liverpool and
Birmingham. A third member was added to each of these cities,
although each elector could exercise only two votes. It was hoped that,
by this device, minority interests would gain representation. In fact, the
capture of all seats in such towns as Birmingham rapidly became one of
the supreme tests of party organisation.

All these developments, coupled with the defeat of 1874, impressed
on Liberals the need for more efficient organisation, The lead in this
field came from Birmingham. There, the 'caucus' of Radical Liberal
politicians had been well known since 1868 for its victories at general
elections and for the constant attention it paid to furthering Liberal
candidates in municipal elections.[13]

The foundation of the National Liberal Federation grew out of the
desire of Birmingham's Liberal leaders to supply from their own
experience the kind of political organisation which the party lacked,
and to provide from a Radical starting-point that cohesion and sense of

---

[13] Considerable historical debate has centred around the origins of the National Liberal Federation. Ostrogorski connected the rise of the NLF directly with the desire of
local Liberals from 1868 to organise the minority vote and win all three Birmingham
seats. But, as Herrick points out, Liberalism was strongly established in Birmingham
before 1868, and was given the impetus to organise itself efficiently as much by the
importance of party in municipal elections and by the presence of organised Nonconformity in the city as by the provisions of the 1868 Act. See F. H. Herrick. 'The Origins of
the National Liberal Federation', *Journal of Modern History* (1945).

purpose among Liberal associations that the Whig leaders at the centre were unwilling or unable to provide. More immediately, the NLF hierarchy grew from the personnel of the Birmingham Liberal Association and the National Education League, a Birmingham-based dissenting pressure group whose members, led by Chamberlain, felt the need for wider horizons and shared the general desire of former rebels to aid the party from within after the defeat of 1874. Thus the NLF centred at the start on Birmingham politicians of national and local note – Chamberlain, Jesse Collings and J. S. Wright. Its first secretary, Francis Schnadhorst, remained secretary of the Birmingham Liberal Association until 1884.

Delegates from 95 local Liberal associations accepted invitations to the first conference of the NLF in May 1877.[14] Chamberlain was elected president and an administrative General Committee appointed which would provide continuous organisation and summon an Annual Council: 46 local associations joined the NLF during the first month of its existence. At this stage the general aim of the NLF was to 'reflect Liberalism in the country'. As McGill has pointed out,[15] the NLF was basically an organisational machine rather than a means whereby the provincial Radicals could dictate party policy. However, Hartington, the party Whips and the managers of the Liberal Central Association in London were bound to see it as a challenge to the power of the centre. Although Gladstone visited the first conference at Birmingham, Hartington withheld approval of the scheme. The main activities of the NLF and its affiliated associations in the early stages were the dissemination of party propaganda, the arrangement of *ad hoc* political meetings, particularly in support of Gladstone's campaigns, and the gradual repair of the vast gaps in Liberal organisation in the counties.[16]

A variety of other Liberal organisations followed in the wake of the National Liberal Federation, The Women's Liberal Federation was founded in February 1887. In Scotland, the North and East of Scotland Association was founded in 1880, followed shortly after by the Glasgow-based Scottish Liberal Federation. In 1887 the two united. Other developments included the establishment in 1887 of the Liberal Publication Department and the inauguration in 1893 of the *Liberal*

[14] R. Spence Watson, *The National Liberal Federation. 1877–1906* (1907) pp. 6 ff.

[15] B. McGill, 'Schnadhorst and Liberal Party Organisation', *Journal of Modern History* (1962).

[16] Watson, *The National Liberal Federation*, pp. 12–13. The Constitution of the National Liberal Federation appeared to be reasonably democratic. The Council, consisting of representatives of the Federated Associations and all Liberal Members of Parliament, met annually. The number of delegates each association might send was apportioned in accordance with the electorate of the constituency.

Magazine under the editorship of Charles Geake. Meanwhile, by the 1890s regional organisations had been set up in such areas as the Home Counties, the Midlands and the West Country.

The restructuring of Liberal organisation after 1877 coincided with two important political events: the re-entry of Gladstone into active politics and the increasing unpopularity of Disraeli's government.

Gladstone's re-entry into politics, with his campaign against the Eastern policy of the government after 1876, marked the moment when the Liberals first regained their vigour and sense of purpose after the defeat of 1874. Gladstone broke his political silence with the pamphlet *The Bulgarian Horrors and the Question of the East.* In this tract, Disraeli was bitterly attacked for condoning Turkish atrocities against the Slav Christians of Montenegro and Serbia, then in revolt against Ottoman rule.

Despite the fact that, in using Turkey as an ally against Tsarist Russia, Disraeli was only pursuing traditional British diplomacy, the fervour and sincerity of Gladstone's attack soon had a decisive impact on public opinion. In Parliament, his Commons resolutions of 1877 were extraordinary in that they did not have the support of Hartington and other Whig leaders. Despite this, and despite Disraeli's return to popularity after the Congress of Berlin in 1878, Gladstone's initiative had given the whole Liberal Party a policy, and had given life and vigour to a somnolent opposition.

Meanwhile the economic depression of the 1870s was eating into the government's popularity. The Farmers' Alliance, founded by James Howard in 1879, rallied the support of many farmers behind the Liberals in the hope that they would make the Land Laws more flexible, and give the tenant farmers more protection during a depression.[17] In addition, the government's reputation in foreign affairs was damaged by the disasters to its 'prancing proconsuls' of empire, defeated at Isandhlwana and Kabul in 1879.

The latter events gave Gladstone an opportunity to attack anew the government's foreign policy during his campaign in Midlothian, This extraordinary progress, undertaken against the Tory Earl of Dalkeith in the winter of 1879, even before the Queen had dissolved Parliament, set a precedent for future election campaigns.[18] Together with the Bulgarian agitation, it also gave the Liberals an example of innovation in political communications to set beside the NLF. Moreover, it gave the Liberals in the constituencies the political fighting spirit which the Whigs in nominal control of the party were quite unable to match, and in destroying the Conservative record it had a material effect upon

---

[17] Hanham, *Elections and Party Management*, p. 30.
[18] R.Kelly, 'Midlothian: A Study in Politics and Ideas', *Victorian Studies*, IV, 2 (1960).

Liberal confidence and upon the result. In Ireland alone the general trend towards Liberalism was upset. There the 37 moderate Home Rule Liberals and 16 Liberals saw emerge a far more potent force, the 24 members of Parnell's militant Home Rule party, dangerous to both Liberals and Conservatives in their desire to use, but not to support, either party.

In the election of 1880, the Liberals gained an overall majority of 54, making inroads into the Conservative preserves in the counties, and winning back many of the urban seats lost in 1874. Wales and Scotland returned 9 Conservatives and 78 Liberals. The NLF, whose total of affiliated associations reached 97 in 1880, was bound to claim the credit for much of this victory.[19]

When the result of the 1880 election was known, the immediate problem for the Liberals was to decide the leadership. Gladstone's resumption of political activity and the wide support he had gained for himself and the party in the Midlothian campaign meant that his claim to be Premier, although not explicitly stated, could not be ignored. Hartington and Granville both acknowledged to the Queen the practical impossibility of forming a government and maintaining it in power without Gladstone's active participation and support. Thus Gladstone's lukewarm promises of independent support for a Hartington administration ultimately guided the Queen's choice in his direction, and he took office at the end of April 1880.

Post-election euphoria was felt in many sections of the party. Gladstone's exclamation, 'The outlook is tremendous', was echoed among young Liberals of Asquith's generation, who saw this as the beginning of an era of promise, and among many Radicals, who hoped that their say in the party's Parliamentary future would now be increased in proportion to their contribution to the Liberal victory. General expectations of Liberal reforming activity were soon shattered by the obstructionist tactics of Parnell and the Irish Nationalists, who eventually succeeded in concentrating Liberal energies upon the Irish question and thus in bringing the party into a new and this time irretrievable schism.

The more specific hopes of the Radicals were immediately shaken by the composition of Gladstone's cabinet. This contained only two Radicals, John Bright and Joseph Chamberlain, and was otherwise of a far more Whiggish character than that of 1868, and still included Lord

[19]As McGill has shown, the main benefit of the NLF efforts cannot be interpreted, as Schnadhorst claimed at the time, in terms of seats gained wherever the NLF was active. This was not true. But the NLF's organisation had been invaluable in dissuading Liberals from standing against each other so that the activities of the NLF were a constant background to Liberal success rather than a major cause of it.

Granville as Foreign Secretary, Sir William Harcourt as Home Secretary and Lord Hartington as Secretary for India.

For a variety of reasons, the high hopes the Radicals entertained of Gladstone's second ministry were rapidly disillusioned. Nor was this attributable solely to the marked Whig dominance in the Cabinet. The disruptive tactics of Parnell, the whole issue of Ireland, together with the activities of the 'Fourth Party', hindered the ministry. More than this, however, was the personal failing of Gladstone's leadership. Certainly, the 1880 Liberal Cabinet needed a stronger control by the Prime Minister than Gladstone cared to exercise.

For whatever reasons, historians have not been charitable on the achievements of Gladstone's second ministry. According to Ensor, never in the modern era had a triumphant majority in the Commons achieved so little. There was truth in this verdict. Four years after the triumph of 1880, the reforms dreamed of by the Radicals remained unfulfilled. Partly this failure after 1880 was due, as after 1868, to factional disputes within the government. All this was aggravated, however, by a series of incidents at home and abroad which served to discredit the government. In colonial affairs, Gladstone's second ministry faced vexing problems in the Transvaal (including a British defeat at Majuba Hill), the revolt of Arabi Pasha in Egypt and a series of tragic mistakes in the Sudan culminating in Gordon's death at Khartoum. At home, the Bradlaugh case, Radical dissent at the lack of social reform, growing electoral unpopularity, but above all the problem of Ireland, overshadowed the ministry.

It was apparent from the start that on the question of Ireland the government would be under pressure from two different directions. The Nationalists under Parnell were unsure of Liberal sincerity over land reform and realised that, however many minor reforming palliatives were directed towards Ireland, it was only by constant agitation that Ireland could remain as a permanent problem for which the politicians at Westminster would have to arrive at a permanent solution. The main opposition to Gladstone's policy of reforming the major causes of Irish discontent came from among the Whigs, but so wide was the disparity of views within the party that when the government fell back upon a policy of coercion in 1882 , an equally sizeable opposition to this policy came from the Radicals, led by Chamberlain and Bright. For the Liberal Party the tragedy was that when Home Rule was put forward as the Liberal solution it at once united men from these formerly quite distinct and different factions in opposition to the policy of the leadership.

The first intimation of the obstacles in the way of Gladstone's policy came in 1880 with the Irish Compensation for Disturbance Bill, empowering County Courts to award compensation to tenants evicted for non-payment of rent. This was thrown out by the Lords, thus precipitating a renewal of outrages against landlords and agents in Ireland. The Land Bill of the following year was more successful, partly because it contained some safeguards for landlords in the form of an accompanying Coercion Bill. The Land Bill promised Irish tenants fair rents, free sale and fixity of tenure and, once the Lords showed signs of delaying its passage, was the occasion for one of the first mass demonstrations organised by the NLF in support of the government's policy. However sincere Gladstone's intentions towards Ireland, as shown in the Land Bill and other measures, it seemed to many Liberals that his policies were playing into the hands of Parnell.

Events seemed to justify these fears. The Kilmainham Treaty (in April 1882) brought Parnell a definite Arrears Bill and the government an indefinite promise of Irish co-operation. Forster, the Chief Secretary and Lord Cowper, the Viceroy, both resigned over this. The murder of Lord Frederick Cavendish, the new Chief Secretary, and T. H. Burke, the Under-Secretary, together with the Nationalist-organised 'boycott' not only of landlords but also of the government's new Land Courts, justified those who were suspicious of Irish sincerity.

The Whig opposition to the Irish measures of 1881–2 (Hartington had refused to give the Land Bill his active support) came at a time when their political and social position was already under attack from members of their own party, in Parliament and in the country. In Parliament they fought in vain against the repeal of the malt tax and against the Game Bill. Although Chamberlain's 1883 attack on the House of Lords, 'who toil not neither do they spin', was primarily directed against the permanent Conservative majority in the Lords, it was seen by many Radicals to apply equally well to the more reactionary members of the Liberal Party. In the country, new Liberal candidates, mainly farmers, were being endorsed by the Farmers' Alliance, and with the promise of popular support were easily able to supplant previous Whig candidates and managers. The organisational drive of the NLF in the counties was inevitably tending to have the same effect.

The most important result of Radical agitation and the most important blow to the Whigs' political future came in 1884 with the Franchise Bill. This was a measure strongly advocated by Chamberlain, Dilke and George Trevelyan, and by Gladstone: it was reluctantly accepted as inevitable by Hartington.

But however strong the delight among Radicals and moderate Liberals at the Bill's passing, the Whigs were appalled by the measure and especially by the calculating Radicalism of the Conservative negotiator, Sir Michael Hicks Beach, on whose supposed reactionary ideas they may have been tempted to rely.[20] The Bill meant the end of Whig political power as it had contrived to continue in Parliament and the country after 1832. The increased electorate and the departure of the small boroughs deprived them of the sources of their power; the 1883 Corrupt Practices Act deprived them of the means whereby they might still have been able to manipulate their way to victory; the single-member seats meant the end of the Liberal practice of running a Whig and a Radical in 'double harness'. It was a sign of the end of the Whig hegemony at the centre that in 1884 Chamberlain prevailed upon Gladstone to reform the Whig-dominated LCA, under the Chief Whip, Lord Robert Grosvenor.[21]

By 1885, despite the Franchise Act and Irish legislation, the government seemed as much a spent force as it had in 1873. Within the Cabinet, factional feeling was heightened by the rejection of Chamberlain's scheme for Irish County Boards and a national council. In the country at large, the mistakes leading to the death of Gordon had reduced the government's popularity yet further. However, the actual defeat of the government in June 1885 on the Budget was to result, not in an immediate General Election but in a short administration by the 3rd Marquis of Salisbury.

---

[20] In its final form the Bill extended the comprehensive occupancy franchise from the boroughs into the counties. At the same time, all parliamentary boroughs of fewer than 15,000 inhabitants were disfranchised; boroughs with a population of 15,000–50,000 were reduced to single-member seats, and this principle also extended to the counties and big cities, which were all divided into single-member constituencies. These provisions were the result of a compromise between Liberal and Conservative leaders after the Bill was at first rejected by the Lords. This rejection had given the NLF another opportunity for a mass protest and demonstration.

[21] McGill, op. cit.

2 Liberalism in Eclipse

The resignation of Gladstone and the subsequent minority Salisbury Government (a caretaker administration until December 1885, when an election could be held on the revised electoral register) inaugurated a period of intense political turmoil culminating in the defeat of Gladstone's Home Rule Bill in 1886. There ensued a period of two decades in which the Liberal Party was firmly eclipsed by the Conservatives.

An important event in the period before the December 1885 election was the launching of Chamberlain's 'unauthorised programme'. In this he advocated free primary education, land reform ('free land') to secure the multiplication of ownership, a revision of taxation to close the gap between excessive wealth and extreme poverty, and the creation of county councils and national councils in Dublin and Edinburgh. Chamberlain claimed that 'about two thirds of the Liberal Party' fought the election on this programme in 1885. Not surprisingly the 'unauthorised programme' bitterly antagonised the Whigs. This cleavage spilt over into the election campaign. The fact that the quarrel took place in the open, and during an election campaign, was a symbolic landmark. It represented a Radical offensive against the established bases of power in the Liberal Party, with the object of creating a truly democratic party in tune with the coming democratic age. During this bitter quarrel Gladstone, still the head of the party, remained aloof. Retirement was in the air, and no doubt Chamberlain saw himself as the successor to the mantle of the GOM. Chamberlain's campaign was not so much a direct attack on Gladstone's leadership of the party as an attempt to secure the type of Liberal Party in which Chamberlain would be the natural heir. Thus, during the 1885 campaign, the Irish issue was secondary to the far more important dispute within the Liberal Party itself, and if the party fought on any programme it was not the pledge to Home Rule (only some 6 Liberal candidates were returned on this issue), but rather the domestic reforms advocated by Chamberlain.

Despite these divisions within the Liberal ranks, there was a general feeling that, even after the stormy events of the previous five years, the enlarged electorate would return Gladstone to power. Not for the first time the verdict of the electorate came as a surprise. The result of the election gave the Liberals 335 seats, the Conservatives 249 and the

Irish Nationalists 86. Parnell was left in the crucial position of holding the balance of power. To this extent, the decisive element in the results was not the election programme of Chamberlain or Gladstone, but the edict from Parnell to the Irish in England to vote Conservative. Although the efforts of the National Liberal Federation and the Farmers' Alliance in the rural seats did result in a Liberal total of 133, against 54 in 1880, in the boroughs the Liberals lost heavily, the Tories winning 118 of the 238 seats, against only 85 of the 287 seats in 1880. No Liberals at all were returned for Ireland.[1]

Despite the success of Chamberlain and Collings, on balance, however, the result was a blow for the Chamberlainites. The promise of free education had proved counter-productive, and the new Liberal Party depended for its majority on men who owed little to the influence of the NLF on their constituencies, and to whom the political reputation of Gladstone was a far more tangible thing than that of Chamberlain. The appeal to the principles of 'progress', as conceived by the Birmingham school, had failed to sweep the country, and the balance in the next Parliament was to be held by Parnell's 86 Irish who were concerned simply and solely with obtaining Home Rule and did not greatly care whether it came from Conservatives, Whigs or Radical Liberals.

It was against this peculiarly indeterminate election result that the political bombshell of the 'Hawarden Kite' burst on to the scene. This leak, by Herbert Gladstone, of Gladstone's conversion to the cause of Home Rule, also signalled the return of Gladstone to the active leadership of the Liberal Party. Prior to the 1885 election, an open 'Home Rule' commitment would have been unthinkable, but in the circumstances of December 1885 Gladstone's action could be seen as an attempt to ensure a working majority for the next reforming Liberal Government – and so many Radicals chose to view it. But the 'Hawarden Kite' served another purpose also, in so far as it thwarted Chamberlain's hopes for an immediate capture of the Party by himself and his followers. Even if the Whigs could no longer be kept within the party fold, Gladstone was unwilling that the party he had done so much to create should fall into the hands of a man for whom he felt so much personal antipathy and whose style and conception of politics were so different from his own.

The effect of the 'Hawarden Kite' at Westminster was immediate. The Conservatives severed their tenuous links with Parnell (which had brought them a small number of seats at the December 1885 election). Parnell, likewise, moved to support the Liberals. The result

[1] B. Goodman, 'Liberal Unionism: The Revolt of the Whigs', *Victorian Studies* (Dec. 1959).

was the rapid demise of the Salisbury Government. The Conservatives were turned out on Collings' amendment to the Address, advocating the creation of smallholdings, a commitment on which the majority of the party was clear.

The defeat of the Salisbury administration on this amendment paved the way for the formation of Gladstone's third ministry. It was, however, a government formed against an unpropitious background. To begin with, the Liberal Party was far from solid in its support of Gladstone. As Hamer has written: '. . . by the end of 1885, Liberals seemed no longer to have a clear agreed understanding as to what made them all Liberals, or what they ought to be doing together in politics.'² This statement was no exaggeration. The Whigs, who had abstained on the Collings motion, refused to take office in Gladstone's Cabinet. Whilst Hartington refused at the outset, such Radicals as Chamberlain and Trevelyan agreed to join but later resigned when Gladstone produced his Home Rule Bill and Land Purchase Bill.

The split of Gladstone and Chamberlain over the issue of Home Rule was one of the cardinal political events of late nineteenth century political development. It reflected a basic and fundamental division between the two men. Chamberlain believed that a truly democratic reform in the domestic sphere would solve the Irish question without the need for political dismemberment of the United Kingdom, while Gladstone and his followers maintained that by returning 86 Parnellites (and, incidentally, eradicating the Liberal representation in Ireland) Ireland had won the right to fulfilment of its Home Rule demands. In fact, however, the differences in outlook on the Irish question were involved with the whole question of the future of the Liberal Party itself, the question being whether the party was to stand for a clear programme of domestic reforms carefully calculated to win electoral support, or to retain its faith in the pursuance of the politics of moral enthusiasm in the tradition of Gladstone. From January until June 1886 Chamberlain was engaged in a tactical battle to persuade the party that he, and not Gladstone, could provide the Liberal Party with the key to the solution of the Irish question that would leave the Liberal Party with a secure future.

The point at which the differences between Gladstone and Chamberlain came to a head was in May 1886, when he resigned from the Cabinet when Gladstone made known the details of his proposed Bill. The only member who left with him was Trevelyan. Chamberlain was forced to base his objections to Gladstone's proposals on specific principles, objecting to the removal of the Irish MPs from Westmins-

² D. A. Hamer, *John Morley: Liberal Intellectual in Politics* (Oxford, 1968) p. 198.

ter. What was even more crucial was the fact that although he could win a declaration of support from the Birmingham Liberals for his own plan for 'Home Rule All Round', Schnadhorst and the rest of the National Liberal Federation had gone over to the support of Gladstone.

This decision of the NLF was crucially important. At the meeting of the General Committee in May 1886 it expressed overwhelming support for the idea of Irish self-government. At this Chamberlain withdrew and six members of the General Committee resigned. But there was no general exodus: indeed 70 Liberal MPs not previously connected with the NLF expressed support for it. No local Liberal associations withdrew but 50 new ones requested affiliation.[3] Apart from his Birmingham base, Chamberlain was almost isolated in the Liberal Party. The NLF, the symbol of the mass of moderate and Radical Liberal support for Gladstone in the country, parted company with its founders.

Despite the loyalty of the NLF to Gladstone, the secession of many Whigs, led by Hartington, Goschen and Sir Henry James, on the Home Rule issue was the more important in Parliament since it gave the Conservatives complete superiority in the Lords. The secession of a small group of Radicals into the Liberal Unionist refuge was also important since it gave strength to the idea that Liberal Unionism was a microcosm of the Liberal Party. It was this secessionist Radical group, led by Chamberlain and faithful to the distant and ambiguous dictates of Bright, which eventually nullified the efforts of Gladstone and Russell and led to the defeat of the Home Rule Bill on its second reading by 343 to 313. A total of 93 Liberals voted against Gladstone.

The struggle over Home Rule between Gladstone and Chamberlain had been fought out among the parliamentary leadership, in the party organisation, and openly in some of the constituencies during the 1886 election. The revealing fact was the totality of the Gladstonian victory, and the ease with which Gladstone was able to split up the potential forces which were apparently secure behind the Radical leader in 1885. Morley declared himself behind Gladstone in December 1885, and when it came to the crisis men like Sir William Harcourt and Henry Labouchère put their faith in Gladstone's political instinct rather than in the potential appeals of Birmingham radicalism. Even extreme Radicals could see reason in the Gladstonian argument that the total removal of the Irish problem would leave the field open for a comprehensive reform of domestic institutions, all the more possible now that the recalcitrant Whigs had removed themselves from the rest of the party. Eventually, the numbers Chamberlain was able to carry into

---

[3] Watson, *The National Liberal Federation*, pp. 84 ff.

the lobby against the Home Rule Bill were small. A section of the hostile vote was made up of 'Hartingtonians' and Conservatives as well as committed 'Radical Unionists'.

Isolated from the bulk of Liberals, Chamberlain now began to establish his own independent organisation in Birmingham, the National Radical Union. Cut off from the party organisation, Chamberlain found himself moving closer to the Hartingtonians, and a large number of those with whom Chamberlain had opposed the Home Rule Bill in the Commons were men who stood closer to Hartington and his 'Committee for the Preservation of the Union' than the Radical politics of the Birmingham Unionist leader.

Meanwhile, despite the failure of the Home Rule Bill, Gladstone (and Schnadhorst) felt confident enough for electoral success to ask for a dissolution on the morrow of defeat. It was not the future of the Liberal Party, but the personal future of Chamberlain, that was in doubt as the 1886 election campaign was waged, The election which followed gave the Conservatives 316 seats and the secessionist Liberal Unionists 78. The Gladstonian Liberals secured 191 and the Irish Nationalists 85, giving the Conservatives an overall majority of 118. Liberal anti-Home Rule candidates had not been bothered by Conservative opponents. In the counties, where the Liberal vote had risen in 1885, the labourers were often moved by dislike of migrant Irish labour to follow Collings and Chamberlain against Gladstone. But the agricultural seats were not the only areas of disaster. In all, the Liberals suffered their largest ever defeat in terms of loss of seats (144 net loss), and the failure of the reversal of the Irish vote in non-Irish constituencies to swing seats to the Liberals, together with the sharp decline in the number of Liberal-held agricultural constituencies, were major features of the result. The reverse was in part due to the demoralisation caused by the defection of Chamberlain, but probably much more to the defects on the party machine caused by the withdrawal of Whig support.

In many respects, the defeat of 1886 marked a divide in the evolution of the party. Despite the loss of office, political Liberalism from 1886 to 1892 was far from static and far from demoralised.[4] A steady tide of by-election successes from 1886 to 1891, and very clear signs that the Conservative–Liberal Unionist alliance was a troubled one, gave hope to Gladstonians that they would soon see the victory of their cause.

The party, however, could not afford to stand still and wait. The 1886 defeat implied the need to develop appeals that went beyond the

---

[4] Hopes of a reconciliation in the party collapsed with the failure of the 1887 Round Table Conference. For this episode, see M. Hurst, *Joseph Chamberlain and Liberal Reunion: The Round Table Conference of 1887* (Newton Abbot, 1967).

cry of 'Justice for Ireland'. While the party was to make valuable political capital out of the unpopularity of Balfour's repressive Irish policy, and the popularity that Parnell won out of his vindication by the Commission set up to investigate the *Times* articles (which had suggested that he condoned the Phoenix Park murders), Liberals were concerned to maintain their image as the party of progressive reform on a wider front – and in ways with which the GOM was not always wholly in sympathy.

The development of a Radical programme was in some ways aided by the events of 1885–86 in so far as the hesitant Whig element had withdrawn from the party, and the promulgation of plans for domestic reform served to cut the ground from beneath Chamberlain, isolating him from the party on the *principle* of Home Rule for Ireland rather than the *tactics* by which domestic reform was to be pursued. With Chamberlain personally there could be no reconciliation while Gladstone remained the Liberal Leader. So much was clear from the failure of the 'Round Table' conferences on the possibility of Liberal reunion in 1887, but the party could still try to win over those who supported Unionism for the sake of Chamberlain's reputation as the leader of the Radical movement.

Hence, after 1886 the progressive image was cultivated to the extent of defending those accused after the 'Bloody Sunday' affair in Trafalgar Square, and inserting a commitment to an Employers' Liability Bill in the party programme, The Liberals ran many working-class candidates where conditions favoured this (notably in Birmingham by-elections against Chamberlainite Unionists), and by 1892 were calling for the payment of MPs to allow further working-class representation in the House. If the withdrawal of the Whigs allowed a resurgence of radicalism in the Party, it also had another interesting consequence: it encouraged the rise of younger men through the party in a most un-Gladstonian fashion. It was during this period of opposition that Asquith, Campbell-Bannerman and R. B. Haldane emerged as competent political figures. These younger politicians were often far more concerned with the issues of social reform than with the traditional Gladstonian Liberal shibboleths. The shake-up given to the party leadership in 1885–6 had done much to speed up their rise within the Liberal Party hierarchy.

However, the most distinctive feature of the internal development of the Liberal Party after 1886 was the growth in influence within the party of the National Liberal Federation, whose offices moved to London in October 1886. Having given important support to Gladstone against Chamberlain in 1886, the Federation saw itself as a power to be reckoned with – a trend which culminated in the declaration of the

'Newcastle Programme' in 1891. This consisted of a series of resolutions advocating measures which the next Liberal Government might
pursue. Both Celtic and Nonconformist enthusiasm were apparent in
the motions in support of Welsh and Scottish disestablishment and a
'direct and popular veto on the Liquor Trade'. But the programme was
most significant as a clear statement of Radical demands for democratic reforms (as in the one man, one vote principle, and the 'mending or
ending' of the House of Lords). In addition, the Newcastle Programme
stressed the need to reform the Land Laws, extend the Factory Acts,
and remodel taxation and rating systems. On the Home Rule issue the
party looked 'with unshaken confidence to Mr Gladstone' to get
through a measure which would leave Parliament 'free to attend to the
pressing claims of Great Britain for its own reforms'. The Newcastle
Programme was thus a bold attempt to commit the Liberal Party to a
designated plan of reform proposed and supported by the 'grass roots'
of the party, and constructed with an eye to electoral advantage. The
tone of the programme, and its apparent acceptance by the party leadership, indicated that Gladstone's personal obsession with Home Rule
had not restricted the instincts of the party for domestic reform. Never
before in British politics had the lower echelons of an organised political party claimed such a positive role in policy-making with such
apparently effective results.

In so far as the 1891 Newcastle Programme was the platform on
which the party fought the 1892 election, the high number of contested
elections (outside Ireland only 23 Conservatives and 7 Liberal
Unionists were returned unopposed) testified to the enthusiasm for the
programme within the party. However, the Liberals were already suffering from financial shortages, and the leadership was well aware of
the need to mollify the demands of the party faithful in the pre-election
period. Significantly, Gladstone himself never fully endorsed the Newcastle Programme.

Prior to the campaign of 1892, the political scene was temporarily
galvanised as the news of the Parnell divorce hit Britain. Massive
Nonconformist pressure from both within the Liberal Party and outside
culminated in Gladstone's repudiation of Parnell. Despite the crisis
blow of the O'Shea divorce the Liberal Party remained confident, and
was eager for the election, which they felt would bring a Home Rule
majority of at least 100. However, the result failed to live up to Gladstone's expectations. The Liberals, with full Irish and Labour support,
had a majority of 40 over the combined strength of 268 Conservatives
and 47 Liberal Unionists. The tenacity of Liberal Unionism in Scotland and the West Midlands had stemmed the tide of Liberal recovery.
The result thus left Gladstone with an unstable majority with which to

redeem the electoral pledges of the previous six years.

The election of 1892 was to usher in a period of confusion within the Liberal Party that was to last at least until the turn of the century. Several factors compounded the difficulties facing the 1892–95 Liberal Government. Firstly, the cause of Home Rule had a priority over domestic reform, at least as long as Gladstone was at the head of the party. This determination at least had the advantage of securing Irish support for the government, and thus allowing it to continue in office; but the dependence on Irish goodwill was constricting and humiliating. While the Home Rule Bill passed the Commons, the Lords rejected it in September 1893, and the futility inherent in the position of a Liberal Government, facing a hostile Upper Chamber, while unable to muster popular enthusiasm for its controversial measures, soon became apparent. Elements in the party who were more interested in reform in a domestic context resented the concentration of the party's legislative effort on the Home Rule issue, and were unwilling to countenance a possible dissolution after the Lords' rejection of the Bill. The electoral appeal of Gladstonian Home Rule could justifiably be questioned after the experiences of 1886 and 1892.

Secondly, it was apparent that the leadership of the party were personally antagonistic towards one another. Stansky's study of this period reveals the almost oriental intrigues that dominated Cabinet decision-making during the administrations of both Gladstone and Rosebery.[5] One basic conflict was between Harcourt and Rosebery. It was a real divergence of principle over the policy of Imperialism and the foreign policy that a Liberal Government ought to pursue. Many members of the Cabinet, however, showed themselves all too eager to conduct their disputes on the lines of personal vendetta. The conflicts that followed the resignation of Gladstone early in 1893 were, in the words of Morley, 'an episode that no one of the prominent actors . . . can pretend to look back upon with unalloyed satisfaction.' The divisions in the Cabinet became worse after the removal of Gladstone, loyalty to whom had at least been a common agreement in the post-1886 party. Thus, while Harcourt objected to the government's handling of diplomatic conflicts over the Sudan, the Armenian massacres of 1895 and the Nicaraguan dispute, Rosebery disliked the death duties which Harcourt made the central feature of his 1894 Budget. By the later stages of the administration the leaders were hardly on speaking terms with one another, and any hope for a concerted policy on which to fight the 1895 election had been abandoned. Each of the leaders went

[5] See P. Stansky, *Ambitions and Strategies: The Struggle for the Leadership of the Liberal Party in the 1890s* (Oxford, 1964).

his own way – Harcourt to press the claims of Local Option, Morley those of Home Rule, while Rosebery sought to build the Liberal campaign on the issue of reforming the House of Lords. By 1895 the chief figures in the Liberal Party felt that they had been betrayed by one or another of their colleagues, and an air of personal recrimination and bitterness was not one which fostered productive legislation or electoral success.

In addition the government found that the Newcastle Programme was frustrated by the tactics of the House of Lords, which rejected or seriously amended government Bills to deal with the liquor trade and education. The antagonism of the Lords over these Bills seriously demoralised the party. But popular enthusiasm for an anti-Lords campaign (mooted by Gladstone in 1893, and openly advocated by Rosebery after October 1894) proved impossible to raise. The NLF had no clear policy on the reform plans to be pursued. The record of by-elections fought when Rosebery was pressing this proposal was not encouraging. Such a programme of legislation undertaken by a government with a slim and declining majority (by December 1894 by-election defeats and withdrawals from the party had reduced the Liberal majority from 40 to 32) in the face of the hostility of the Parnellite section of the Irish, who had gone into open opposition to the government when it refused to press Home Rule after the 1893 defeat, proved unprofitable. It served only to highlight the impotence of the Liberal Government.

Finally, the Cabinet seemed to have lost touch with its supporters. Dissent was rife within the party, most particularly among the Celtic Radicals at Westminster who were bitterly disappointed at the seeming inactivity of the administration over reforms for Scotland and Wales. In 1893 one Scottish MP resigned his seat (subsequently lost to a Liberal Unionist candidate) in protest against the government's failure to introduce legislation to protect the crofters. In 1894 Lloyd George, already the most vocal of the Welsh Radicals, resigned the Liberal whip along with three of his colleagues. Meanwhile other Radicals, such as Labouchère, did not hesitate to make trouble for Rosebery after he had become Prime Minister. Nor were relations between the Cabinet and the National Liberal Federation very close. Indeed, when the Cabinet chose to resign in June 1895, it was against the clearly expressed advice of the NLF secretary to carry on 'by hook or by crook'.

All these difficulties were aggravated by the loss of working-class support for the Liberals. The handling of the Featherstone strike, together with the low priority given to industrial legislation at a time of worsening industrial relations, all served to alienate the trade union and working-class supporters within the party. It was, perhaps, symbolic that Keir Hardie's Independent Labour Party was formed in 1893.

It was hardly surprising, against this background both in Parliament and in the country, that Rosebery's administration was short-lived. When, due to a ruse by the opposition Whips, the government was defeated in the Commons (early in 1895) over the Campbell-Bannerman army reforms, it was with a certain sense of relief that the Cabinet determined to leave office.

Whilst the Liberals could point to some successful legislation – the establishment of parish councils, Harcourt's important fiscal innovation of graduated death duties, Henry Fowler's Indian legislation, together with the competent records of Asquith at the Home Office and Rosebery at the Foreign Office – the overall state of the party was one of confusion and disunity. The party lacked both finance and enthusiasm, with the result that in the election of 1895 many Conservative-held seats went uncontested. In addition, the party lacked anything resembling a coherent unified policy.

The outcome of the election was a crushing Liberal defeat. The Conservatives, with 341 seats, gained a majority of 152. The Liberals were reduced to 177. In addition, there were 70 Liberal Unionists and 82 Irish Nationalists. The extent of the Liberal disaster was evident when both Harcourt and Morley were defeated in their own constituencies. It was a defeat which took the Liberals, in an atmosphere of bitter mutual recrimination, into a period in opposition which was to last for ten years.

The 1895 election in fact marked a watershed in the development of the Liberal Party. Not only did it lead to a decade of opposition, but it also marked quite firmly the end of the Gladstone era. In a different way, the 1895 defeat also marked the beginning of a reaction against the power of the National Liberal Federation.

The departure of Gladstone from political life had a double impact on the party. It deprived the Liberals of his political acumen and his immense reputation, but at the same time prepared the way for the party to shed the more constricting, negative elements of the Gladstonian creed. These years saw the growing influence of a more 'constructivist' Liberal philosophy, represented by such people as C. T. Ritchie. In due course these ideas provided the basis for the programme of social reform of the 1905 to 1914 era.

The reaction to the power of the National Liberal Federation which set in after 1895 was hardly unexpected. By 1898 the NLF was ready to disavow any claim to be the policy-making centre of the party. Its resolutions recognised that the Federation was not to 'interfere with the time or order in which questions are taken up'. Similarly, the Federation agreed that its relationship with the official leadership was purely advisory. There were no more 'omnibus' resolutions proposing specific measures for a Liberal Government to undertake. The heyday of the caucus was over.

Although the Liberals had been soundly defeated in the 1895 election, the party remained a potent force at Westminster. Despite the crippling divisions among the party leaders, the Liberals were able to prevent the Conservatives getting their education proposals through the Commons. At the same time, however, there were optimistic signs of reviving Liberal fortunes in a series of by-election victories in such seats as Southampton and Reading after 1895.

Overshadowing these encouraging signs, however, were the changes and struggles within the leadership of the party. As Stansky has appropriately labelled the period, it was an age of ambition and strategy. Rosebery resigned as leader of the party in November 1896. Harcourt stayed as leader of the Liberals in the Commons, with Lord Kimberley becoming leader in the Lords. It was an unhappy arrangement. Harcourt rapidly encountered difficulties, most particularly from within the party at his failure to condemn the government more vigorously during the inquiry into the Jameson Raid. This, in fact, was one element which caused Harcourt to resign in 1899. The party, divided and in opposition, was once again faced with the necessity to select a leader of the Liberal Party within the House of Commons. It was in this situation that Sir Henry Campbell-Bannerman became leader of the party. With Campbell-Bannerman as leader, the Liberal Party was to enter the new century.

3 The Liberals in Opposition: 1900–1906

Campbell-Bannerman became leader of the Liberal Party in the Commons in February 1899. He was hardly the most obvious candidate to be leader of a party – indeed, in 1895 he had nearly become Speaker of the House, a post which would have removed him from active party politics. Nor had Campbell-Bannerman many of the characteristics of charisma or dynamism likely to set him as an obvious leader. Although he had first experienced Cabinet office in 1886, and had been Secretary of State for War under both Gladstone and Rosebery, his ministerial experience was relatively narrow. Yet Campbell-Bannerman had qualifications much needed by the party: good-humoured, upright, a man of character and principle, he had just the temperament required to hold the party together. Indeed, the many difficulties facing the new leader were soon to be greatly compounded by a serious division within the Liberal ranks over the situation in South Africa. From early 1899 onwards, the position grew increasingly tense as conflict with the Boers appeared nearer. Appropriations were increased for the Army in Cape Colony and plans were under way to send out additional troops. These appropriations were criticised by Campbell-Bannerman on 21 April in the Commons. By June, the Liberal leader's criticism of British intentions had significantly increased.

Speaking at Ilford on 17 June, in the most effective speech Campbell-Bannerman had made since becoming leader, he made a forceful plea for a peaceful settlement between Britain and the Transvaal. Three days later, on 20 June, Joseph Chamberlain assured Campbell-Bannerman that war was not intended, but that the military plans for the Cape were merely to reinforce the diplomacy of the Colonial Office. Clearly, Chamberlain wanted the support of the Liberals to remove the issue above party politics. After consulting his colleagues, Campbell-Bannerman refused to agree to Chamberlain's request. From this time on, the Colonial Secretary increasingly began to use the theme which dominated the political debate over the next years – namely, that the government's critics were in fact the enemies of peace and friends of the Boer enemy.

It was unwise that, against a deteriorating situation, Campbell-

Bannerman went on vacation to Marienbad in mid-summer, ignoring the bad news which followed him from England. The net result was that, by September, the Liberal front bench was taking widely divergent lines over the issue of Kruger and the Transvaal. There had always been considerable tensions within the party between the ardent 'Little Englanders' and those who looked with favour on a humanitarian and benevolent Imperialism. This conflict had been a feature of the 1892–5 government. During the 1890s these fundamental divisions widened further as the prospect of conflict with the Boer Republics grew. The outbreak of war, following the ultimatum from Kruger and the invasion of Natal and Cape Colony, brought these divisions to a head.

Stanhope's motion of October 1899, censuring the government, split the Liberal Party forces. While Campbell-Bannerman, Asquith, Haldane and Sir Edward Grey abstained, 186 Liberals went into the opposition lobby. The crisis became more serious when Rosebery (together, with Asquith, a member of the Imperial Federation League) seemed to be emerging from retirement in order to mount a campaign that would unite the pro-Imperialist elements in a breakaway party. In July 1900 some 41 Liberal MPs actually voted with the Unionists against the 29 members of their own party who supported Sir Wilfrid Lawson's 'pro-Boer' amendment. The Liberal Imperialists gained control of the *Daily Chronicle* from anti-war Liberals, and there was a clear division between the *Manchester Guardian* and *Westminster Gazette* (anti-war) and those Liberal newspapers which followed a more Imperialist line (e.g. the Roseberyite *Daily News*).

Campbell-Bannerman's own position was sympathetic to the Radicals. He had all along been convinced that the conflict had been unnecessarily provoked, both by Chamberlain and the Cape Government. He accepted the war, declaring that he would not in any way hinder the efforts of British arms, but also repeated that he would not withdraw any of his previous criticisms of British policy. As the war progressed, Campbell-Bannerman increasingly leaned to the Radical position, especially after he learned of the civilian concentration camps being used in the Transvaal.

On the right of the party, a powerful minority of leading Liberals, including Asquith, Grey, Haldane and Fowler, were in support of Rosebery's Imperialist position. They urged Liberals to forget past events and join whole-heartedly with the government in full support of the war. At the opposite extreme of the party were the Radicals such as John Morley and David Lloyd George, for whom the war was a clear case of the rights of a small nation against the power of an aggressive empire. Although the actual outbreak of war made the anti-Imperialist position difficult to sustain (for it was Kruger who had invaded Natal, not Britain the Transvaal), as the war progressed support for the pro-Boer position in the party rose.

The divisions in the Liberal ranks were soon followed by a sharp reversal of Liberal by-election performances. Prior to the outbreak of war, Liberals had secured several by-election gains from the government. In the first two by-elections of the war (at Bow and Bromley and at Exeter) Liberals performed extremely badly. In both seats the government increased its majority.

With these obvious divisions in the Liberal ranks, and with public opinion strongly on the side of the government, the Conservatives under Salisbury took advantage of the opportunity to call an election for July 1900. Shortly before the dissolution, a Liberal Imperial Council had been formed with Lord Brassey as chairman. This organisation subsequently began 'approving' Liberal candidates whose attitudes were certainly not in line with the views propounded by Campbell-Bannerman. There were signs that, once again, the party might be faced with a breakaway group.

With so many advantages on the Conservative side, under difficult circumstances the Liberals made a better fight than many expected in July 1900. Partly they were helped by the Conservative campaign which attempted to brand all Liberals as 'pro-Boer' (which was ludicrously untrue) rather than concentrate on the real and undeniable divisions within the party. The outcome of the July 1900 'Khaki election' was a triumph for Salisbury. The Conservatives secured 402 seats to the 186 of the Liberals. The Liberals had thus improved their position very marginally compared with 1895, although their representation was less than when Parliament had been dissolved. The Liberals lost ground in the English counties and in Scotland, but improved their position in Wales, where opposition to the war in South Africa was strongest. Scotland and the large cities showed most enthusiasm for the war.

The result was of little comfort for Campbell-Bannerman, who now found himself in the unenviable position of an opposition leader who had led his party to a crushing electoral defeat, and whose most able colleagues openly followed the lead of a rival statesman. And yet, although the election had exposed Liberal divisions, curiously the result of the election was to make the chances of a real breakaway from the party less likely. Both Chamberlain and Salisbury had sought to brand the entire party with the pro-Boer label; yet the Liberals had not lost ground in terms of their parliamentary representation. The electoral assets of Liberal Imperialism were still dubious, and in some constituencies it had proved a distinct disadvantage (as it did at

Merthyr where Keir Hardie was returned against a Liberal who had supported the government in its conduct). The election of July 1900 had effectively demonstrated that a reunion of the forces of 1885, of which Rosebery was thinking, was not a viable programme.

With Chamberlain himself uninterested in a cross-party alliance, Liberal Imperialism did not have enough strength to stand on its own, a fact which was appreciated by Asquith if not by Rosebery. As long as Campbell-Bannerman held the centre of the party and the National Liberal Federation behind him there was little chance of an internal *coup d'état*. Indeed, in July 1901 the official leader was able to secure a unanimous vote of confidence at a meeting of the parliamentary party.

Such an apparent display of unanimity, however, did not end the conflict within the party. Most obvious was the antagonism between Rosebery and Campbell-Bannerman which was displayed quite openly. In his Chesterfield speech of 15 December 1901, Rosebery came out with an appeal for a total revision of the objects of the party. Instead of the 'fly-blown phylacteries' of the old Liberal creed (notably the commitment to Home Rule, but by implication extending to the rest of the Gladstonian programme) the party must build up a new programme from a 'clean slate'. Rosebery talked of a government based on 'national efficiency', and an ending of the old party antagonisms. The Liberal League, formed in 1902 and involving Rosebery (as president), Asquith, Fowler, Haldane and Grey (as vice-presidents), served to maintain these divisions, but the younger Imperialists saw its function as an internal pressure group within the party rather than as a separatist body.

By May 1902, however, the Treaty of Vereeniging ended the war. At home the tide of public opinion began to swing more noticeably against the government. Liberal criticism of the government's handling of the conflict (Campbell-Bannerman's 'methods of barbarism' had proved a telling phrase) became a viable political platform, and the Liberals were able to capitalise on the criticisms put forward by the Commission of Inquiry into the war.

Meanwhile, other events were to aid the reviving fortunes of the Liberal Party. The most important was the Education Act of 1902. This legislation was to provide the first glimmering of a Liberal dawn. It not only opened up divisions within the Unionist Cabinet (Chamberlain found the approach adopted by the government particularly unpalatable), but also roused the grass-roots of the Liberal Party in defence of the control of primary education by the school boards. Nonconformist anger was brought to a level not seen since the Bulgarian atrocities. Both Campbell-Bannerman and Asquith sank their differences over the Boer War in defence of the Liberal principles now under attack. The Education Act of 1902, followed by the argument over the tax on the importation of corn and later by the 1904 Licensing Act, represented attacks on Liberal principles that had been part of the party's heritage. In the face of these measures the party found a new unity. Rosebery's call for a review of the basic philosophy of the party could be forgotten. Liberal enthusiasm to fight in defence of its old principles was rekindled. By mid-1903 only a handful of constituencies lacked Liberal candidates eager to give battle on the 1902 Education Act.

From 1901 onwards, the effect of the government's growing unpopularity was revealed in successive by-election reverses. It rapidly became clear that this was something more than the 'swing of the pendulum'. When, in January 1903, the Newmarket constituency was lost, the seventh by-election defeat since the passing of the Education Act, it was perhaps understandable that the Liberals believed the long winter of their discontent was drawing to an end.

The unpopularity of the government, however, was not the only lesson of the by-elections. Liberals were attracting not merely Nonconformists outraged by the Education Act, but also gaining support from the political wing of the Labour movement, now indignant at the outcome of the Taff Vale decision. By turning the interest of the Labour movement to events in Parliament, the Taff Vale decision acted as a much-needed fillip for the Labour Representation Committee. Since its birth in February 1900 the LRC had hardly been a triumphant success. Only two 'Labour' candidates (R. Bell and Keir Hardie) had been elected in July 1900, whilst the trade unions had often been difficult to interest in parliamentary action. Taff Vale dramatically changed that attitude.

By 1903 both the LRC and the Liberals were united in opposition to the government. Given that past relations between the Liberals and the Trades Union Congress had been good (Henry Broadhurst, the TUC General Secretary, had been a Liberal candidate in 1895), and given that neither group had found much advantage in their lack of unity during the 1895 and 1900 elections, there were powerful figures on both sides who saw the considerable advantages that might come from some sort of accommodation.

Early in 1903, significant moves towards an 'entente' between Labour and Liberals were made. Speaking at Belmont on 2 January, Campbell-Bannerman expressed his keen sympathy for more Labour representatives in the Commons. A month later, Lord Tweedmouth, the chairman of the Council of the Scottish Liberal Federation, told the Edinburgh annual general meeting that a Liberal–Labour alliance was greatly to be desired. In fact, it was Ramsay MacDonald who made the first approach to the Liberals through George Cadbury, by pointing out to Gladstone's secretary, Jesse Herbert, the dangers that the Liberals would face by opposing any LRC candidates. MacDonald went on to promise that, on almost every issue, LRC members would support a Liberal Government, but that given hostility by the Liberal Party, the LRC would oppose Liberal candidates throughout the country.

This threat soon became more meaningful when, on 21 February 1903, the fourth LRC annual conference at Newcastle passed a resolution providing for a Parliamentary Fund for Labour candidates, to be raised by contributions from affiliated societies at the annual rate of one penny per annum. This, together with the 'Newcastle Resolution', had important consequences for the negotiations. The Parliamentary Fund gave the LRC a decisive power for electoral action which it had not previously possessed. Meanwhile, a month later, on 11 March 1903, Labour won the Woolwich constituency, a seat in which in 1900 a Conservative had been returned unopposed. Will Crooks owed much of his victory to the support of the local Liberal association and the by-election seemed yet further proof of the advantages to be gained by co-operation.

Against this background, Jesse Herbert strongly warned Herbert Gladstone of the advantages of co-operation with Labour, most particularly since he believed the LRC could 'influence the votes of nearly a million men'. Herbert feared that, if the LRC vote went against the Liberals, the party would be trounced in the boroughs, and in the county divisions of Lancashire and Yorkshire. In addition, there was the important consideration that any entente which provided for straight LRC–Conservative contests in 35 constituencies would not only save the Liberal Party £15,000 but win 10 seats from the Conservatives. After detailed discussion and negotiation between Herbert Gladstone and Ramsay MacDonald, by March 1903 the agreement was settled. On 13 March, Gladstone provided Campbell-Bannerman with a detailed memorandum outlining the terms of the secret alliance.[1] An agreed number of Labour candidates were to fight the next election with Liberal support. In return, Labour would not contest Liberal-held seats.

On one point, however, Gladstone had been insistent: the local constituency Liberal associations must retain freedom of choice. This clause was subsequently to provide a constant thorn in the side of the

---

[1] Herbert Gladstone's memorandum of 13 March 1903 is printed in full in F. Bealey, 'Negotiations between the Liberal Party and the Labour Representation Committee before the General Election of 1906', *Bulletin of the Institute of Historical Research,* XXIX (1956) 269 f.

entente, causing some rival by-election candidates. Thus in the Barnard Castle contest in July 1903, the local Liberal association refused to allow Arthur Henderson, the LRC candidate, a straight fight with the Conservative. Despite pressure from Headquarters, a Liberal candidate was fielded, although Henderson subsequently went on to win by 47 votes over the Conservative, with the Liberal a poor third.[2]

A further example of the lack of goodwill at constituency level was displayed in the Norwich by-election of January 1904. G. H. Roberts, the Socialist-sponsored candidate, refused to stand aside and, although finishing at the foot of the poll, took 2,444 votes, not sufficient to deny the Liberals victory, but nonetheless a strong showing. Although both by-elections had demonstrated the dangers of splitting the progressive vote, local Liberal associations often continued reluctant to accede to outside pressure to come to a local accommodation with Labour – particularly in Scotland, South Wales and the industrial North-East.

Fortified by the opposition to the Education Act, and with the Gladstone–MacDonald entente securing the flank against Labour, the Liberals were already, by 1903, well in the road to recovery. Meanwhile the greatest blow to the government came from a different quarter. On 15 May 1903 Joseph Chamberlain launched his campaign for Tariff Reform and Imperial Preference in a speech at Birmingham. It was a rallying-cry from which the Liberal Party never looked back.

The raising of the issue of Tariff Reform brought all Liberals together in defence of Free Trade. With the exception of Rosebery, who became increasingly isolated from the Liberal leadership, Free Trade acted as a tonic to party unity. Asquith was brought into close co-operation with Campbell-Bannerman. During 1903, as Liberals attacked the Chamberlain heresy, something of the old Gladstonian crusading spirit returned to the party. The tone of Asquith's speeches moved the Liberals firmly towards a policy of social reform. The party was on the march again.

The impact of Tariff Reform on Conservative fortunes was disastrous. Chamberlain, who had split the Liberal ranks in 1885, split the Conservative Cabinet in 1903. The Free Traders led by the Duke of Devonshire, were in revolt. A small group of back-benchers, including Winston Churchill and Sir John Dickson-Poynder defected to the Liberals. In Parliament, Free Trade Conservatives voted with the Liberals against the Address in 1904. For a time, it seemed that the government might collapse and an election be imminent. The Liberals, in fact, were

---

[2] For this contest, see R. Douglas, *The History of the Liberal Party, 1895–1970* (1971) pp.71–3.

to be disappointed, both in their expectation of an early general election and in their hopes of an alliance with the Conservative Free Traders. Although negotiations took place between Devonshire, Earl Spencer and Asquith in December 1903 and January 1904, they eventually collapsed over the vexed question of the 1902 Education Act.

But though Liberals were disappointed in their hope of an early general election, the by-elections continued to bring them fresh victories. A severe government defeat at Norwich was followed by similar catastrophies at Gateshead in January 1904 (a Labour gain) and Oswestry, normally regarded as safe Conservative territory, in June 1904 (won by the Liberals). The nadir of the government's fortunes came in March 1905, when Buteshire was lost, followed a month later by Brighton.

During 1905, however, Balfour began a counter-offensive aimed at what appeared to be the Liberal's weakest points: the Liberal League and Ireland. The Liberal League (formed in February 1902 as the official organisation of the Liberal Imperialists) was still, despite Campbell-Bannerman's hostility, a potentially powerful organisation. But Balfour's attempts to woo the League, and thereby reopen the party split, came to nothing. If for no other reason, the Liberal Imperialists realised that their best hope of office remained with the Liberal Party.

Balfour's failure with the Liberal Imperialists seemed as if it might be offset by a revival of Liberal divisions over Home Rule. On 14 November, at a breakfast meeting with John Redmond and T. P. O'Connor, Campbell-Bannerman convinced the Irish leaders that he was still strongly committed to Home Rule. He promised to outline, in his next major speech, a policy committing Liberals to Home Rule in gradual stages. In a carefully-worded speech at Stirling on 23 November 1905, Campbell-Bannerman fulfilled his pledge. Two days later, in a speech at Bodmin, Rosebery made a strong attack on Campbell-Bannerman's 'Stirling Declaration'. Most Liberals decried Rosebery's attack, whilst Asquith calmed the situation. A potentially divisive issue then subsided, but before it was totally quietened, Balfour took the opportunity to resign. On 4 December, Balfour offered his resignation, no doubt hoping to embarrass the Liberals.

In fact, Balfour's hope of creating disunity in the Liberals over taking office was soon doused. On 24 November, when rumours of Balfour's impending resignation were circulating, Herbert Gladstone wrote to Campbell-Bannerman arguing that, on tactical grounds, he should refuse office. Gladstone was supported in this argument by Asquith, Grey and the editors of the *Westminster Gazette* and *Spectator*. However, the thought that swayed Campbell-Bannerman was the danger of who the King might ask to form a government. The Marquis of Ripon warned Campbell-Bannerman of this on 28 November. The prospect of the Marquis of Lansdowne, Joseph Chamberlain or, worse still, Rosebery forming a government decided the issue. The net result was that when King Edward sent for Campbell-Bannerman on 5 December the offer was speedily accepted.

The one problem that remained on 5 December concerned whether it should be Asquith or Campbell-Bannerman who led the party in the House of Commons. This had already been the subject of intrigue by Asquith, Grey and Haldane at a meeting at Relugas (Grey's fishing lodge in north-east Scotland) as early as September 1905. It had been agreed at this meeting that Asquith would become Chancellor of the Exchequer, and would lead the party in the Commons. Campbell-Bannerman, although Premier, would be removed to the House of Lords. In this plan, which effectively removed Campbell-Bannerman from the real seat of power, Haldane would become Lord Chancellor, and Grey Foreign Secretary. Events, however, failed to materialise in this way. Campbell-Bannerman stood firm in his resolve to stay in the Commons. Grey and Haldane, despite earlier protestations to the contrary, accepted the position and the Relugas compact collapsed.

The main task facing Campbell-Bannerman's administration was to prepare for victory in the forthcoming general election. With the party machine, under Herbert Gladstone, very much in preparedness, and with Campbell-Bannerman's own position both in the party and in the country very much stronger than in 1900, Liberals prepared for the election in a mood of confidence. Although the campaign proper did not begin until after Christmas, the opening broadside was delivered by Campbell-Bannerman in a speech at the Albert Hall on 22 December. Its contents were fairly predictable, with the emphasis on Free Trade, but also references to trade union law reform, land, the question of the Chinese coolies in South Africa and payment of members of the House of Commons. Other proposed reforms included site value taxation, smallholdings legislation, modernisation of the Poor Law, relief of overcrowding and action to end 'sweated' labour. In a later speech at Stirling, although again stressing Free Trade, Campbell-Bannerman promised 'a course of strenuous legislation and administration, to secure those social and economic reforms which have been too long delayed'. The message, or so it appeared, was that the Liberals were to be the party firmly committed to social reform. However, on the details of this forthcoming social legislation, Campbell-Bannerman was fairly silent. Instead, the bulk of the Liberal offensive was directed at the record of the Balfour administration, the obvious divisions of the Conservatives on the fiscal question and the potential dangers if Chamberlain were returned to power.[3]

Liberal enthusiasm for the battle was apparent in the nominations. Only a few avowed Conservative Free Traders were allowed an unopposed return. Except for two seats (Oxford University and Mid-Cumberland), every constituency was contested by a Free Trader, whether Liberal or Labour. Liberals contested 121 more seats than in 1900. The Liberal press enjoyed the support of such Conservative Free Trade journals as the *Spectator*. Meanwhile, with the exception of Scotland, the MacDonald–Gladstone pact worked extremely well; and outside Scotland only two Liberal-held seats were attacked by Labour.

Though many factors combined to favour the Liberals, the landslide victory of the election came as a stunning surprise. On 12 January the Liberals gained their first victory in Ipswich. The following day Arthur Balfour lost Manchester East.

The defeat of Balfour was the prelude to a Liberal landslide in industrial Lancashire. Even the staunchest of Conservative citadels, in the hitherto safe rural shires, fell to the Liberals. In all, 1906 was a landslide comparable only with the victory of the 'coupon' candidates in 1918, or the National candidates in 1931 and Labour in 1945. The full results were as follows:

	Seats	Total votes	% of total
Unionist	157	2,463,606	43·7
Liberal	375	2,583,132	45·9
Labour	54	528,797	9·4
Nationalist	83	35,109	0·6
Others	–	21,557	0·4
	670	5,632,201	100·0

Few Conservative seats escaped the landslide of 1906. The only important exceptions were West Lancashire, the stronghold of Birmingham and Sheffield. Even the South-East of England, usually a Conservative monopoly, saw normally safe seats fall to Liberals. Although a few rural seats in the West Midlands, rural Lincolnshire and the East Riding stayed Conservative, the electoral map of Britain had been almost totally redrawn.

The greatest single disaster for the Conservatives came in the textile districts of East Lancashire and the West Riding, where 29 of the 30 seats won in 1900 were lost. In Wales 28 of the 34 constituencies

[3] For the 1906 election, see A. K. Russell, *Liberal Landslide: The General Election of 1906* (Newton Abbot, 1973) *passim*.

returned Liberals; only one Conservative survived, while in Scotland, for the 70 seats, only 6 Conservatives and 5 Liberal Unionists survived against 57 Liberals.

The Liberals had a further reason for elation at the results of 1906. For the election had seemed a total vindication of the Gladstone–MacDonald entente. In virtually all the English constituencies, Liberal–Labour co-operation had worked well. Such Liberal organisers as Jesse Herbert were delighted at the results.[4] A major exception, however, was to be found in Scotland. Here, the pact was not operated since the Scottish Liberal Federation, considerably to the right of English Liberalism, refused any compromise with Labour. North of the Border, no Labour candidate enjoyed a straight fight against a Conservative. In ten constituencies, three-cornered contests occurred. Significantly, in these ten contests, while Labour only won two, the Liberals forfeited six seats they might otherwise have won.

Outside Scotland, however, in only five constituencies did Liberals contest recognised Labour seats, with Labour taking four of them nonetheless. It was a tribute to the working of the pact that in only two constituencies were Liberal seats lost as a result of Labour candidates. In all, 29 LRC representatives were elected and almost all were dependent on Liberal votes.

With the Liberal election triumph, the almost unrelieved Conservative massacre, and the harmonious working of the Gladstone–MacDonald pact, 1906 saw the Liberal Party at its zenith. The euphoria of the results had now to be translated into the reality of government.

---

[4] See Jesse Herbert to Herbert Gladstone, 16 Feb. 1906, quoted in Douglas, *History of the Liberal Party*, p. 76.

4 The Liberal Ascendancy: 1906–1910

With the triumph of the election behind him, Campbell-Bannerman found himself in a position of strength unequalled by any Liberal leader in recent history. He was head of the largest anti-Conservative majority for over eighty years. If the Liberal back-benches were filled with men new to Parliament, there was no lack of capable and indeed brilliant men seeking the higher positions of office. Hence the Cabinet chosen by Campbell-Bannerman proved to be one of the strongest and most gifted of any peacetime administration. It was a blend of the outstanding intellectual power of Asquith, who became Chancellor of the Exchequer, Haldane at the War Office, Augustine Birrell as President of the Board of Education and James Bryce as Chief Secretary for Ireland, together with the dynamism and drive of Lloyd George at the Board of Trade and Winston Churchill as Under-Secretary at the Colonial Office. The Foreign Office was entrusted to the much respected Sir Edward Grey.

Despite the inclusion of such obvious young Radicals as Lloyd George, the Cabinet retained a strongly Gladstonian flavour. Such men as Lord Loreburn, the Lord Chancellor, Morley, Herbert Gladstone, Bryce and Ripon all belonged to the Gladstonian tradition. In addition, Lord Crewe as Lord President of the Council, Lord Tweedmouth as First Lord of the Admiralty and Lord Elgin as Colonial Secretary were all moderates unlikely to ruffle the placid waters of Whitehall.

It was hardly surprising, armed with such a massive majority and with a Cabinet of undoubted strength, that Radicals had high hopes of reforms to come. The early days of the new government lent strength to these Radical hopes. There were persistent rumours that Campbell-Bannerman was moving increasingly to the Left. The King's Speech, in February 1906, tended to reinforce this optimism. It promised a reduction in armaments and a major legislative programme of twenty-two Bills for the new session.

However, despite so many factors in its favour, the Campbell-Bannerman administration never really fulfilled the high hopes of the early days of 1906. What, then, had gone wrong? Partly the explanation was to be found in the personality of the new Premier. For whilst

Campbell-Bannerman soon established an undisputed command over
the Commons, proving himself an able parliamentarian, he was a weak
leader of a government. His policy was to allow each Minister to care
for the problems of his own department. At no time did Campbell-
Bannerman play the part of a leader or Prime Minister. Indeed, as his
private secretary recorded, 'he was continually forgetting that he *was*
Prime Minister'.[1] Hence, lacking leadership, the Liberal Party lacked
also both impetus and direction.

A second factor in the equation lay in the character of the Parliamentary Liberal Party elected in the 1906 landslide. An analysis of the 377
Liberals in the new Parliament soon dispels the myth that the Liberals
represented left-wing reforming radicalism. The occupational background (by group) was: barristers, 64; service officers, 22; 'gentlemen',
69; established businessmen, 80; self-made businessmen, 74; solicitors,
21; writers and journalists, 25. The remaining 22 were made up of 9
teachers, 8 trade unionists and 5 doctors. Thus the Parliamentary Liberal Party was not composed of the wild Radicals that its enemies
sometimes supposed. Politically, the party was dominated by 'centre'
Liberals. Its social composition was preponderantly middle-aged
men from the commercial and professional middle class. The real
Radicals were few and far between: 'The dangerous element does not
amount to a dozen', reported Herbert Gladstone to Campbell-
Bannerman early in 1906 with undisguised relief.[2]

Compared with the Conservative opposition, the relative strength of
barristers, solicitors, writers and businessmen was greater in the Liberal Party. The officers and country gentlemen were less numerous
than in the Conservative opposition. The Liberals were still not a party
catering to any significant degree to the parliamentary ambitions of
working men: on the contrary, 125 of the 377 Liberals were public-
school educated, 135 had attended Oxford or Cambridge and more
than one in four were men of great wealth. Not surprisingly, the social
composition and political outlook of the parliamentary party acted as
no great spur to radical reform.

Apart from this restraining force among the Liberals themselves,
part of the failure of the Campbell-Bannerman administration to
achieve even greater measures of social reform lay with the House of

[1] Lord Ponsonby's notes on Campbell-Bannerman in Francis W. Hirst, *In the Golden
Days* (1947) p. 259, quoted in José F. Harris and Cameron Hazlehurst, 'Campbell-
Bannerman as Prime Minister', *History*, Vol. 55, No. 185 (Oct. 1970) pp. 360–383.

[2] Gladstone to Campbell-Bannerman, 21 Jan. 1906, quoted in Harris and Hazlehurst,
op. cit.

Lords. Balfour had already declared, in his Nottingham speech, his intention of blocking social reform in the Upper House. The Lords faithfully carried out that pledge. During 1906 the Lords destroyed Birrell's Education Bill, designed to remove Nonconformist objections to the 1902 Education Act. A Bill to abolish plural voting met a similar fate. During 1907 a variety of land reform measures were similarly blocked, including the Small Holdings Bill, the Evicted Tenants (Ireland) Bill, the Small Landowners (Scotland) Bill and the Land Values (Scotland) Bill. By mid-1907 it was already clear that Balfour and Lansdowne intended to use the power of the Lords for purely party-political purposes – although it was noticeable that the hostility of the Lords to Liberal legislation was tempered by the electoral popularity (or otherwise) of the Bill concerned. Thus it was significant that the Lords were careful to avoid blocking the Trade Disputes Act.

1907 was thus a year of frustration and anger for Liberals. The outcome of the government's legislative programme in 1907 was minimal. There was truth in Lloyd George's reference to a bundle of sapless faggots fit only for the fire. Of the nine major Bills which the Liberals had hoped to carry, only the Territorial Army Act, the Small Holdings and Allotments Act and the Patents Act became law.

Meanwhile other factors, in addition to the wrecking tactics of the House of Lords, were helping to undermine the popularity and esteem of the government as the euphoria of 1906 died away. By 1907 the economic prosperity of the previous year had given way to a worldwide trade recession. Nor had the Liberals any cause for optimism on the electoral front. The party lost three of the 16 contested by-elections during 1907, while in the municipal elections of November 1906 there had been heavy losses to the Conservatives.

Two of the by-elections, at Colne Valley and at Jarrow, were both significant for the increased support shown for Labour. In the Colne Valley, Victor Grayson, an avowed Socialist who in fact refused to join the Labour Party, won the seat despite Liberal and Conservative opposition. In the Jarrow division, the death of the Liberal member produced a four-cornered by-election in July 1907. The result was a triumph for Labour, whose candidate, the trade unionist Peter Curran, topped the poll with 4698, compared with the 3930 of the Conservative, 3474 for the Liberal and 2122 for the Nationalist. It was significant that the Liberal polled only half the 1906 total.

The advent of 1908 brought new electoral setbacks. Three more Liberal seats were gained by Conservatives early in 1908. The municipal election results were equally depressing, with such traditional Liberal council strongholds as Coventry and Nottingham falling to Conservatives. Added to these electoral difficulties was the rapid decline in the health of the Prime Minister. The strain of office, and the illness and death of his wife, proved too much for Campbell-Bannerman. From the spring of 1908, ill-health confined him to his home at 10 Downing Street. On 6 April 1908 he resigned; he died later the same month.

The administration that had begun with such high hopes in 1906 was over. With its demise, the feeling was one of disillusion. For although Campbell-Bannerman's two years in office were in many ways impor- tant and constructive, his ministry as a whole never really constituted a real success. Whilst it had brought self-government to South Africa, initiated far-reaching Army reforms, pursued a successful détente with Russia and repaired the damage done by the Taff Vale decision, it was open to fundamental criticism. Essentially, the ministry had been con- cerned with the issues of the past, not of the future. It had been repair- ing the damage and omissions of the previous decade, not preparing new or enlightened attitudes towards the social problems of the future.

Yet Campbell-Bannerman's administration had achieved a success of a different kind. It had given experience and office to men who were to prove themselves in later years. Indeed, the administrative success of many of the individual Ministers in the Campbell-Bannerman ministry was remarkable. This was particularly true of Haldane, the Secretary of State for War. He created not only the General Staff, but by the Territorial and Reserve Forces Act of 1907 revised the whole organisa- tion of the Army. Haldane's energy was at least equalled by the dynamism of Lloyd George at the Board of Trade. His most construc- tive achievements were the Merchant Shipping Act of 1906 and the Port of London Authority Act which, although it did not become law until Lloyd George had moved to the Treasury, had been prepared by him. A third source of energy came from Winston Churchill, the Under-Secretary at the Colonial Office. Churchill's abilities were given greater scope than usual because Elgin, the Secretary of State, was among the weakest members of the government. Churchill's achieve- ments at the Colonial Office included the establishment of self- government in the Transvaal, followed by similar status immediately afterwards for the Orange Free State.

The departure of Campbell-Bannerman from the political scene marked a significant event in the evolution of the Liberal Party. With his disappearance, John Morley warned, 'will arrive a critical hour for our Party and our Principles'. And so it proved.

The successor to Campbell-Bannerman as Prime Minister was Her- bert Asquith. At 56, Asquith was a natural choice. He had been in Parliament for twenty years, and had served both Gladstone and Rosebery as Home Secretary, before becoming Campbell-Bannerman's

Chancellor of the Exchequer. Although, late in 1907, there had been talk of a move to draft Sir Edward Grey, the Foreign Secretary, no one challenged Asquith's succession in 1908.

The new Premier entered office with two important advantages. He was, as one early biographer wrote, outstanding among Liberal statesmen as the one politician who most united the party.[3] Secondly, he inherited from his predecessor an exceptionally talented ministry. Indeed, Asquith's first act was to strengthen the team even further. Elgin was replaced at the Colonial Office by Lord Crewe. Tweedmouth, whose faculties were fast fading, was removed from the Admiralty to the less onerous position of Lord President of the Council. Much the most significant appointment, however, was the advancement of David Lloyd George to be Chancellor of the Exchequer. It was an appointment that changed the course of the ministry and indeed the history of the country.

Born in Manchester in 1863, Lloyd George's upbringing and background were rooted in Welsh radicalism. In 1890, at the age of 27, he had won a dramatic victory by 18 votes in a by-election at Caernarvon Boroughs, the constituency he was to retain at thirteen successive General Elections. Lloyd George's preoccupation in his first years in the Commons was with the objectives of Welsh radicalism – the need to attack and destroy the established church, the destruction of the power of landlords, the creation of a University of Wales and the establishment of a Welsh Parliament.

Lloyd George was above all, though, the champion of conscience; he was the voice of the underprivileged. And his oratory was, perhaps, unsurpassed in modern British politics; it was the oratory to move men and inspire movements. In 1900 his outspoken sympathy with the Boers had made him a Radical hero. His period at the Board of Trade after 1906 showed his administrative ability. By 1908 Lloyd George's journey into Liberal politics had brought him from the mists and hills of North Wales to 11 Downing Street.

The reconstructed ministry under Asquith faced a troubled political outlook. In the last days of the Campbell-Bannerman Government, the party had suffered a severe blow in the Peckham by-election on 24 March 1908, when a Liberal majority of 2300 was easily overturned. The popularity of the government seemed to be ebbing fast, and the advent of Asquith failed to halt this trend.

The elevation of Churchill to the Presidency of the Board of Trade necessitated a by-election in Manchester North-West. When polling took place on 24 April, Churchill lost the seat to the Conservatives by

---

[3] J. P. Alderson, *Mr Asquith* (1905) p. 268, quoted in Harris and Hazlehurst, op. cit.

29 votes. Churchill had subsequently to be moved to the safer territory of Dundee, where he was returned to Westminster on 9 May despite Conservative and Labour opposition. The result in Manchester North-West, if the most dramatic, was not isolated. Of the 15 Liberal-held seats which saw by-elections in 1908, the Liberals retained only 9.

Against this electoral background, 1908 saw the introduction of an important Liberal social reform. The 1908 Budget, prepared by Asquith as Chancellor and introduced by him as Prime Minister, provided old-age pensions at 8s. per week for married couples.

The winter of 1908–9 found the Liberal Government at the nadir of its fortunes. The by-elections were still running strongly against it. The government's legislative programme had been mutilated by the Lords. Powerful interests had been alienated by its attempts at reform. A deepening trade recession gripped the country. Moreover, the party itself had been torn by a back-bench rebellion over naval expenditure which forced Tweedmouth to reduce the estimates by £400,000.[4]

These difficulties, though important, were part of a more fundamental weakness. In 1908, as in 1906, the Liberals had still to formulate a policy of social reform that would move the party away from nineteenth-century political Liberalism – the mixture of the freedom of the individual, the absolute necessity of free trade, an acceptance of capitalist economics and a somewhat vague and haphazard social empiricism – on which the party was still living. The Liberals had yet to find the policies to tackle the grave social problems in the country that had been highlighted by Charles Booth's study of London and Seebohm Rowntree's survey of York. It was against this background that the 'New Liberalism' was born. At the centre of this movement were a group of writers centred round the *Nation*, including J. L. Hammond, Henry Brailsford, L. T. Hobhouse, C. F. G. Masterman and J. A. Hobson. An articulate spokesman of the new creed was Winston Churchill, whose agile brain was already devising schemes for labour exchanges, wage boards, and a 'Committee of National Organisation' to counter fluctuations in unemployment. To this extent, Churchill was singling out for attack the issues which aroused the *Nation* group – casual labour, unemployment, undernourishment and poverty.

Within this new radicalism, Asquith was never really at home. As Hazlehurst has written: 'Although he continued the work of social reform begun under Campbell-Bannerman, Asquith's radicalism went little deeper than that of his predecessor. His speeches on the constitutional crisis in 1910 and 1911 were a revelatory reminder of his own

[4] For a detailed discussion on this theme, see A. J. Dorey, 'Radical Liberal Criticism of British Foreign Policy, 1906–1914', unpublished D.Phil. thesis (Oxford, 1964) pp. 120–2.

fundamental conservatism.'[5] Asquith, indeed, though assenting to the
new departures, gave them neither inspiration nor passion and
remained lukewarm about state intervention. Yet despite Asquith's
lack of zeal for social reform, the new Liberalism made rapid and
tremendous strides. By 1910 the Liberal Government had put on to the
statute book measures creating wage boards, labour exchanges, public
provision for the development of natural resources, old-age pensions,
new measures to control town planning and major policies to develop
smallholdings. Even such enthusiasts of the new Liberalism as J. A.
Hobson were impressed. To Hobson, the new legislation constituted
'an organic plan of social progress, which implies a new consciousness
of Liberal statecraft'.[6]

As if to crown these measures of social reform, there came the introduction of Lloyd George's 'People's Budget'. But there were some iron-
ical features of this measure. The Budget that Lloyd George claimed
was a 'War Budget' to wage implacable war against poverty and
squalidness was also to pay to construct the Dreadnoughts; the Budget
that was eventually to provoke the peers towards constitutional rebellion was introduced as virtually the only radical measure not likely to be
rejected by the Lords.

These things aside, the text of Lloyd George's speech on 29 April
1909 to the Commons saw his radicalism at its most perfect. He ended
his peroration by looking to 'that good time when poverty, wretched-
ness and the human degradation which always follows in its camp will
be as remote to the people of this country as the wolves which once
infested its forests'.

Faced with the need to raise an additional £16 million in revenue,
Lloyd George produced proposals which to his opponents seemed little
short of revolutionary. Income tax was raised from 1s. to 1s 2d. in the
pound, while for those with incomes over £5000 a supertax of 6d. in the
pound was introduced. The tobacco duty was increased by ½d. an
ounce, whisky duty was up 6d. a bottle (a measure that not unnaturally
was strongly opposed by the government's Irish Nationalist allies).
New taxes were introduced on cars and petrol, with the pledge that the
revenue raised was to be devoted to road-building. The proposals that
produced most political apoplexy, the land taxes, were strangely
enough to survive only a few years, and were abolished by Lloyd
George when Prime Minister.

The full realisation of the radical nature of the Budget dawned on the

[5] See C. Hazlehurst, 'Asquith as Prime Minister', *English Historical Review* (1972)
p. 513.
[6] J. A. Hobson, *The Crisis of Liberalism* (1909) p. xii. quoted in Hazlehurst, op. cit., p.
514.

Conservative benches only slowly. When it did, the parliamentary battle commenced: in all, 70 parliamentary days and no fewer than 554 divisions were needed to push the Budget through the Commons – Lloyd George himself voting in 462 of them, Asquith in only 202.

Outside Parliament, an equally vehement debate raged in the country – a debate memorable for Lloyd George's outspoken speech at Limehouse, a speech which actually provoked the King so far as to dispatch a letter of rebuke. In a less restrained manner, the Duke of Beaufort declared that he would like to see Lloyd George (and Winston Churchill for that matter) put in the middle of twenty couple of dog-hounds.

Despite the outcry of the peers, the tide of public opinion was flowing in support of the Budget by August 1909. The High Peak by-election (of July 1909) had been a comforting result for the Government. Meanwhile, the Budget Protest League was increasingly seen to be ineffective. At the same time, the issue was rapidly switching from the fiscal merits of the Budget proposals to the much more dangerous ground of whether the peers were entitled to reject a Finance Bill – an event that had not occurred for 250 years.

Before July, such a possibility was hardly mentioned; now the crisis of the Budget had become a crisis of the Constitution. Through the folly of his opponents Lloyd George saw his wish fulfilled: the implacable war against poverty had extended to war against that most obvious target of political reform, the Lords.

Speaking at Birmingham in September, Asquith had warned the peers, in the vein of a Victorian headmaster, of the perils of rejection. Only a bold man, declared Asquith, could forecast or foresee the consequences. Lloyd George was by now well aware of the obvious advantages of an outright rebellion by the peers. At Newcastle-upon-Tyne on 9 October Lloyd George waxed lyrical, asking of his audience 'who ordained that a few should have the land of Britain as a perquisite; who made 10,000 people owners of the soil, and the rest of us trespassers in the land of our birth?'

These were radical, challenging speeches. The Lords, in their anger, fell into the trap Lloyd George had prepared. At the beginning of November Asquith had warned the King that rejection of the Budget by the Lords was now probable. On 30 November his warning was fulfilled. The Finance Bill was rejected by the Lords by 350 votes to 75. Two days later, a resolution moved by Asquith was carried in the Commons declaring that the action of the House of Lords was a 'breach of the constitution and a usurpation of the rights of the Commons'. The following day Parliament was dissolved; the general election was fixed for polling to begin on 14 January 1910.

The election found the Liberals in confident mood. At last, the party had an issue on which to fight, and an issue on which public opinion seemed on the side of the government. The Liberals were entering the battle as a united party, but the Conservative ranks were still divided between the Tariff Reformers and the Tory Free Traders grouped as the 'Centre Party'.

The Liberal campaign also started well. Asquith's major opening speech was delivered at the Albert Hall on the 10 December. His most significant theme, apart from repeating the need of the Commons for absolute control over finance, the maintenance of Free Trade and the curtailment of the legislative powers of the House of Lords, was his declaration of future strategy. Asquith declared:

> I tell you quite plainly, and I tell my fellow countrymen outside, that neither I nor any other Liberal Minister supported by a majority of the House of Commons is going to submit again to the rebuffs and the humiliation of the last four years. We shall not assume office, and we shall not hold office, unless we can secure the safeguards which experience shows to be necessary for the legislative utility and honour of the party of progress.[7]

These were attacking words. Yet it was by no means certain that the electorate would follow Asquith's call. Indeed, the first results, showing 18 Conservative gains on the first day, suggested hope for the Opposition. It soon became clear, however, that whilst the Conservatives had recovered some lost ground, the Liberals, with Labour and Irish Nationalist support, would easily retain office.

The returns in January 1910, with the 1906 figures in parentheses, were as follows:

	MPs	Votes	%
Liberal	275 (377)	2,880,581	43·2
Unionist	273 (157)	3,127,887	46·9
Labour	40 (53)	505,657	7·6
Nationalist	82 (83)	124,586	1·9
Others	0 (0)	28,693	0·4
	670 (670)	6,667,404	100·0

Compared with the 1906 election, the Liberals had lost over 100 seats, with corresponding Conservative successes. At the same time, the Liberals recovered most of the by-election losses they had suffered (regaining Churchill's old constituency of Manchester North-West, and recapturing the Colne Valley seat lost in 1908 to Victor Grayson). Most

---

[7] Quoted in P. Rowland, *The Last Liberal Governments: The Promised Land, 1905–10* (1968) p. 243. This is a detailed and excellent account of this period.

of the Liberal losses were in the areas won in the landslide of 1906, particularly in the agricultural seats of the South Midlands, in the suburbs of London and in the usually Conservative strongholds of Surrey, Kent and Sussex.[8]

The Conservatives made no net gains either in Wales or Scotland, both areas returning to the pattern of 1885. Nor did Conservatives make many gains in the textile areas of East Lancashire or in West Yorkshire, whilst the North-East remained equally strongly Liberal.

Far more than the landslide victory of 1906, the results in January 1910 were a fair representation of the geographical areas of Liberal strength in the Edwardian period. Generally, the Liberals were weakest in the major cities, but strongest in rural Scotland and Wales and in the mining regions. The Liberals were weakest of all in the four largest cities, namely Glasgow, Birmingham, Liverpool and London. In January 1910, for example, the party won none of the seven seats in Birmingham and only one of the nine in Liverpool. The exceptions to this general rule were such cities as Edinburgh, Leeds, Bradford and Bristol. The Liberals were also weak where the middle-class suburban vote was strongest, most particular in Kent, Surrey and parts of Middlesex.

Although the mining constituencies constituted a solid base of Liberal support, there were indications as early as 1910 that this loyalty was to some extent being eroded by Labour. Labour were making definite headway in South Wales and West Yorkshire and to a lesser extent in the North-East, although the Liberals still remained entrenched in the Derbyshire–Nottinghamshire coalfield.

Liberal support in the rural areas varied from region to region. Wales was an impregnable stronghold; eastern Scotland was equally secure. Both East Anglia and the West Country had strong Liberal representation, while the party won most of the West Yorkshire seats. On the other hand, the Liberals never dislodged the Conservatives from their local strongholds around York, Exeter, the South Coast and parts of Kesteven.

Given the controversial measures of the 1906–10 government, the Liberals had cause to be pleased with the 1910 results. But the January 1910 election was, in fact, to be the prelude to a period of peculiar difficulty and grave crisis in Liberal history.

---

[8] For details of the January 1910 election, see M. Kinnear, *The British Voter: An Atlas and Survey since 1885* (1968). See also N. Blewett, *The Peers, The Parties and The People: The British General Elections of 1910* (1972).

5 The Crisis of Liberalism: 1910–1914

The election of January 1910 had returned Asquith to power. In this sense, it was a Liberal victory. But Asquith had won a battle, not a war. In the four years after 1910, the Liberals were to endure crisis after crisis, as the problems of Ireland, the suffragettes, industrial militancy, relations with the Labour Party, and above all the gathering world storm, loomed over a minority Liberal Government.

In January 1910, however, the most immediate problem lay in the conflict with the Lords. On this question, Liberal confidence had suffered a somewhat severe blow. For, prior to the January 1910 election, Asquith had given the impression that he had a guarantee from the King to create sufficient peers to pass the Budget into law. When it was revealed that no such assurance had been given, disappointment and frustration among Liberal supporters went very deep.

Both in the constituencies and in the back-benches, there was considerable disillusion. Many constituency associations were faced with the resignations of senior officials; back-benchers, so confident in the January campaign, found they had much explaining to do. At Westminster, Asquith seemed totally to have lost his nerve and there were rumours that, if the situation were not saved promptly, Churchill and Lloyd George might be tempted to resign and lead a party revolt.[1] By April, however, the government had recovered its nerve; the main lines of the Liberal attack had been drawn up. In mid-April, three resolutions were submitted to Parliament. These three resolutions proposed:

(i) That the Lords should no longer have the power to reject or amend a money Bill;

(ii) That Bills passed by the Commons in three successive sessions of Parliament should become law despite the opposition of the Lords; and

(iii) That the maximum length of Parliament should be reduced from seven years to five.

[1] See Hazlehurst, 'Asquith as Prime Minister', p. 523.

On 14 April a Parliament Bill containing these proposals duly received its first reading. Meanwhile the Budget passed the Commons on 27 April. The following day it passed the Lords without a division.

It was at this stage, with the Budget now passed and the wider constitutional battle about to begin, that the death of King Edward VII occurred on 6 May. This further complicated an already delicate position. The ensuing Constitutional Conference, an attempt to agree on a compromise solution and reduce the pressure on George V, eventually collapsed in failure in November.

However, at times it had come nearer to success than was then realised. Lloyd George, one of the four Liberal delegates at the Conference, had gone so far as to propose the establishment of a full party coalition to settle the major political issues. It would seem that this idea (not of course, known to the general public) was at first sympathetically received by several leading Conservatives and by such Liberals as Sir Edward Grey and Lord Crewe. However, the Conservatives rapidly abandoned the idea, The prospect of coalition, like the Conference itself, collapsed.

On the day the Conference finally collapsed (10 November 1910) Asquith asked the King for an immediate dissolution. The King refused to grant this request until the outcome of the House of Lords vote on the Parliament Bill was known. Since the Lords then promptly proceeded to adopt the Rosebery proposals in place of the government's recommendations, the dissolution of Parliament was only delayed until 28 November.

For the second time within a year the country was again faced with a general election. For the Liberal Party, the contest was a regrettable necessity. The main lines of the Liberal election campaign were laid down by Asquith in a speech at the National Liberal Club on 19 November. The Liberals would fight on the issue that the Lords had systematically thwarted the wishes of the House of Commons elected in 1906.

To a large degree, the election of December 1910 was a repeat performance. And as such, the argument and appeal had to some extent already been heard before. But the Liberals still possessed a major advantage: they were able to face the electorate as a united party. The Conservatives still remained with the millstone of Tariff Reform round their necks.

From the first results, it became clear that whilst the Conservatives were picking up the occasional seat, they would not gain the necessary 62 seats to ensure them a majority. Indeed, the final results showed little overall change from January.

	Total Votes	%	Seats
Unionist	2,426,625	46·4	274
Liberal	2,290,020	43·8	270
Labour	374,409	7·1	42
Nationalist	131,720	2·5	84
Others	11,509	0·2	·
	5,234,283	100·0	670

The small net turnover in seats in fact disguised considerable real changes. In two areas, the North-West and the extreme South-West, the Conservatives made substantial gains, whilst the Liberals improved their position in the agricultural constituencies of the South Midlands. Wales and Scotland remained the stoniest of soil for the Unionists. Only 3 of the 34 Welsh seats, and 9 of the 70 Scottish constituencies, returned Unionists or Liberal Unionists.

The Liberals also benefited to some extent, in such seats as Whitehaven and Cockermouth, by local arrangements with Labour.[2] In all however, though the trends of the December 1910 election indicated that a few parts of the country were moving away from the Liberals, the verdict of the electors was as clear as in January. The Liberal Government was to continue. But though Asquith was to continue in power, the election had not diminished the number of problems facing the party.

The immediate task for the government following the verdict of the December 1910 election was to settle the question of the House of Lords. The election itself had not solved the passage of the Parliament Bill. It still remained possible that it would be necessary to create a sufficiently large number of peers to overcome a recalcitrant House of Lords. In fact, George V had given a secret pledge prior to the December election to create the necessary peers if Asquith so requested him. The pledge was reluctant – but definite. In July 1911, when it seemed that the Conservative majority in the Lords would try to make serious amendments to the Bill, Asquith formally informed Balfour of the King's pledge. In the face of this threat, the Unionist leaders backed down. Landsdowne, the leader of the Unionist peers, advised his followers to abstain.

---

[2] Labour fielded only 56 candidates in December 1910, 22 fewer than in January. Labour returned 42 members, gaining five seats (Fife West, Bow and Bromley, Sunderland, Whitehaven and Woolwich) but losing three (St Helen's, Wigan and Newton), all in straight fights with Conservatives. As in January, the party's *independent* strength was conspicuously absent. The great bulk of the 42 members had been returned without Liberal opposition, some of these running in harness in double-member seats (with the Liberal almost invariably polling more votes than Labour).

The position was, however, gravely complicated by the revolt of the die-hard peers, headed by Lord Halsbury. The seriousness of the revolt lay in the fact that it was soon clear that the diehards would outnumber the Liberal peers, even with the Lansdowne moderates abstaining. Once again, the prospect of a mass creation of Liberal peers seemed very likely.

In the event, after delicate negotiations between Lord Crewe and Lord Cromer, the government narrowly won on 10 August 1911, with a majority of 17. The Liberals, aided by the votes of a variety of cross-bench peers together with 37 Conservative peers, had very narrowly scraped home. Eight days later the Parliament Bill received the royal assent.

The struggle with the Lords, though ending with a triumph for the Commons after a bitter struggle, did not end the conflict. Subsequent controversial Liberal legislation was to suffer under the terms of the Parliament Act. Two such measures concerned Welsh Church disestablishment and the abolition of plural voting. The Welsh Church Disestablishment Bill, introduced into the Commons in April 1912, was twice rejected by the Lords. In 1914, when the Bill again passed through the Commons, the Parliament Act was invoked. By this time, however, the outbreak of war led to the suspension of the operation of the Parliament Act. A very similar fate befell the Plural Voting Bill.[3]

Meanwhile, the most important Liberal legislative achievement of the 1910–14 period was the National Insurance Act of 1911, aimed at providing state insurance against both sickness and unemployment. Although the Bill provoked much outcry in the country, the Conservative opposition did not seriously question the principle of the legislation whilst the Lords let the Bill through without a debate.

The Government's Franchise Bill, introduced in June 1912 against a background of mounting suffragette militancy, met a less happy fate. Although the aims of the Bill were confined to universal male suffrage, the abolition of plural voting and the abolition of university constituencies, the Bill would have provided the opportunity to allow the Commons to extend the vote to women if it so wished. Three different amendments were proposed at committee stage to this end. These plans seriously miscarried when the Speaker (much to Asquith's annoyance) ruled these amendments out of order.

The Bill was then withdrawn and a Private Member's Bill introduced shortly afterwards. Whilst this would have enfranchised many women, it would not have given them equal franchise. This was lost by 292 votes to 245. It was opposed by Asquith, Churchill and Herbert Samuel and supported by Grey, Lloyd George and Walter Runciman.

[3] See Douglas, *History of the Liberal Party*, pp. 55–6.

These divisions (on a free vote) over women's suffrage were not the only evidence of a growing lack of unity in the parliamentary party. There was evidence of a growing disquiet over defence policy. In March 1911, 37 Liberal MPs voted for a reduction of military and naval expenditure. In July 1912, 23 voted against the Naval Supplementary Estimates and a further back-bench revolt occurred in March 1913. Although these radical critics of the government's foreign policy never constituted a serious threat to the government, even at the peak of their influence, they were evidence of the strains the party was later to face during the war.

An equally embarrassing issue for the government arose over the 'Marconi' affair, in which allegations were made that both Lloyd George and Sir Rufus Isaacs had derived a personal gain from certain government dealings with the British Marconi Company. These allegations were later modified so that the issue centred round whether the two Ministers should have disclosed certain private transactions to Parliament. The Marconi affair, itself very much a small storm in a large teacup, was of more interest in revealing the degree of party bitterness existing in 1912.

This party bitterness was itself a reflection of the climate in the country. The strikes of 1912, centred round the 'Triple Alliance' of railwaymen, miners and dockers, were evidence of the new dimensions of industrial militancy. The violence of the suffragettes and the militancy of the strikers seemed to contemporaries and historians alike to mark the beginning of the end of the old era of politics.

But overshadowing events in England lay the growing menace of civil war in Ulster. With the passing of the Parliament Act, a new element was introduced into the question of Ireland. No longer could the opposition rest assured that, whatever the Liberal Government might attempt, the Lords would inevitably veto it. By 1912 the opponents of Home Rule, faced with the prospect of Home Rule within the lifetime of a single Parliament, had become increasingly desperate. And at the head of the Conservative opposition was Andrew Bonar Law, himself a man with strong Ulster connections.

In 1912 the House of Commons saw the introduction of the Government of Ireland Bill, providing for an Irish Parliament which would legislate on most Irish affairs, but with overriding power vested in Westminster, in which a reduced contingent of Irish MPs would sit. The Bill passed the Commons; almost inevitably, it was then rejected by the Lords. The next session of the Commons again passed the Bill; once again the Lords duly rejected it. The Bill, now being prepared for submission to Parliament once again, would become law whatever action the Lords might take.

At this juncture, an attempted compromise was introduced. On 9 March 1914 Asquith proposed an amendment whereby Protestant Ulster could opt out of Home Rule for a six-year period, a proposal bitterly attacked by the opposition as a 'delay in execution'. This attempted compromise was followed shortly afterwards by the 'Curragh Mutiny'. This in turn led to the resignation of J. E. B. Seely, the Secretary for War, a position which Asquith himself took on.

Asquith continued attempts at compromise, including a Buckingham Palace conference with representatives from each party – a move which caused much anger among the Liberal rank-and-file who saw the government's prestige and authority visibly disintegrating. On 25 June 1914 the conference collapsed, confirming that events in Ulster were passing out of the control of the politicians. The growth of the Ulster Volunteers and, in the South, the National Volunteers was unmistakably clear evidence. The problem of Ireland, so near to explosion in July 1914, was itself to be engulfed in a wider and more devastating event. On 28 June the Archduke Franz Ferdinand was assassinated at Sarajevo; the approaching civil war in Ulster was overshadowed by a world becoming engulfed in war.

By the summer of 1914, the Liberal Party had entered a very different political climate from the *annus mirabilis* of 1906. The crises on the industrial front, suffragette militancy and deep Cabinet divisions had all shaken the party. Equally, the by-election record of the government, especially in such seats as Leith and Midlothian, was depressing in the extreme. And yet there were signs of hope. Liberal organisers, such as Herbert Gladstone, were optimistic that opposition to the Insurance Act was fading. Lloyd George and Percy Illingworth, the Chief Whip, received glowing reports of the reception of the Land Programme. That there were signs of decay at the grass-roots, and increasing divisions at the top, were undeniable. Yet it was far from certain that the Liberals would not be able to fight back in time for the next general election, most particularly as the Conservatives remained deeply divided, both over Tariff Reform and the party's leadership.

There was, however, a fundamental problem facing the Liberals which would not disappear – the question of the party's relations with Labour. Whether, as Trevor Wilson has written, this was the most menacing problem facing the Liberal Party before 1914 is at least debatable.[4] But that the problem was there is undeniable. And it was an issue which deeply divided the party. On the one side were the Radicals who favoured co-operation with Labour. They had firmly supported Herbert Gladstone's policy of accommodation in the years

---

[4] T. Wilson, *The Downfall of the Liberal Party* (1966) pp. 16–17.

before 1906, and welcomed the new Labour representatives in Parliament as the allies of a vigorous Liberalism. At the opposite extreme was the right of the party, the industrialists and businessmen, who wanted no dealings with Socialism at any level.

The 1910 election had demonstrated the fact that the Liberal Party was not prepared to make concessions for any further Labour expansion beyond the mark already established in the 1906 election. Most of the by-election clashes in the period from 1911 to 1914 were fought in this context. Between the general election of December 1910, and the outbreak of war in 1914, Liberals suffered a depressing series of by-election reverses. As the table indicates, no fewer than 15 Liberal-held seats were lost to the Conservatives. At the same time Labour lost four seats, two to the Liberals (Hanley, 13 July 1912; Chesterfield, 20 August 1913) and two to the Conservatives (Bow and Bromley, 26 November 1912; North-East Derbyshire, 20 May 1914).

Date of by-election		Constituency	From	To
28 Apr.	1911	Cheltenham	Lib.	Con.
13 Nov.	1911	Oldham	Lib.	Con.
21 Nov.	1911	S. Somerset	Lib.	Con.
20 Dec.	1911	N. Ayrshire	Lib.	Con.
5 Mar.	1912	Manchester S	Lib.	Con.
13 July	1912	Hanley	Lab.	Lib.
26 July	1912	Crewe	Lib.	Con.
8 Aug.	1912	Manchester NW	Lib.	Con.
10 Sept.	1912	Midlothian	Lib.	Con.
26 Nov.	1912	Bow & Bromley	Lab.	Con.
30 Jan.	1913	Londonderry	Con.	Lib.
18 Mar.	1913	S. Westmorland	Con.	Ind. Con.
16 May	1913	Newmarket	Lib.	Con.
20 Aug.	1913	Chesterfield	Lab.	Lib.
8 Nov.	1913	Reading	Lib.	Con.
12 Dec.	1913	S. Lanarkshire	Lib.	Con.
19 Feb.	1914	Bethnal Green SW	Lib.	Con.
26 Feb.	1914	Leith	Lib.	Con.
20 May	1914	NE Derbyshire	Lab.	Con.
23 May	1914	Ipswich	Lib.	Con.

Although such Liberal seats as Cheltenham, North Ayrshire, South Somerset and Newmarket were lost in straight fights with Conservatives, and although these straight fights showed a fairly consistent swing away from the Liberals, much the most serious feature was the effect of the intervention of Labour candidates at other by-elections. In no fewer than 11 formerly safe Liberal seats, Labour candidates intervened in by-elections, causing five seats to fall to the Conservatives. These Liberal losses as a result of Labour's intervention comprised Oldham (13 November 1911), Crewe (26 July 1912), Midlothian (10 September 1912), South Lanarkshire (12 December 1913) and Leith (26

February 1914). Not only had the Liberal vote in these seats collapsed but, even more alarmingly, the Conservative vote had held steady or even increased.

Though bitterly frustrating to Liberals, these Labour candidates had hardly provided convincing evidence of Labour's popularity. All had come bottom of the poll; none had obtained over 30 per cent of the votes cast. Nor had Labour fought any rural or residential seats; its candidates had come forward only in such areas as Durham, industrial Scotland or industrial towns such as Crewe, Oldham and Keighley. Yet this is not to deny that in some areas Labour's advance was both definite and impressive.

Of these parliamentary by-elections, the position has been admirably summarised by McKibbin:

> In all these constituencies the Labour vote had increased compared with the last contest. In Holmfirth it was much more than doubled; in Crewe it was nearly doubled. In N.E. Lanarkshire and Leith the Labour vote rose absolutely in reduced total polls. In Keighley it was static. Plainly Labour was not doing worse than in 1910, let alone faring abysmally.[5]

Though Labour had not gained a seat, its advance in industrial areas seemed to many contemporary observers one of the most noticeable features of these by-elections. These contests, however, were important in a different way, for Labour's intervention had raised the whole question of Liberal–Labour relations. If Labour intervention in such seats as Leith or Midlothian had embittered the Liberals, equal anger had been caused by Liberal intervention in three particular contests: Hanley in July 1912; Chesterfield in August 1913; and North-East Derbyshire in May 1914. These three by-elections highlighted the problems of Liberal–Labour relations. The Hanley contest was particularly significant for it threatened, more than any contest since 1906, the whole working of the Lib–Lab entente.

In the summer of 1912 Enoch Edwards, the 'Lib–Lab' miners' leader and M.P. for Hanley, died. Despite having signed the Labour Party Constitution in 1909, Edwards had continued to work with the local Liberals; the miners' money continued to be placed, as of old, at the disposal of the Liberals.[6] From the start, both sides claimed the seat as their own. And both adopted candidates. As the campaign developed, the relations between the two parties became even more bitter. In the event, the Liberals retained the seat, Labour came second and the Conservatives third.

[5] R. McKibbin, *The Evolution of the Labour Party* (Oxford, 1975) p. 84.
[6] R. Gregory, *The Miners in British Politics, 1906–14* (Oxford, 1968) p. 171.

The Hanley by-election was followed a year later by a by-election in Chesterfield caused by the death of James Haslam in July 1913. Haslam had in fact announced his retirement in April, with the result that the local Labour Party set about finding a successor. Barnet Kenyon, the Assistant Secretary of the Derbyshire Miners' Association, seemed the most likely choice. The real problem here arose over Kenyon's close links with the Liberals. Kenyon had attempted to find a position acceptable to both sides, by assuring Labour men that he would support the Labour Party and by letting the Liberals know that he remained essentially a Liberal. This stance was not acceptable to Labour. On 12 August the National Executive of the Labour Party refused to endorse his candidature; the Miners' Federation of Great Britain retracted its support.

Kenyon's subsequent campaign, using a Liberal agent and the Liberal organisation, proved embarrassing. Whilst many miners' MPs spoke during his campaign, MacDonald denounced as 'ridiculously absurd' the idea that he should give platform assistance. Although Kenyon won at Chesterfield, the incident had demonstrated again that the miners' links with political Liberalism were becoming more and more tenuous. And no sooner had the rancour at Chesterfield died away, than a by-election in North-East Derbyshire raised the whole problem again.[7] The significance of these by-elections was not lost on progressives: as the *Nation* warned, on 23 May 1914, the real fight in the constituencies was coming to be more and more a contest between Liberalism and Labour. Even in areas of the country where Liberal–Labour relations had previously been warm, a new hostility was arising.

Other by-elections revealed the same situation. Thus, the Holmfirth by-election of June 1912 had led to the final severing of the once-close links between the Yorkshire Miners' Association and the Liberal Party.[8] A similar conflict between Liberal and Labour occurred in the summer of 1912 when the Master of Elibank's elevation to the English peerage occasioned a by-election in the strongly Liberal citadel of Midlothian.[9]

Not surprisingly, by the spring of 1914 the problem of Liberal–Labour relations had reached serious dimensions. Speaking at Ladybank on 4 April 1914, Asquith bemoaned the fact that virtually every by-election lost during the previous two years was the result of three-cornered contests. This was a theme taken up two months later by Lloyd George, in the wake of C. F. G. Masterman's defeat in the

[7] For the North-East Derbyshire contest, see Douglas, *History of the Liberal Party*, pp. 80–2.

[8] Gregory, *The Miners in British Politics*, p. 117.

[9] For Midlothian, see Douglas, *History of the Liberal Party*, p. 83.

Ipswich by-election where once again the progressive vote had been split.

The problem of Liberal–Labour relations, highlighted in this rather dismal Liberal by-election performance, was repeated in the municipal elections of this period. After the sweeping municipal successes of the years up to 1905, the period after 1906 saw the Liberals not merely on the defensive, but suffering some severe reverses. Thus in 1908 Liberals suffered heavy losses throughout Lancashire as well as losing control of a variety of provincial boroughs, including Sheffield, Nottingham and Leicester. These were serious defections, for Leicester had been in Radical control since 1835, Nottingham for forty years. They were joined by others: in 1909 Coventry fell to the Conservatives for the first time in twenty years. In 1911 Burnley was won by the Conservatives for the first time in its history, whilst in 1912 Liberals lost control of Bradford.

At the same time that these former Radical citadels were falling to Conservative control, Labour appeared to be increasing its council base each year. The party registered net gains in each year up to the outbreak of war. Certainly, by 1914 Liberal strength in the major provincial boroughs had been considerably eroded. In such towns as Liverpool or Birmingham, Liberalism was already a much depleted force. In London, the Progressives (the name the Liberals used to contest local elections) were in marked decline. In some of the working-class wards in such towns as Leeds and Bradford, Liberals were already beginning to form anti-Labour alliances with the Conservatives.

The evidence of both the by-elections and the municipal elections shows clearly that the Liberals were in electoral difficulties prior to 1914. Yet, as we have seen, many of their senior organisers remained confident of the prospects for the next general election. The Land Programme, in particular, was seen as a potential vote-catcher.

If the Liberals were in difficulties prior to 1914, neither MacDonald nor the Labour Party was facing the future with any great confidence. Certainly, MacDonald was only too aware in 1913 of Labour's electoral weakness. As McKibbin has written, MacDonald was very probably keen to maintain the electoral alliance with the Liberals and was under no illusions of Labour's weakness in the country.[10] Nor was MacDonald alone in his pessimism – or political realism. Philip Snowden was realist enough to calculate that Labour could win only 'half a dozen' seats on its own account.[11] The events of Sarajevo meant that Labour's resolve was never put to the test. To that extent, the Liberal

[10] McKibbin, *Evolution of the Labour Party*, p. 80.
[11] Philip Snowden, *An Autobiography*, (1932) pp. 217–18.

fate in the general election of 1915 will never be known.

But of the debate on the downfall of Liberalism a few points can be said. In 1914 the Liberal Party was certainly not dead, nor indeed dying, despite the arguments propounded by George Dangerfield, who saw in the political and industrial crisis prior to 1914 symptoms of the oncoming 'Strange Death of Liberal England'.[12] As McKibbin has aptly stated, in a short but impeccably devastating phrase, Dangerfield's work is a literary confection which does not attempt serious analysis.[13]

In short, a breakdown of the Gladstone–MacDonald pact for 1915 would have meant probable major reverses for the Liberals and the possible total elimination of independent Labour representation. For the evidence of 1910–14 is conclusive on one point: Liberals and Labour had either to hang together or they would hang separately. In the event, however, the most direct threat to the Liberals once war was declared came not from the external threat of Labour, but from internal factors. For the First World War was to put to the ultimate test not only the conscience of Liberalism but also the leadership of Asquith.

---

[12] George Dangerfield, *The Strange Death of Liberal England, 1910–14* (New York, 1961).

[13] McKibbin, *Evolution of the Labour Party*, p. 236. For a critique of Dangerfield, see also H. Pelling, *Popular Politics and Society in late Victorian England* (1968) pp. 102–3.

6 Liberals at War: 1914–1918

The coming of war in August 1914 transformed the political climate in the country. Indeed, the decision to go to war produced severe strains in the Liberal Cabinet. On 2 August the Cabinet decided that any substantial violation of Belgian neutrality would compel the British Government to take action. The same day, Germany issued her ultimatum to Belgium, demanding passage for her troops into France.

On 3 August the British Cabinet took its fateful decision to enter the war. The decision was not unanimous. Morley, John Burns, Sir John Simon and Lord Beauchamp were all reported to have offered their resignations. In the event, Asquith was able to win over Simon and Beauchamp. Only Morley and Burns resigned from the Cabinet. Among the junior Ministers, they were joined by C. P. Trevelyan.

These resignations were symptoms of a deeper concern within the Liberal ranks in Parliament. Only after Sir Edward Grey's speech to the Commons on 3 August did the majority of the party acquiesce reluctantly in the decision taken by their leaders in the Cabinet. Only one Liberal voice was raised in support of the war in that debate, whilst there was a group of some thirty 'pacifists', mainly left-wing Radicals, who bitterly attacked Grey in the debate and remained critical opponents of the government throughout the war.

The coming of war affected the parties in varying degrees. Whilst both Conservatives and Irish Nationalists pledged full support for the war, the Labour ranks were split, with Ramsay MacDonald (chairman of the Parliamentary Labour Party) heading the pacifist opposition. It was within the Liberal Party, however, that the dilemma was greatest. By tradition, the Liberals contained a strong and powerful Nonconformist and pacifist wing that might be expected to create problems. Again – and much more fundamental – the Liberals' philosophy was likely, even where it could support war, to stop short of the methods of waging total war. On such issues as conscription the Liberal conscience was likely to be put on the rack. This is not to say that the Liberal Party could not have successfully fought a war, but it would have been a war waged with aversion. As it was, the very totality of the First World War had a profound and disastrous impact on the party. For whatever reasons, the Liberal Party was never again to be the same after 1914 as it had been before.

In August 1914, however, this dark future still lay mercifully hidden.
The most immediate impact of the war was the electoral truce between
the parties and the run-down in Liberal organisation. The party's most
able administrators moved to other causes. Thus Sir Robert Hudson
was to become chairman of the Joint War Finance Committee and Sir
Jesse Herbert devoted much energy to the Parliamentary Recruiting
Committee. Far more significant, in the longer term, was the suspension at constituency level of even a skeleton organisation.

Although the Liberals entered the war relatively united, the first
months of war soon proved an unhappy time. This was particularly so
for the intellectuals within the party. As Joseph Henry of Leeds wrote
to Herbert Gladstone, the 'war lords' were vermin, the war itself was a
dreadful thing, but the whole thing had to be seen through.[1] Before
very long, it became apparent that the Liberals would indeed find that
the war was to test their conscience on a variety of issues. The Liberals
had soon to fight to preserve a whole gamut of established and
cherished ideals: 'Free Trade'; individual freedom of conscience; freedom of the press; the voluntary principle of recruitment. For the party
faithful, these were the very constituents of their political philosophy,
and many Liberals were determined that these must not be violated,
even in the cause of national victory.

At the opposite extreme was the hawkish group of Liberals, men
such as Henry Cowan, Sir Henry Dalziel and F. G. Kellaway, who
formed a 'ginger group' for a more vigorous prosecution of the war.
During late 1914 and early 1915, as general dissatisfaction with the war
developed, these men led the growing right-wing criticism of the government over such issues as lax treatment of enemy aliens, inefficiency
in government contracting for war supplies and the need for a Ministry
of Munitions. These divisions and doubts within the party were important and significant.

But they were less important than the cardinal result of entry into
war: namely, that the fortunes of British Liberalism were to be placed
for the duration of the conflict in the hands of the Conservative Party.

These wider implications of the war, however, were not the thoughts
uppermost in the minds of politicians as the first year of the war ended.
The most significant development was the rise of public disquiet and
discontent at the conduct of the war. The generals, the politicians and
the press were at loggerheads, the people bitterly frustrated with the
bloody stalemate on the Western Front following the Battle of the
Aisne. Meanwhile, the government suffered a heavy personal blow with

[1] Henry to Gladstone, 5 Sept. 1914, Gladstone MSS, BM Add. MSS 46,038, f.99.,
quoted in Hazlehurst, 'Asquith as Prime Minister', op. cit.

the death of Percy Illingworth, the highly respected Chief Whip, of whom all sections of the party approved.

This discontent with the progress of the war was to have vital and far-reaching consequences. Whilst there had been no demand at the beginning of the war for a Coalition, as 1915 progressed, calls to change to a Coalition intensified. It became increasingly clear that, without a more broadly-based government there would be damaging public controversies in Parliament and a lack of confidence in the country. The resignation of Lord Fisher, the First Sea Lord, at the same time as a parliamentary storm gathered over the alleged shell shortage, made it impossible for the Conservative leaders to keep their followers in check. Open attacks on the government, and especially the running of the Admiralty, developed. With reluctance, Asquith agreed with Bonar Law and Lloyd George that a Coalition was imperative, however much they disliked the prospect. On the evening of 17 May 1915, Asquith wrote to Lord Stamfordham, the King's private secretary: 'After much reflection and consultation today with Lloyd George and Bonar Law, I have come decidedly to the conclusion that, for the successful prosecution of the war, the Government must be reconstructed on a broad and non-party basis.'[2] Two days later, on 19 May, Bonar Law formally signified his agreement. The last Liberal Government had ended.

In the political circumstances of May 1915, a more broadly based Coalition was probably inevitable. Yet the secrecy with which it was born caused both anger and dismay among Liberals. Asquith, very typically, took the onus of the decision on reconstruction himself. Crewe, for example, later complained that 'with no preliminary discussion with one of us, even the most intimate and influential . . . he decided on reconstruction'.

Whatever the secrecy surrounding the birth, the new infant was not welcomed by Liberals. The Coalition appeared to be a disguised concession to Toryism. Back in 1914, Simon had felt that a Coalition would be 'the grave of Liberalism'[3] Provincial Liberal sentiment, voiced by such spokesmen as Joseph Henry, warned of the dangers of embracing the tainted Conservative Party. Not all, perhaps, echoed Margot Asquith's degree of bitterness (she referred to 'this d—d Coalition which I loathe') but there was considerable disquiet as to the future.

Despite much Liberal resistance to the formation of a Coalition, it was overborne by Asquith. Both Conservatives and Labour joined the new government, although there was no Irish representation. The fil-

---

[2] Asquith Papers, Box XXVII. ff. 162–3, quoted in Roy Jenkins, *Asquith* (1964) p. 360.
[3] C. Addison, *Four and a Half Years* (1934) I, p. 35.

ling of the new Cabinet posts was a matter of some delicacy. Both Churchill and Haldane had to be sacrificed to placate Bonar Law. Lloyd George agreed to move to the Ministry of Munitions, a newly-created office. On Liberal insistence that a member of their ranks should be Chancellor, Reginald McKenna was allocated the office. Eight Conservatives joined the Cabinet, with Bonar Law as Colonial Secretary. Arthur Henderson, the sole Labour member of the new Cabinet (and the first member of the party to hold Cabinet office) became President of the Board of Education.

The formation of the Coalition in May 1915 was only the first of a series of tribulations that was sorely to try Liberal sentiment. For as 1915 progressed, the issue of compulsory service (which had seemed remote in January 1915) assumed more and more attention. By the summer, alarm in the Liberal ranks was widespread. At the end of May, one Liberal went so far as to warn Lloyd George that such a step would break up both the Liberal and Labour Parties and wreck progress for a generation.[4]

In fact, the whole conscription crisis was a perfect example of a virtually hidebound Liberal Party forced to follow the Conservative lead. To begin with, Conservative pressure for conscription was largely channelled into spurring on the efforts of Lloyd George at the Ministry of Munitions – the Ministry in closest touch with the recruitment problem. But by August, as Lord Curzon, the Conservative Lord Privy Seal, wrote to Lloyd George, it was apparent that the Cabinet could not continue to evade the subject.

But before the conscription crisis came to a head, another issue had arisen which bitterly divided Liberals. This was the McKenna Budget of September 1915. Its proposal for a 33⅓ per cent *ad valorem* tariff on a wide-ranging variety of luxury goods, roused the wrath of Free Trade Liberal back-benchers. Although McKenna was able to defeat a substantial Liberal revolt, some thirty Liberal and Labour back-benchers opposed the government. It was an ominous sign of the storms about to break over conscription. As the autumn of 1915 progressed, the foremost Liberal advocates of the compulsory conscription campaign were such back-bench figures as F. E. Guest, Sir Alfred Mond and Ellis Griffith. Lloyd George and Churchill were the two Liberals in the Cabinet most in favour. But the Cabinet, however, was itself deeply divided. Asquith was personally opposed to compulsion, but was prepared, so Lloyd George informed C. P. Scott, editor of the *Manchester Guardian*, to accept it as a last resort to maintain his position. Those lining up against conscription included such leading figures as Sir John

[4] E. R. Cross to Lloyd George, 30 May 1915, Lloyd George Papers, D/20/1/6.

Simon, the Home Secretary (who resigned over the issue), McKenna at the Exchequer and Walter Runciman at the Board of Trade. Their opposition centred not merely on their attachment to individualism but because they believed the economy could not take the strain.

The failure of Lord Derby's scheme of voluntary enlistment finally decided the issue in favour of compulsion. At the beginning of January 1916 the Conscription Bill was introduced to the Commons. Within the Cabinet, Sir John Simon had already resigned as Home Secretary. Only strong persuasion from Asquith halted other departures from the Cabinet. McKenna, Birrell, Walter Runciman and even Sir Edward Grey were all reluctant to accept conscription.

If Asquith contained the rebellion in the Cabinet, he was less successful with the Liberal back-benchers in the Commons. 35 Liberals, 13 Labour members and 59 Irish Nationalists voted against the government. The debate in the Commons fully revealed the bitterness felt within the Liberal ranks. Simon, in his resignation speech, attacked the government for imitating one of the most hateful institutions of Prussian militarism, whilst Liberal back-benchers argued that it was a violation of England's tradition of liberty.

The significance of the conscription issue cannot be underestimated. It had tested the conscience of the party severely. It had nearly brought about the disintegration of the government. Even after the crisis of December 1915 had passed, Asquith still seriously feared a split in the Cabinet. And it had confirmed deep divisions at the highest level in the Cabinet.

The conscription issue was important for another reason. It demonstrated that, by the beginning of 1916, two very distinct camps were emerging within the Parliamentary Liberal Party: there were the doves, unhappy about the Coalition from the beginning, but now also increasingly unhappy about the many fundamental Liberal beliefs that were being attacked and eroded. To these, conscription was the negation of all they believed in. At the opposite extreme were those Liberals, increasingly a clearly defined group, to whom the winning of the war exceeded all else. To these, old shibboleths might have to be abandoned in the new covenant of total war.

Already, this split was a portent of things to come. As Hankey succinctly observed in his diary, the people who wanted compulsory service did not want Asquith, whilst the supporters of Asquith did not want conscription. Here was the genesis of the great Asquith–Lloyd George split of December 1916. Meanwhile, during 1916, the advocates of a more rigorous prosecution of the war gained ground steadily. This movement was to some extent mirrored in the formation of the Liberal War Committee in January 1916. This growing cleavage in the Liberal

ranks was further widened by the events of the Easter Week rising in
Dublin, which was to produce the resignation of Augustine Birrell as
Chief Secretary for Ireland and the politically disastrous executions in
Dublin. These events persuaded Asquith to pay a personal visit. On his
return, Lloyd George was given the delicate task of negotiating a solution.[5] Meanwhile, the divisions within the Liberal ranks were exposed
once again in May 1916 when the government proposed to extend
conscription to married men. Another back-bench revolt ensued, with
28 Liberals voting against the second reading. These divisions over
conscription were themselves forced into the background when another
crisis faced the government. On 5 June 1916 Lord Kitchener, the Secretary of State for War, was drowned when the *Hampshire* struck a mine
shortly after leaving for Russia.

Asquith had clearly to offer the vacant War Office to Lloyd George,
once an attempt had failed to persuade Bonar Law to accept the office.
Yet Lloyd George (whose acceptance Asquith *had* to secure) was naturally reluctant to accept an office under the conditions which had so
limited his predecessor. In this battle for power, Lloyd George was the
clear victor. On 6 July Lloyd George finally accepted the post of Secretary of State for War virtually on his own terms. Asquith's position
was becoming more and more untenable.

It was against this background that the great split of December 1916
between Asquith and Lloyd George must be seen. However, the crash
of 5 December 1916 did not come without some warning. Long before
Asquith resigned, powerful pressures had been building up within the
Asquith–Unionist Coalition for a reconstruction of the government.

The two issues most affecting the stability of the government concerned, firstly, the relations of the Unionist back-benchers with their
party leaders in the Cabinet and, secondly, Lloyd George's relations
with the generals. This latter issue had become acute since July 1916,
when Lloyd George had gone to the War Office and subsequently been
locked in conflict with General Sir William Robertson.

In November 1916 the famous Nigeria debate clearly exposed the
marked dissatisfaction of many Unionist MPs not only with Bonar
Law but with the Coalition generally. The outcome was to spur
Unionist Ministers into pressing more vigorously their demands for a
reconstruction of the Government. The climax of the growing opposition to Asquith was not long delayed. Asquith resigned as Prime Minister on the evening of 5 December, the day after the critical leading

---

[5] Lloyd George's proposal, though gaining the support of John Redmond and also of
leading Ulster Unionists, soon foundered on the opposition of Lansdowne and Walter
Long. On this issue, the Conservatives in the Cabinet were totally split.

article in *The Times* and the same day that Bonar Law informed him that he was unwilling to continue in the government unless the War Committee proposal, as agreed earlier, was adopted. Since Asquith knew that other Conservatives would not serve in an administration without Lloyd George or Bonar Law, the King asked Bonar Law to form a government.

The following day, 6 December, was a crucial time. Amid numerous political discussions on this day, the Liberal members of the old Cabinet (without, of course, Lloyd George) agreed that Asquith should not accept a subordinate position under Bonar Law. Consequently, Bonar Law abandoned his attempt to form a government, and Lloyd George was asked to form one. On 7 December, Lloyd George became Prime Minister.

The destruction of the last Liberal Government, leading as it did to the fatal split in the party, rapidly produced a wealth of historical mythology, most notably in the conspiracy theory which lay most of the blame at Lloyd George's hands. Recent historians have changed the parameters of the debate. A. J. P. Taylor has argued that, rather than being manoeuvred out of office, Asquith deliberately resigned office as a manoeuvre to rout his critics.[6] A more recent view has been put forward by Hazlehurst, who has argued that, essentially, the destruction of the last Liberal Government and the fall of Asquith was the outcome, not of the machinations of Lloyd George, but of a Tory Party crisis. In their desire to prosecute the war more efficiently, the aims of the Conservatives coincided with those of Lloyd George. This did not mean that Lloyd George necessarily went over to the Tories, nor indeed that he intrigued with them to *oust* Asquith, but that Lloyd George, in company with Bonar Law and Sir Edward Carson, worked together to persuade Asquith to change the political direction of the war. As Dr Hazlehurst rightly argues, neither of the two prime movers, Bonar Law or Lloyd George, had any desire to remove Asquith from the Premiership. Indeed, the replacement of Asquith was not considered as a practical proposition by those later accused of conspiracy.

Why, then, did the crisis of December 1916 end with the resignation of Asquith and Lloyd George's assumption of the Premiership? It is now clear that this was the result of something akin to a nervous breakdown on Asquith's part after the compromise agreement of 3 December. By this compromise, it was agreed that Lloyd George should head a small three- or four-man War Commission under the

---

[6] For a fuller discussion of the crisis, see Lord Beaverbrook, *Politicians and the War, 1914–16*, pp. 287–534. See also C. Hazlehurst, 'The Conspiracy Myth', in Martin Gilbert (ed.), *Lloyd George* (Englewood Cliffs. NJ., 1968).

supreme, though not immediate, control of Asquith, to whom all disputed decisions would be referred. This compromise in fact marked a very wide area of agreement. Henceforth, Lloyd George would have borne daily responsibility for the conduct of the war, without the supreme authority to force through decisions.

There was no need, following this agreement, for anything that called for Asquith to resign. However, it was Asquith himself who, in a brief moment of mental and emotional exhaustion, lost the will to go on ruling. A combination of a deterioration in Asquith's relations with Lloyd George, at a moment of great nervous strain, propelled the Premier into a temporary capitulation. By the time Asquith had recovered his balance, it was too late.[7]

Lloyd George's first task as Prime Minister was the construction of a Cabinet. At least in terms of those Liberals to be included, it was a difficult task. Asquith had made it clear he would not serve under him. Other Liberals followed Asquith's lead. Although Christopher Addison agreed to serve as Minister of Munitions, no senior Liberals joined the new administration, whilst Churchill, who was keen to serve, was kept out by Conservative opposition.[8] The key posts in the new Coalition were thus filled by Conservatives. Lloyd George had thus become Prime Minister on 7 December 1916 in the most difficult circumstances. Equally as serious were the problems now facing the divided Liberal Party. As Trevor Wilson has written: 'During the last two years of the war, the difficulties facing the Liberal party moved to a climax. Threatened by disruption within and attack on two fronts from without, the party wilted visibly before the dangers encompassing it.'[9]

In these last years of war, the Asquithian Liberals' policy towards the conflict seemed to be less positive or coherent than ever before. The party was divided over Lloyd George's struggle with the generals and equally split over Lansdowne's plea for a negotiated peace. Not only on issues of policy, however, were the Asquithian ranks divided: their position vis-à-vis the new Lloyd George Coalition was hopelessly unclear. Since they had not joined the government, they clearly did not fully support the new administration. Yet did this mean they were its outright opponents? Or, expressed differently, was there still a single Liberal Party, or had it split into two separate and hostile wings?

In a sense, after December 1916, the party had already split. One group of Liberals sat on the government benches, another on the opposition front bench. There were also two sets of Whips: one serving Lloyd George, the other Asquith. Yet the lines of division were still blurred.

[7] Hazlehurst, ibid.
[8] Churchill was eventually brought back in July 1917 – as Minister of Munitions.
[9] Wilson, *Downfall of the Liberal Party*, p. 104.

The respective Whips still canvassed *all* Liberals, not distinct groups of Liberals, whilst in the *Liberal Magazine* Asquith announced that, far from being an opposition leader, he would offer the government 'organised support'.[10] However, though these official platitudes tried to conceal the bitterness which the events of December had created, the divisions in the party grew more obvious. In the Derby by-election, following the resignation of Sir Thomas Roe on 21 December 1916, Asquithian resentment at the choice of Joseph Davies, a leading Lloyd Georgeite, led to the personal intervention of Geoffrey Howard, the Liberal Whip, to secure a different candidate.

In Parliament, however, the bitterness of the two ranks was muted by Asquith's refusal to oppose the government and his adoption of a nebulous policy of 'general support from the outside'. Such a policy, however idealistic it might appear, left the mass of Asquithian back-benchers politically impotent.

With Asquith providing no leadership, the parliamentary debates assumed a somewhat unreal appearance. Such back-bench Liberals as J. M. Hogge, William Pringle and Leif Jones would bitterly denounce the Lloyd George Government. But the opposition front bench would be deserted and silent.[11]

However, as 1917 progressed, a series of divisions in the Commons showed that the ranks of the respective Lloyd George and Asquithian supporters were becoming more clearly defined. One such division occurred in March 1917, when the government altered the established duties on Indian cotton goods, an action regarded by many Liberals as a move to a protectionist tariff. Despite Asquith's failure to give any lead, 46 Liberals opposed the government and 59 followed the Coalition whip. The Liberal divisions were hardening. As Haldane wrote to his sister, the Liberal Party was already 'much disintegrated'.[12]

A further split in the Liberal ranks occurred later in 1917 in divisions over the Representation of the People Bill. Many of the more extreme Coalitionists sought to retain the system of plural voting in borough constituencies and to disfranchise conscientious objectors. Both proposals offended Liberal tradition, with the result that Herbert Samuel, who led the opposition, was able to take 106 Liberals into the opposition lobby. A later debate on the disfranchisement of conscientious objectors (on 21 November) was carried on a free vote only by 209

---

[10] *Liberal Magazine* (1917) quoted in Wilson, ibid., p. 106.

[11] For details of these debates, see E. David, 'The Liberal Party Divided', in *English Historical Review* (1972).

[12] R. B. Haldane to E. S. Haldane, 2 Mar. 1917, quoted in Wilson, *Downfall of the Liberal Party*, p. 104.

votes to 171. This debate again demonstrated how a hard-core of unre-
lenting 'war to the finish' Coalitionists was developing. Their ranks
included Ellis Griffith, Frederick Crawley, Sir John Cory, F. G. Kellaway, Sir Alfred Mond and Sir Courtney Warner.

By mid-1917, Liberal back-benchers were up in arms against the
Lloyd George Coalition. Yet the reticence of Asquith and the Liberal
front bench to oppose Lloyd George was a constant irritant. It was
hardly surprising that frustrated Liberal MPs were becoming more
exasperated with Asquith and his colleagues for their apathy than with
Lloyd George, despite the error of his ways. Indeed, Asquith's apathy
led him to fail even to oppose the Irish conscription measure in April
1918. The extent of his protest was merely to head a mass abstention by
the Liberal Party on the second reading of the Military Service Bill.[13]

The significance of these bitter debates, as far as the Liberal Party
was concerned, lay in the crystallisation of the supporters and opponents of the Government. The line of demarcation was steadily becoming clearer. The respective supporters of Asquith and Lloyd George fell
rather distinctly into two camps. Lloyd George's support among the
back-benchers had owed much to the unstinted work of Christopher
Addison and David Davies during the summer and autumn of 1916.
On the evening that Lloyd George was commissioned by the King to
form a government, Addison made his famous statement that there
were 49 out-and-out supporters of Lloyd George and a further 125 who
would support him if he could form a government. After December
1916, a definite Lloyd George group of Liberals grew up. In the main,
Lloyd George drew his support from those Liberals who were willing to
sacrifice everything in order to win the war. It was no coincidence that
30 of the 40 Liberals who served on the Liberal War Committee followed Lloyd George. If analysed by class and wealth, by and large
these Lloyd George supporters were self-made Radical Nonconformists, men in wool or engineering who were also doing well out of the
war. Asquith, on the other hand, can almost be said to have taken with
him the Liberal conscience.

The divisions over the Military Service Bill had confirmed these
main divisions between the followers of Asquith and Lloyd George. On
9 May 1918, a further important event took place, the now famous
Maurice debate. The significance of the Maurice debate was not that it
was an isolated example of Liberals dividing against the Government –
for it most certainly was not – but rather that it was the only occasion
on which Asquith gave the division his official blessing.

[13] The Military Service Bill became law on 18 April 1918. However, the Coalition
Government never actually applied its provisions to Ireland.

The Maurice debate was occasioned when, in May 1918, Major-General Frederick Maurice, former Director of Military Operations at the War Office, had alleged in the press that Government statements concerning the numbers of British troops in France were untrue. Asquith, always ready to take issue with Lloyd George over interference in the control of military strategy, refused Bonar Law's offer of a two-man judicial inquiry and instead demanded the establishment of a Select Committee of the House of Commons. Asquith insisted his motion was not a vote of censure. Lloyd George, however, treated the issue as a vote of confidence. On the vote the Government won by 295 votes to 108 – a much larger majority than had appeared likely at the time. Some 71 Liberals had supported the Government, but 98 had voted against.

The Maurice debate, though hardly a vote on a vital point of Liberal principle, marked a significant stage in the growing separation and hostility of the two Liberal sections. And it came at a time when the prospect of a general election was coming nearer. Before the spring of 1918, Lloyd George had no compelling need to make plans for an election, nor had he particular need to contact and conciliate the Conservative Central Office.

However, the passing of the Representation of the People Bill on 6 February 1918, with its extension of the franchise and major redistribution of seats, provided an urgent reason for proceeding with an election. Lloyd George, by this time, also had special reasons for an electoral arrangement with the Conservatives, for by 1918 many Lloyd George Liberals were far from happy at the support they would obtain in their own constituencies. The advantages of an electoral understanding with the Conservatives, and the formation of a separate Coalition Liberal Party, increased steadily. Prior to the setting up of a separate party, Lloyd George's support, as we have seen, was limited to the forty or so members of Sir Frederick Crawley's 'Liberal War Committee', together with other shifting blocks of supporters. As late as the end of 1917, the Coalition Liberal Whip (Guest) advised against the formation of a separate Lloyd George Liberal Party. At that time, hopes of reunion were still alive and there was considerable sympathy for Asquith. By 1918 the position had changed. On 12 July a number of Lloyd George's supporters, at a meeting chaired by Addison, discussed the question of an election and the programme the party might adopt. The following day, Guest wrote to Lloyd George urging an agreement with Bonar Law over candidates and policy. By September, Lloyd George had decided on an election in harness with the Conservatives, although he was still negotiating with Asquith (via an intermediary, Lord

Murray) for the former leader to return as Lord Chancellor, an offer Asquith duly rejected.

By October the essential arrangements over the famous 'coupon' had been made (this was the nickname given to the letter jointly signed by Bonar Law and Lloyd George stating that the holder was the officially recognised Government candidate). Under the agreement, despite much pressure from Lloyd George, it was agreed that only some 150 seats would be allocated to 'couponed' Liberals; elsewhere, Liberals would support Coalition Conservatives. For those Liberals without the coupon, the electoral prospects were likely to be bleak. On 14 November a formal announcement of the dissolution was made; on 22 November the Coalition manifesto was issued.

As part of a deliberate policy, Lloyd George not only sent many of his former Liberal Cabinet colleagues and back-benchers to face a highly uncertain electoral future, but even found it impossible to reward all the loyal followers of his own wing. Faithful supporters such as George Lambert, the veteran member for South Molton, were denied the coupon, while others such as Colonel Josiah Wedgwood, later to join the Labour Party, received the coupon, even though they protested that they had no wish to have it.

Clearly, the deciding factor in these allocations was not personal loyalty, nor was it the voting record on the night of the famous Maurice debate of 9 May 1918: the essential and crucial factor was the limit of 150 Liberals who were to receive the coupon as arranged in the alliance with Bonar Law and Sir George Younger, the chairman of the Conservative Party organisation. In the event, 541 coupons were eventually issued, the Liberals receiving 159, the Conservatives the lion's share with 364, while 18 were allocated to the ephemeral National Democratic Party.

The 'coupon' election of 1918 was fought both on different constituencies and with a much enlarged electorate from the previous general election in December 1910. Under the Representation of the People Act, which became law in February 1918, the electorate had risen to 21,392,322. The 'coupon' election of 1918 was thus the first election in this country fought on the basis of universal adult male suffrage for those over 21.

This very important extension of the franchise in 1918 was accompanied by an equally far-reaching redistribution of constituencies. Such a redistribution – the first since 1885 – was long overdue. This redistribution, however, was mainly to the advantage of the Conservatives. The areas of greatest population growth after 1885 were the urban centres of London, Birmingham, Liverpool and Glasgow – areas in which the Conservatives were relatively strong compared with the Liberals. Meanwhile the areas of relative population decline had been rural Scotland and Wales (where the Liberals were entrenched) and Southern Ireland (by now solid Nationalist territory). Any redistribution was therefore of direct benefit to the Conservatives. It has been calculated that if the election of December 1910 had been fought on the redistributed constituencies of 1918, the Conservatives would have gained between 25 and 30 seats. This bonus enjoyed by the Conservatives at the 'coupon' election was one factor – albeit slight – in the Coalition landslide.

The election results of December 1918 were nothing short of a complete triumph. It was a Coalition landslide greater than the Liberal victory of 1906 and as sweeping a success as the National Government in 1931. No fewer than 332 'couponed' Conservatives, together with 127 Coalition Liberals, were returned. Together with 4 Coalition Labour MPs and 9 National Democratic supporters, the full strength of the Coalition numbered 472. In addition to this total, a further 47 uncouponed Conservatives and 3 Ulster Unionists gave the Coalition general support. In contrast, the opposition benches presented a sorry state of disarray. The largest group, the 73 Sinn Fein members, never took their seats. Labour could muster only 60. The remnant of 'Wee Free' Liberals numbered a mere 36, while a further 17 assorted 'Independents' also generally voted against the Government.

The landslide of 1918 was quickly attributed by the Independent Liberals to the allocation of the coupon. This judgement was mistaken. The overwhelming success of the couponed candidates (472 out of 541 were returned) has disguised the exact nature of the Coalition victory. The idea that success was due to the coupon was in fact mistaken. The 1918 victory was essentially a victory of the right, and couponed Liberals were successful, not so much because they possessed the Coupon, but because they were guaranteed no Conservative opposition. Thus, in such areas as Liverpool and Manchester, even uncouponed Conservatives gained easy and substantial victories.

Even this explanation is only half correct. The paradox of 1918 was that, at a time when the electors were in an unusually radical mood, Lloyd George and his Conservative allies, by exploiting the wave of patriotic sentiment that followed the end of the war, persuaded them to return a massive majority of Conservatives and Coalition Liberals to Parliament.[15]

The circumstances of the 'coupon election' disguised the true electoral strength of the Lloyd George Liberals in December 1918. Of the

[14] M. Kinnear, *The British Voter* (1968) p. 70.
[15] C. Cook and J. Ramsden, *By-Elections in British Politics*, p. 17.

127 Coalition Liberal seats secured in 1918, many were concentrated in industrial working-class areas that would be highly vulnerable to any Labour advance. They had been won in 1918 on a patriotic campaign in the absence of Conservative opposition. By 1922 one – and sometimes both – of these factors had been removed. Except for rural North Wales, and to a lesser extent parts of East Anglia, Devon and Cornwall and some London seats, the Coalition Liberals were dependent on Conservative votes. This was most true in such areas of Coalition Liberal strength as industrial West Yorkshire, the North-East, South Wales, the mining seats in Derbyshire and North Staffordshire.

If the strength of the Coalition Liberals was less than it appeared, for the Independent Liberals led by Asquith the results were both a rout and a humiliation on a scale almost unparalleled in British politics. A mere 36 uncouponed Liberals had survived the massacre. Virtually all the leaders of the pre-1914 party were defeated. Asquith, Sir John Simon, Walter Runciman, Reginald McKenna, Herbert Samuel and the Chief Whip, J. W. Gulland, all failed to return to Westminster. Two ex-Ministers, Sir Charles Hobhouse in Bristol East and T. McKinnon Wood in the St Rollox division of Glasgow, both suffered the added humility of a lost deposit at the foot of the poll in a three-cornered contest. McKenna, Runciman, Samuel and H. J. Tennant were all similarly placed in three-cornered contests.

Fewer than twenty Asquithians defeated a Coalition opponent. Fewer still had withstood a three-cornered contest, whilst the Liberal pacifists were totally obliterated. Even the most traditional of Liberal strongholds fell before the onslaught. In Frome, the sitting member, who had represented the division since 1892, obtained less than 9 per cent of the total votes. Nor were the 36 survivors of the election based on any firm regional or geographical basis. Indeed, as Roy Douglas has written, even among the tattered band who did scramble home, good luck played a large part.

Within the space of a single election, the unity and strength of the pre-war Liberal Party had been shattered.

7 A Party Divided: 1918–1923

The 'coupon' election of December 1918 had given Lloyd George his triumph. Or so, at least, it appeared on the surface. What the results of 1918 disguised was the shallowness of both Lloyd George's own personal position and that of his party. For his party (as is discussed on pp. 79–80) lacked real roots or any established power base.

In December 1918, however, these problems still lay in the future. Lloyd George's immediate task centred on the policy of reconstruction which the country so desperately needed. Although the most senior posts in the Cabinet were in Conservative hands, the Liberals retained a remarkably strong voice. In the reconstituted Cabinet of October 1919 they possessed seven members, apart from Lloyd George himself. Among these were Ronald Munro at the Scottish Office, Edward Shortt at the Home Office and Edwin Montagu at the India Office. Only two of the Coalition Liberal Ministers, however, can be said to have been near the centre of power: Winston Churchill and H. A. L. Fisher. However, outside the Cabinet there were other proponents of Liberalism, as well as the Prime Minister's own secretariat or 'Garden Suburb'.

Despite all this, the influence of the Coalition Liberal party on post-war events was far from unimportant. To begin with, they were largely responsible for the government's imaginative new departures in social reform. Despite the mismanagement of finance, Christopher Addison supplied much of the momentum behind the housing programme. T. J. Macnamara played an important part in combating unemployment, whilst Mond also pressed for employment policies. In education, H. A. L. Fisher, together with his Welsh colleague Herbert Lewis, fought a long battle to save such items as teachers salary scales from drastic economies. The important extension of national insurance in 1920 was also to their credit, whilst Edwin Montagu introduced important reforms over India.

It was significant that, when the Geddes recommendations threatened almost the entire social policy of the government, it was the Liberal ministers, headed by Fisher, Mond, Montagu and Churchill, who led the counter-attack in the Cabinet – although the battle they fought was largely lost and the government's social policies were left in ruins.

Over Ireland, the Coalition Liberals again acted as the voice of protest – however ineffective – against the atrocities of the Black and Tans. Such ministers as Shortt, Addison and Fisher fought hard in 1919 for a more moderate policy – a battle again lost with the arrival of Hamar Greenwood at the Irish Office in April 1920.

Whilst the Coalition Liberals' front benches possessed a variety of talent, with such figures as Montagu, Addison and Hilton Young, the great failing of the Coalition Liberals was their anomalous political position.

Throughout 1919 and 1920, Lloyd George's political objective was the creation of a 'Centre Party' which would, by uniting the Coalition Liberals and Conservatives at all levels, provide a permanent base to fight off Socialism. The idea had been mooted with H. A. L. Fisher and Christopher Addison as early as September 1919. At that time, Lloyd George believed it would be the Unionists who would provide the main obstacle. However, after some persuasion both Bonar Law and Younger agreed. Lloyd George took the acceptance of his own party for granted.

In this, however, Lloyd George was to be rudely awakened. Whilst such Liberal Ministers as Churchill and Addison were enthusiastic for fusion – although for different reasons – they were isolated voices. When, on 16 March 1920, Lloyd George faced his Liberal colleagues at a crucial meeting intended to be the preliminary to public fusion with the Conservatives, he met firm opposition. The net result was that when Lloyd George met the Coalition back-bench MPs two days later, he made only vague appeals for 'closer co-operation' in the constituencies, rather than demanding fusion. Even this mild appeal met angry criticism.

The result was that, unable to deliver his party's own support, Lloyd George could clearly not approach the Unionists. As Morgan has written, the Coalition Liberals remained Liberals still and, whether he liked it or not, so did Lloyd George.[1]

The decision to create a Coalition Liberal Party, which became necessary after the 1920 Leamington Conference (see p. 80) never really became translated into political reality. The Coalition Liberals always remained an organisation of too many Chiefs and too few Indians. The further away one came from Downing Street, the more peripheral was the influence of the Coalition Liberal Party. This weakness centred round two vital factors; the party lacked (as was seen

[1] K. O. Morgan, 'Lloyd George's Stage Army', in A. J. P. Taylor (ed.), *Lloyd George: Twelve Essays* (1971) p. 247.

earlier) a secure electoral base and, perhaps even more crucially, lacked organisation at the grass-roots.

After the Leamington conference, the Coalition Liberals began the creation of a separate party organisation in the constituencies and federations. Despite lavish expenditure from the Lloyd George Fund, the party organisation never really provided the Coalition Liberals with firm roots. Although, in name at least, some 224 constituency Lloyd George Associations were established, few of these maintained an active existence.[2] Most had a mere propaganda value and lacked real local activity. Certainly, nothing resembling a comprehensive constituency network ever existed, and even in such areas as Scotland or Wales little constituency activity took place.[3]

The precarious electoral base of the Coalition Liberals was increasingly revealed in the by-elections from 1918 to 1922. During 1919, Coalition Liberals lost a variety of seats to Labour; and this continued during 1920 on an even greater scale. When Labour won Dartford on 27 March and South Norfolk on 27 July, the scale of the rot was obvious to all. The loss of South Norfolk produced considerable despair among Conservative supporters of the Coalition at the fate of their Liberal allies. Sir George Younger, the party chairman, wrote to Bonar Law;

> This constant loss of C(oalition) L(iberal) seats becomes serious and I see no chance of any improvement. With poor candidates and no organisation of their own, the attrition is bound to go on and the indecision of the Downing Street staff does no good. They arrive, spend money lavishly, but cut little ice.[4]

With each by-election disaster, dreary reports came in of the lack of any Coalition Liberal organisation. In a general review of the dismal Coalition Liberal performance at by-elections, F. E. Guest wrote to Lloyd George: 'New methods will have to be adopted, and many of our old methods will have to be scrapped, if the new and vast electorate is to be got at.'

However, if the Coalition Liberals faced severe problems, they were relatively light compared to the difficulties facing the Asquithian Liberals. For this forlorn group, led by Sir Donald Maclean until Asquith returned to Parliament in the Paisley by-election of February 1920, the political future seemed doubtful and uncertain.

---

[2] See M. Kinnear, *The British Voter* (1968) pp. 88–91.
[3] See Chris Cook, *The Age of Alignment*, pp. 43–5.
[4] Quoted in M. Kinnear, *The Fall of Lloyd George: The Political Crisis of 1922* (1973).

And yet some Liberals were able to put a brave face on the events of 1918. There were exceptional factors about the election – the electoral pact, the low turnout, the inadequate register, the emotional tone of the campaign – which helped explain the disaster. One defeated Liberal candidate wrote to his constituency secretary that there was no need for undue Liberal depression, since in 1918 'conditions were so peculiar that it cannot be regarded as representing the normal views of the electorate.'

These views were possible consolations for the disaster of the 'coupon' election. No such comforting explanations were possible, however, as the continued party split after 1918 revealed just how much damage the party had suffered.

In fact, the Asquithian Liberals were slow to realise that Lloyd George intended a permanent separation. During 1919, however, as Lloyd George continued to employ the 'coupon' in by-elections, the nature of his intentions became clearer. The defeat of Sir John Simon in Spen Valley marked an important step in this process of separation. The final break – and the establishment of a separate Coalition Liberal organisation – came with the failure of Lloyd George's attempts to create a 'Centre Party' by fusing the two wings of the Coalition.

This attempt at fusion, though it ended in failure, had important consequences. In March 1920 the Asquithian Liberal Party declared war on the Coalition Liberals. This declaration was echoed from constituency to constituency, as Liberal Associations passed resolutions condemning both the Coalition and the policy of close co-operation with the Conservatives.

This growing animosity came to a head at the general meeting of the National Liberal Federation at Leamington in May 1920. Several Coalition Liberal MPs attended the gathering. However, when the Coalition case was argued from the platform, interruptions steadily mounted. T. J. Macnamara, who had spoken against Simon in the Spen Valley by-election, received a rowdy reception. This was nothing, however, compared with the general pandemonium which occurred when F. G. Kellaway declared that during the Boer War Asquith had been unfaithful to Liberalism. As tempers mounted Sir Gordon Hewart, the Attorney-General, stated that, in protest at these unruly proceedings, the Coalition Liberals would withdraw. Amid loud cheers, they did. The divisions in the party had become finalised; and it was at the constituency level that they were often felt most disastrously. After 1918, many local Liberal Associations suffered an almost total collapse of organisation, membership and activities.

The gravity of the situation facing the local Liberal Associations in the constituencies after 1918 was not lost on leading members of the party. Herbert Gladstone, the director of Liberal headquarters, had no illusions. He was later to write of the position after the débâcle of the 'Coupon':

> . . . The result of 1918 broke the party, not only in the House of Commons but in the country. Local associations perished or maintained a nominal existence. Masses of our best men passed away to Labour. Others gravitated to Conservatism or independence . . .

As Gladstone continued, the remnants in the constituencies neither held meetings nor maintained even elementary electoral organisation.

Nor was Gladstone alone in his pessimism. Thus the secretary of the Midland Liberal Federation reported after the 1922 general election that 'the most dreadful feature of our work during the past four years had been the difficulty of arousing any interest whatsoever'. Constituencies were left without agents; local branches withered away; propaganda lapsed entirely. Perhaps even more significantly, Liberals failed to field a major challenge in municipal elections.

In the decade after 1918, the Liberals never fielded a full team of municipal candidates. Only 19 per cent of those seeking election in 1921 were Liberals, while 35 per cent were Labour. By 1929, less than one in eight of those fighting provincial borough elections were Liberal.

In the first post-war municipal elections, in November 1919, Liberals suffered a major reverse at the hands of Labour. In radical towns with a Liberal tradition, such as Bradford, Leicester, Nottingham and Wolverhampton, formerly secure Liberal wards fell to Labour. The débâcle of 1919 not only greatly increased Labour representation, but also precipitated the formation of numerous Liberal–Conservative 'anti-socialist' municipal pacts. Examples of these, which in some cases lasted for the whole inter-war period, were Sheffield (where the two parties combined to form the Sheffield Citizens' Association), Bristol, Derby and Wolverhampton.

This Liberal decline at local level was most marked on the London County Council. Here, the decline of the Progressive Party had already been strongly in evidence before the First World War.[5] From 83 representatives on a Council of 118 in 1904, the Progressive strength had been reduced to 50 by 1913. In 1919, Progressive representation was reduced to a mere 40; by 1925, with only six representatives, the party had virtually disappeared as an independent force in London politics. Indeed, there were no Progressives at all after the 1934 elections.

Partly cause, partly a consequence of this collapse of local Liberal organisation at the grass-roots was the disastrous by-election record of

[5] See P. Thompson, *Socialists, Liberals and Labour: The Struggle for London* (1967).

the Asquithian wing of the party from 1918 to the fall of the Coalition in 1922. Ironically, the first by-elections after the Coupon Election seemed to suggest better things. Asquithians won Leyton West (1 March 1919), Hull Central (29 March) and Central Aberdeenshire and Kincardine (16 April). Of these results, J. M. Kenworthy's victory in Hull Central on a swing of 32·9 per cent was the most sensational.

These results, however, proved to be a false dawn. After April 1919 the by-elections suddenly, but consistently, showed that the initiative in the constituencies had passed from the Liberals to Labour. During the remainder of 1919, in the three contests fought by Conservative, Liberal and Labour, the Liberals came bottom in all three. Up to the 1922 general election the Independent Liberals won only two other by-elections. These were in Louth, a traditional rural Nonconformist seat that had returned a Liberal at virtually every election since 1885, and Bodmin, a similarly traditional Liberal West Country stronghold.

The greatest disappointment for the Independent Liberals came in three-cornered contests. In such constituencies as Manchester Rusholme, Plymouth Sutton and Ilford, Labour forced Liberals into third place. In the 24 three-cornered by-election contests between 1918 and 1922, the Independent Liberals could poll only 24·8 per cent of votes cast, compared to 35·1 per cent for Labour and 40·1 per cent for the Coalition. Indeed, much the most significant feature of the by-elections during the lifetime of the Coalition was the advance of Labour, whose victories against both Coalition Liberal and Conservatives were often dramatic.[6] In the longer term, however, the significance of the by-elections was the extent to which (outside the old Nonconformist rural areas) protest votes were finding their home with Labour rather than with the Asquithian Liberals. In part this was due to the large number of seats left uncontested by Independent Liberals at by-elections. No Independent Liberals were brought forward at by-elections in such seats as Bromley, Woodbridge, Dover or Taunton.

The disintegration of Liberal organisation and morale at constituency level was a reflection of a wider malaise in the party. For after 1918, the Independent Liberals lacked two crucial weapons: distinctive policies and effective leadership. After 1918, it was difficult to determine even in broad terms what the Liberal Party stood for. Was it a party of radicals? Or anti-Socialists? Or had it become a loose Free Trade moderate centre party? The Asquithian Liberals had made few attempts to answer that question. The first – and basic – task for the Liberal Party was to decide where it stood in relation to Labour. This, in the six years after 1918, Asquith and his supporters never estab-

---

[6] See Chris Cook and John Ramsden, *By-Elections in British Politics* (1973).

lished. As Kinnear has written, Asquith himself declared that he was 'not in the least alarmed by the Red Spectre', whilst Simon (not even on the left wing of the Party) had stated that Labour ought not to be treated as the common enemy.[7] Yet these declarations were oddly at variance with the *Liberal Magazine* (the official Asquithian journal) which had stated that 'under socialism, individual freedom would practically disappear' and that the Labour Party 'is a morbid political coalition held together by insincerity'.

These basic contradictions in the philosophy of the party were exposed whenever fairly advanced radical ideas were discussed. Thus, when some Liberals toyed with the idea of nationalisation early in 1920, the party immediately witnessed yet another split. A 'Liberal anti-nationalisation committee' (consisting largely of the wealthier Liberal industrialists) ran a scare campaign. As Kinnear comments, such internal disputes over economic policy would not, in normal times, have greatly hurt the party – they were indeed a healthy sign of intellectual debate – but occurring as they did in a divided and leaderless party they assumed an importance out of all proportion. It was doubly ironic that the party's failure to adopt a distinct policy and programme coincided with the institution of the Liberal Summer Schools, an important inter-war development in Liberal education. Under the inspiration of Ramsay Muir and Walter Layton, the first Summer School was held at Grasmere in 1921. Subsequent Summer Schools were held annually either at Oxford or Cambridge.

One common denominator in the Liberal misfortunes after 1918 lay in leadership; or rather the lack of it. And, in large measure, the blame lay with Asquith. In the period after the Paisley by-election of 12 February 1920 and the Leamington Conference of May 1920, vital years went by (particularly in the run-up to the 1922 election) with the Liberal leader giving neither lead, direction nor policy. Asquith, who was 70 in 1922, was becoming a shadow of his former self.

Lack of positive leadership over policy from Asquith was clearly one factor. Another – allied with it – was the fact that, even before 1918, dissident radical Liberals could now look for an alternative party in Labour. This process had begun during the war; several Liberal MPs and candidates, including such figures as C. P. Trevelyan and Charles Roden Buxton had already joined Labour. Some of these seceders might have returned to the Liberal fold if Asquith had adopted a constructive and radical programme. As it was, the long-term effect was to siphon off the many advanced social reformers and make the party perhaps less open to radical ideas than before.

[7] M. Kinnear, *The Fall of Lloyd George* (1973) p. 201.

Whilst the Independent Liberals faced serious problems of policy, organisation and leadership, the Coalition Liberals faced problems of a different order. The Coalition Liberals were finding their political world beginning to crumble about them. Lloyd George himself was becoming the most unloved of politicians. His own personal position was becoming increasingly difficult. Coalition Liberal discontent was rife, yet Lloyd George did little about it. The Liberal back-benchers were treated with complete indifference. With the exception of Churchill, Lloyd George's main colleagues and confidants were all Conservatives. Those Liberals left in the government were becoming increasingly isolated.

Meanwhile, in the Conservative constituency associations, the movement to sever the Coalition links was rapidly rising. On 2 June 1922, 11 Conservative peers and 30 MPs published a manifesto in the press declaring that 'to drift further with ever-changing policies must quickly produce chaos, disaster and ruin'. The signs of revolt were becoming more evident.

With all these portents, it was remarkable that it was not until August 1922, when an imminent general election seemed likely, that Lloyd George set up a committee, consisting of Mond, Kellaway and Macnamara, to investigate the Coalition Liberal Party Machine.

By the autumn of 1922, against a long background of by-election reverses, Coalition Liberal morale had all but disappeared. Lloyd George's bellicose handling of the Chanak affair did nothing to calm the party. It was the political crisis of Autumn 1922, which, by threatening the Coalition with a new rebellion anyway, decided the Cabinet to take the plunge and hold an immediate election.

Meanwhile, the Conservative MPs were summoned to the Carlton Club by Austen Chamberlain, in an effort to secure their consent to fight the election as a Coalition. The meeting at the Carlton Club resolved that the Conservatives would not be the allies of the Coalition Liberals at the next election; it thereby destroyed the Coalition.

Lloyd George resigned as Prime Minister the same afternoon. On Monday 23 October, Bonar Law was unanimously elected leader of the Conservative Party to succeed Austen Chamberlain – who had himself replaced Bonar Law only nineteen months previously. Three days later, Parliament was dissolved. The date of the general election was fixed for 15 November.

The fall of the Coalition left both Lloyd George and his Liberal supporters without a power base. Despite a plea by Mond that the Coalition Liberals should fight during the subsequent election as Liberals desiring a reunited party, the bulk of the Coalition Liberals decided to act with any sympathetic Conservatives during the campaign.

With the fall of the Coalition, Lloyd George was left without any clear direction in which to try to lead his followers. In a speech at Leeds on 21 October, he was palpably engaged in an exercise to buy himself time. He offered no positive programme, and he carefully avoided defining his relations with the other parties. A similar lack of positive policy was again apparent when he spoke at the Hotel Victoria on 26 October. For once, Lloyd George was in the rare and unhappy position of a leader with nothing to say.

Indeed, to some extent he was also a leader with nothing to lead. For, with the fall of the Coalition, the Lloyd George Liberals now discovered what had long been a political fact: they were a party without roots. The coming of the election meant that they must fend for themselves. Such electoral arrangements as they could make with other parties would have to be at constituency level.

Apart from North Wales, where Coalition Liberalism was strong in its own right, the most fortunate were the Lloyd George Liberals in Scotland. Feeling in the Scottish Unionist ranks was strongly in favour of a continued Coalition. As it was, the Eastern Division of the Scottish Unionist Association formally decided not to oppose sitting National Liberal Members. In return, the Scottish National Liberals agreed not to oppose sitting Conservatives. Apart from such isolated constituencies as Perth and Glasgow Cathcart, the National Liberals in Scotland enjoyed a Coalition in 1922.

South of the Border, however, Coalition Liberals were forced to make such arrangements as they could to secure local Conservative support. So, in London, Macnamara in Camberwell North-West, as well as Arthur Lever in Hackney Central and Lt-Col. M. Alexander in Southwark South-East, received official Conservative support only after they had given specific pledges of support to a Bonar Law Ministry. Others were less fortunate. Despite repeated attempts to secure Conservative support in Sunderland, Sir Hamar Greenwood was faced with two Conservative opponents in this double-member constituency.

The rapid increase in the number of Conservatives coming forward to attack Coalition Liberal seats was likely to produce electoral disaster for Lloyd George's supporters. Yet Lloyd George was powerless to prevent it. His threat to bring forward candidates against sitting Conservatives was hardly practical politics. Though urged to adopt this course by Mond and Rothermere, nothing came of the 'phantom host' of candidates promised by C. A. McCurdy, the Chief Whip. As

Churchill rightly observed, nothing was to be gained, and much would be lost, by spreading the war.

In the event, moderation prevailed. Only 144 Coalition Liberals were eventually adopted. Only 24 of these were in constituencies that had not been allocated to Coalition Liberal or National Democratic candidates in the 'coupon' election. Only seven of these 24 fought against sitting Conservatives. The bulk of the attack was directed at Labour. In addition to Scotland and the East End of London, the Coalition continued virtually undisturbed in such towns as Bristol and Newcastle. Some 121 Coalition Liberals (Churchill among them) escaped any Conservative opposition. Compared to the 144 Coalition Liberals, the Asquithians launched a determined challenge with 333 candidates. The Conservatives brought forward 482 candidates. Labour fielded 414, its largest contingent so far.

The outcome of the election was a triumph for Bonar Law, a major advance for Labour, a meagre return for Asquith and a total humiliation for the Lloyd George Liberals.

1922 General Election Result

	Total votes	% share	Candidates	MPs elected	Unopposed returns
Conservative	5,502,298	38·5	482	344	42
Liberal	2,668,143	18·9	333	60	6
National Liberal	1,412,772	9·4	144	53	4
Labour	4,237,349	29·7	414	142	4
Others	571,480	3·5	68	16	1
	14,392,330	100·0	1,441	615	57

For the Asquithian Liberals, the results were a bitter disappointment. Admittedly, their numbers elected rose to 62, but this was only a meagre success. Yet even this advance could hardly disguise several disturbing features. Fourteen of the seats won in 1918 had been lost, nine of them to Labour. The Liberals fared particularly badly in the mining areas. In Durham the three remaining Liberal constituencies were all lost. Other traditional Liberal mining strongholds lost included Peebles and South Midlothian (Sir Donald Maclean's constituency), Leigh, and North-East Derbyshire.

On the other hand, the Independent Liberals managed to gain 43 seats. Of these, 10 were won from Coalition Liberals, 32 from Conservatives and Independents, but only one from Labour. It was significant that the best results for the Asquithian Liberals were in the traditionally Liberal rural seats lost in the 1918 débâcle.

However, the most disturbing feature of this partial revival, outside the occasional area such as rural Scotland or the West Country, was its lack of a secure regional base. Very many traditional Liberal seats, especially in the cities, had not been recovered, while several of the Liberal victories were in areas which had not returned Liberals for a generation. In Oxford, Frank Gray's success was the first Liberal victory since 1885. Likewise, the Liberal gain in Bootle was the first victory after forty years in the wilderness. In fact, one Liberal Federation Secretary noticed that party organisation bore little relation to success. In many cases, the worse the organisation, the better the party fared. The explanation seemed to lie in the fact that, in 1922, the Liberals gathered the protest votes at the shortcomings of the Coalition.

This was particularly true of the series of Liberal victories in rural seats which had rarely, if ever, returned Liberals before 1922. Typical of Liberal gains in these areas were the victories in Grantham, Horncastle, Holderness and Taunton.

A further disturbing feature for the Liberal Party was that its best results were, almost without exception, in straight fights against the Conservatives. In the 31 constituencies in which Independent Liberals enjoyed straight fights with Conservatives in 1918 and 1922, the Liberal share of the vote increased by over 10 per cent. These seats, however, were almost exclusively rural or residential. In the 54 constituencies in which the three major parties contested in 1918 and 1922, the Liberals increased their share of the vote by only 4·5 per cent from 22·7 per cent to 27·2 per cent. The Liberal recovery in industrial working-class seats was, in general, conspicuously absent. The occasional exception, such as Walsall, which Pat Collins won for the Liberals, only made the general pattern more obvious. In the rural seats, however, the presence of Labour candidates had less effect, and in such seats as Westbury and Chippenham the Liberals were still able to regain lost territory.

If the results of the 1922 election were disappointing for the Asquithians, they were utterly disastrous for the Coalition Liberals. Many of the leading Lloyd George supporters went down to defeat: Churchill was beaten at Dundee, Hamar Greenwood at Sunderland and Freddie Guest in East Dorset. Whereas, in 1918, 138 Coalition Liberals had been returned, only 60 survived the 1922 election. No fewer than 81 seats were lost, 21 of which had even lacked defenders. Whilst 57 seats were retained, only three new seats were won.

In the industrial areas the rout assumed the proportions of a massacre. In Sheffield, only the Park division survived as the lone outpost of Coalition Liberalism. Attercliffe was lost to Labour on a swing of

33·5 per cent; Hillsborough fell on a similar huge swing. South Wales
was the scene of a similar débâcle. Neath was lost on a swing of 24·3 per
cent, while Labour also captured Aberdare, Llanelli, Merthyr, Aberavon and Swansea East, which the Coalition Liberals had narrowly
retained in the by-election of July 1919. In Scotland, despite the con-
tinuation of local Conservative–National Liberal agreements, it was the
same story of industrial Liberal seats swamped by a Labour tide. Eight
of twelve seats in industrial Scotland were lost.

Only in its stronghold of rural North Wales was Coalition Liberalism
able to survive unaided against Conservative and Labour attacks. The
net result of 1922, as far as the Coalition Liberals were concerned, was
a disaster.

Faced with the dramatic increase in Labour support, and with the
Conservatives under Bonar Law secure with a comfortable overall
majority, it is hardly surprising that the Liberal Party found little
comfort in the verdict of November 1922. Over breakfast with C. P.
Scott, the editor of the *Manchester Guardian*, Lloyd George asked him for
his views on the result. Scott replied that the election constituted a
worse disaster for the Liberal Party than 1918 because there was less
excuse for it.

The return of Bonar Law to power, with its promise of a period of
political tranquillity, seemed at least to offer the Liberals a breathing
space to put their house in order. And the first prerequisite to this was
the question of reunion. Throughout 1923, the Liberals spent much
effort grappling with the problem of reunion. Unlike the other difficulties facing the party, it was a problem about which they might do
something. However, the circumstances and conduct of the 1922 election had hardly given reunion a good start. With the notable exceptions
of such areas as Manchester and Leeds, the two Liberal factions had
spent the 1922 election fighting each other.

And, as Trevor Wilson wrote, for most Independent Liberals, including Asquith, the only satisfaction to be derived from the election results
was to 'gloat over the corpses which have been left on the battlefield'.[8]
After the election, memories of these bitter scenes presented a major
obstacle to reunion. Yet, to members in both wings, it seemed a vital
and pressing question. Many Coalition Liberals saw reunion as giving
them a more definite place in politics, most particularly in the light of
Labour's advance. Here, indeed, was the crunch. Lloyd George, more
than Asquith, could see the realities of the political situation after
Labour's advance in 1922. And yet, a lingering pride prevented submission, whilst Asquith seemed to want nothing less than just that.

[8] T. Wilson, op.cit., p. 243.

This position, in spring 1923, continued unchanged as summer approached. At the same time, growing evidence of the desire for reconciliation in the constituencies became apparent. In two by-elections, in Anglesey and Ludlow, local reunion was achieved. But throughout the spring and early summer of 1923, National Liberal reconciliation initiatives were summarily brought to a halt. Thus, the Welsh National Liberals held a meeting in March to consider the reunion position and appointed nine delegates with full power to meet Independent Liberals in any conference. This was communicated to a meeting at Shrewsbury of the Welsh Liberal Federation. The response to this friendly gesture was not encouraging. The Federation passed the following resolution: 'That the consideration of the letter from the National Liberal Council be deferred for six months.' A further major speech by Lloyd George – on 28 April at Manchester – again produced only a frosty reception from Asquith. Supplied with an opportunity of accepting the hand of friendship, Asquith chose as an alternative, in a speech at Bournemouth, to catalogue some of the difficulties, stressing particularly that the Coalition Liberals had been voting with the Conservatives.

May produced no further real moves towards Liberal reunion, except in the constituencies, where the *Lloyd George Liberal Magazine* reported:[9]

> The month has seen a considerable increase in the number of resolutions from rank-and-file organisations throughout the country advocating co-operation and consultation between the Party leaders as the first step towards complete reunion.

It was against this background that the Annual Conference of the National Liberal Federation took place at Buxton. It was a moment of crucial importance for the success of Liberal reunion attempts. The concrete results of the conference in terms of Liberal reunion were virtually nil. It was true that the delegates put on record their satisfaction with the growing desire for party union. It was also the case that the friendly reception given to such National Liberals as Mond and McCurdy contrasted very favourably with the hostility shown at Leamington in 1920 to Hewart and Addison. Nevertheless, the Conference rejected the crucial amendment to a pro-reunion resolution calling on the Independent Liberal leaders to discuss with the National Liberal leaders the best means of promoting party unity. The *Manchester Guardian*, in its comments on the Buxton proceedings, declared that the blunt truth revealed by the gathering was that the party was so dangerously preoccupied with its internal problem that it had little time for

[9] *Lloyd George Liberal Magazine*, June 1923, p. 697.

the external problems of policy, especially domestic policy. How, it asked, can Liberal leaders hope to rouse enthusiasm until they have themselves enough enthusiasm to endure one another for the good of the cause?

There is little doubt that Buxton was the moment of lost opportunity for Liberal reunion. Despite an insistent call from the constituencies for reunion, Conference had turned an almost deaf ear. This was reflected in a growing number of associations such as Thornbury and Ashton-under-Lyne making their own local arrangements for reunion.

But with the exception of these few local arrangements, the continued party split led to an even further deterioration in party morale at constituency level. This loss of morale had both cause and effect in a depressing Liberal by-election record between 1922 and 1923. Although the party gained Willesden East and Tiverton, in general its vote had failed to make any marked improvement. The main significance of the by-elections was Labour's ability to consolidate and extend its 1922 advance in industrial areas, mainly at the expense of the Liberals, and Labour's slow but definite advance in rural areas, once again hitting hardest at the Liberals.[10]

At the same time that the moves towards reunion at local level were increasing, there is strong evidence to suggest that Asquith's intransigence in ever readmitting Lloyd George to real power within a reunited party was increasing. If this is correct, the sad paradox of Liberal history stands out: Asquith succeeded in keeping out Lloyd George until October 1926, but at a cost of seeing the party destroyed. Lloyd George became leader when only a rump was left for him to lead. And Simon – whom perhaps Asquith saw as heir apparent – repaid his former chief by leading a breakaway Liberal National Party after November 1930.

Meanwhile, to add to the multitude of political cross-currents at work in July 1923, Lloyd George was once again – having despaired of Liberal reunion – refusing to abandon his contacts with the Conservatives.

With the months of August and September relatively empty of political activity, the position regarding reunion remained unchanged. With the exception of local reunion in Bradford (largely caused by the raising of Tariff Reform by Baldwin), so the position rested when in September 1923 Lloyd George set off for what was to become a triumphant lecture tour of America. By the time he returned, Baldwin's unexpected announcement of his conversion to protection had transformed the political climate.

[10] For the by-elections of this Parliament, see Chris Cook and John Ramsden, op.cit., pp. 44–8.

8 Revival and Decline: 1923–1926

Baldwin's decision to call an immediate election over the issue of Protection transformed the position of the Liberal Party. At one stroke, the road to Liberal reunion lay open. Baldwin succeeded, where every Liberal had failed, in reuniting the two warring factions.

Although there had been rumours that Lloyd George was planning to abandon Free Trade, these doubts were removed when, on his return to Southampton from the United States, the former Prime Minister declared himself unreservedly against Baldwin's fiscal departure.

The main essentials of reunion were settled at a meeting on 13 November attended by Asquith, Lloyd George, Vivian Phillipps and Mond. It was agreed to fight the election as a united party, with a united Liberal Campaign Committee (chaired by Lord Beauchamp) and a single campaign fund. All candidates were to stand as 'Liberals', without any prefix or suffix.

The most interesting discussion centred on the Liberal campaign strategy. Free Trade presented no problems, for Lloyd George spoke as an unqualified Free Trader. Regarding unemployment, Lloyd George suggested the use of National Credit during depression, while the Asquithians proposed an extended Unemployment Insurance Scheme. On foreign policy, it was decided to launch a major attack on the government's handling of the Ruhr question and reparations. These lines of attack, on Free Trade, unemployment and foreign affairs, were to be expected. Nothing very radical or new was proposed. The meeting agreed that nothing corresponding to a 'Newcastle Programme' could or ought to be attempted, but that what was wanted was 'a limited number of bold but effective pronouncements'. A manifesto on these lines was drafted the same evening by Mond and Phillipps. This decision was of vital significance, for the whole Liberal campaign was subsequently to centre on a negative defence of Free Trade.

The ease with which reunion seemed to be accomplished, and a campaign policy agreed on, in fact disguised several factors. It certainly disguised the extent to which Lloyd George retained control not only over his money, but also over his Coalition Liberal organisation.

The financial arrangements soon caused considerable acrimony. At the 13 November meeting, Lloyd George had promised considerable financial support, although no record of the exact amount has survived. It was left to Herbert Gladstone to be responsible for collecting Lloyd George's contribution from Sir Alfred Cope. After more discussions, it was agreed that a contribution of £100,000 from the Lloyd George wing and £50,000 from the Independent Liberal headquarters would be sufficient. But actually getting the money out of Lloyd George proved a source of conflict.

The possibility of future conflict between Lloyd George and Asquith stemmed also from another source. In taking up the cause of Free Trade, and rejoining the Liberal ranks, Lloyd George had effectively become Asquith's second. As Beaverbrook expressed it, 'he really had a choice between death and surrender on fairly easy terms'.[1] The Free Trade Liberal Party was in Asquith's control, not Lloyd George's. Lloyd George's position after the election, when his National Liberal followers were decimated, only reinforced the realisation upon Lloyd George.

Meanwhile, Lloyd George had not entirely abandoned the old Coalition. At a meeting at Cherkley on 12 November, a somewhat unreal plot had been hatched to secure a Free Trade victory followed by a new Coalition, but the details were soon leaked to Baldwin. The plot subsequently collapsed.

Although rumoured in the press, Lloyd George's intrigues with his old Coalition partners did not mar the galvanising effect of Liberal reunion on constituency morale and activity. Hitherto dormant associations were brought by the onset of Free Trade and a reunited party into hurried activity. The net result was that the Liberals were able to field 457 candidates, compared to 536 Conservative and 427 Labour.

The ease with which Liberal reunion was achieved at this national level was not so easily repeated in the constituencies. Five years of division were not healed overnight. Indeed, in two constituencies (Camborne and Cardiganshire) rival Liberal candidates were adopted in 1923. In addition, in several constituencies, particularly in Highland Scotland, local faction continued with the Asquithian Liberals refusing active support to sitting National Liberals.

Despite the old battle-cry of Free Trade, even in the optimistic atmosphere of 1923, local associations in many industrial areas failed to generate sufficient energy to field a candidate. This was particularly

[1] A. J. P. Taylor, *Beaverbrook* (1972) p. 219.

true of such areas as Durham, South Wales and the Clyde. Even in 1923, local co-operation with the Conservatives was one factor at work, together with the difficulty of attracting good candidates and the problems of raising sufficient finance.

If the nominations provided evidence of Liberal decline, the campaign itself favoured the Liberals. For the Liberals were fighting on their home ground in defending Free Trade. The tone of the Liberal campaign was firmly set by Asquith. It was, essentially, the orthodox defence of Free Trade that had been debated twenty years before. Asquith set himself out to establish that Protection would raise food prices and that neither nationalisation nor the capital levy could be introduced without damaging the economic system. If the Liberals had a programme other than this, it was hardly spectacular. Speaking on 23 November, Asquith went on to outline some other Liberal aims: he called for a remodelling of the Insurance Act, courageous use of national credit, development of Imperial resources and the full operation of the Trade Facilities Act.

Nor, except for occasional remarks by Lloyd George, did the Liberal leadership think they needed anything more radical or constructive in terms of policy. As Cowling observes, although Lloyd George declared that Liberals would be as successful in the future in introducing major social reforms as they had been previously, the details of this future legislation were left to look after themselves.[2] The radicalism of April 1923 had vanished from Lloyd George's speeches. In the campaign, little distinguished Lloyd George, Asquith or Grey. The emphasis, again and again, was on the negative virtues of Free Trade.[3]

It was ironic that much of the Liberal success in 1923 was the result of the party fighting on an essentially conservative policy, with the party portraying itself as the party of common sense and established right.

Despite this negative campaign, the Liberals achieved a marked electoral revival in December 1923. The first results, from Free Trade Lancashire, seemed to confirm the worst fears of those Conservatives who had argued against Baldwin's electoral strategy.

The Liberals swept to victory in no less than five Manchester constituencies, in addition to taking both the Wavertree and West Derby divisions of Liverpool, constituencies with a consistent Conservative tradition since 1885. Even in such areas as Nottingham, where the Conservatives might have expected to benefit from high unemployment

---

[2] M. Cowling, *The Impact of Labour* (Cambridge, 1971) p. 346.

[3] Much the best discussion of the main speeches of the Liberal leaders is to be found in R. Lyman, *The First Labour Government* (1957) pp. 42–52.

and severe foreign competition, the Protectionist platform made little
impact. The final results were as follows:

	Votes	%	Candidates	Members	Unopposed
Conservative	5,514,541	38·0	536	258	35
Liberal	4,301,481	29·7	457	158	11
Labour	4,439,780	30·7	427	191	3
Communist	39,448	0·2	4	—	—
Nationalist	97,993	0·4	4	3	1
Others	154,452	1·0	18	5	—
	14,547,695	100·0	1,446	615	50

The Liberals, although doing well, had not achieved an unqualified
success. Although, on balance, they had gained 53 seats from the Conservatives, they had suffered a net loss of ten to Labour.

The party did particularly well in three areas. In the South-West, the
Liberals secured twelve gains. The South Midlands and northern
Home Counties produced another six victories, while in Lincolnshire
and East Anglia Liberals took a further six.

The party also gained a few semi-industrial county divisions such as
Nuneaton, Bosworth and Cleveland, all with a strong Nonconformist
vote. Much the most curious series of Liberal victories, however, were
the large number of normally 'safe' Conservative seats which fell to the
Liberals. Such constituencies as Basingstoke, Blackpool, Chelmsford,
Chichester, Lonsdale and Shrewsbury, never previously Liberal, were
captured.

At the other extreme, the most disappointing feature of the Liberal
revival was the failure to make substantial inroads into the Labour
vote. Indeed, in the majority of industrial areas with the partial exception of North-East England, the Liberals suffered a further loss of
ground. Whereas the Liberals took 69 seats from the Conservatives,
losing only 16 themselves, *vis-à-vis* Labour the party gained only 13 for
the loss of 23.

In several industrial areas which the Liberals had long regarded as
their own preserve, the results were further proof of the rapidly fading
Liberal support amongst the working classes. In South Wales, the
party lost further ground. But perhaps the most disheartening was the
series of losses to Labour in such Midland seats as Northampton,
Wellingborough, Derby and Leicester.

The result of the 1923 election left the Liberal Party holding the
balance of power. Protection had been rejected with no uncertain voice.
But what government should take the place of Baldwin? Should the
Liberals put MacDonald into office? Or should some other formula be
found to avoid the experiment of a Labour Government?

The occasion found the party deeply divided. On the right, opposition to the policy of putting Labour into office was most strongly voiced by Churchill. He was supported by such right-wing Liberals as Freddie Guest, Sir Beddoe Rees, the Member for Bristol South, and Brigadier-General Spears.

The *Liberal Magazine*, however, together with the constituency and federation organisations supported the experiment. Fear of the renewal of any form of tacit or open Conservative alliance far outweighed the dangers that might result from a Labour Government.

It was against this background of a divided party that the Liberal leadership had to adopt its course of action.

When the Liberal leaders first met to discuss their future course of action, Asquith's own immediate idea, which received the support of Simon, was to turn the Conservatives out as soon as possible, then to do the same with Labour through a combination with the Conservatives.[4] Lloyd George strongly opposed this plan with the argument that any such minority Liberal Government so dependent on Conservative votes would be entirely without freedom of action.

However, the feeling of the meeting was against him: Lloyd George then proposed an adjournment. Asquith, always ready to adjourn anything, agreed. When the leaders met again, Asquith had changed his views: Asquith now wanted a policy of total independence. Lloyd George, who was clearly envisaging a period of co-operation with Labour, accepted this as a first step in the right direction.

Thus, at a crucial moment in the history of the party, the Liberal leaders had been divided. The net result of all this was that the Liberals voted Labour into office without ever having considered how they would fare if Labour refused to co-operate. In this vital respect, Asquith's policy was without reality from the start. The Liberal Party would *not* be able to judge Labour on its merits. Either the Liberals would have to support Labour measures or vote against. To vote against meant an election which the Liberals could not, for financial reasons, contemplate. It was to prove to be a policy without room to manoeuvre. But the decision had been made. On 18 December Asquith made it clear, in a speech to the Liberal Parliamentary Party, that the Liberals would not keep the Conservatives in office or join in any combination to keep Labour out. If a Labour Government were ever to be tried, Asquith declared, 'it could hardly be tried under safer conditions'. Asquith went on to add that, whoever might be in office, 'it is we, if we really understand our business, who really control the situation'.

---

[4] See Chris Cook, *The Age of Alignment* (1975) pp. 180–96.

The outcome was that when, on 21 January 1924, the Labour amendment to the Royal Address was put, it was carried by 328 votes to 256. Rumours of a large revolt by back-bench Liberals to maintain Baldwin in office failed to materialise. Only ten Liberals voted against the Labour amendment.

The following day, Baldwin tendered his resignation to the King. Shortly afterwards, following a meeting of the Privy Council, at which MacDonald was sworn a member, the King invited Ramsay Mac-Donald to form a government. The first Labour Government had arrived. With its advent, the Liberal Party was about to be launched on the disastrous course which culminated in the débâcle of October 1924.

The decision to install a Labour Government was both a vital and crucial decision for the Liberal Party. For such a decision to succeed, it was imperative for the Liberals, whilst the minority Labour Government remained in power, to achieve several targets. To begin with, strong leadership was essential. And this meant a complete healing of the Asquith–Lloyd George split, as opposed to the hurried coming-together that Baldwin's Tariff Election had brought about.

Secondly, it was imperative to use the coming months to develop constructive policy proposals – in social reform, industry, unemployment and foreign affairs – so that in any subsequent general election the Liberals could offer a distinctive, constructive and wide-ranging manifesto. Further, so that the party could fight on as broad a front as possible, derelict constituencies would have to be revived, candidates recruited and finance made available.

United and purposeful leadership was the prerequisite for new policies, revived organisation and sustained morale. It was essential if, in the changed order of British politics after the advent of Labour to office, the Liberals were to have a powerful and central position on the political stage. Although, nominally, the party was united, in reality it remained as divided as ever. The nearer one came to the centre of Liberal Power, the greater the divisions that were evident.

Nor, perhaps, was this so surprising. The reunion brought on by the Tariff Election had been both sudden and incomplete. During the election campaign, Lloyd George's Coalition Liberal headquarters were still operating, and were not finally disbanded until February 1924. Moreover, many Asquithians found it difficult to accept the return of the Prodigal Son with his hankerings after Coalitionism so recently buried. Indeed to a large extent, it was not so much personal animosity between Lloyd George and Asquith (Lloyd George insisted he could get on well with 'the old man') which marred reunion, but the bitter distrust of Asquith's close colleagues such as Donald Maclean, Herbert Gladstone, and Vivian Phillipps – to say nothing of Margot.

However, the real cause of suspicion and distrust during 1924 centred much more on the realities of political power rather than on lingering personal animosities – although personalities exacerbated the problem. The root of the problem lay in the weakened position of Lloyd George and his supporters after the results of 1923 were known. During the campaign, Lloyd George had very much played 'second fiddle' to Asquith – not because he wanted to, but because there was no alternative. The results of 1923 had decimated the ranks of the former Coalition Liberals, leaving the balance of power within the new Liberal Party undeniably in Asquith's favour. Yet Lloyd George retained one asset of unrivalled value: his Fund. Virtually bankrupted by two successive general elections, the Independent Liberal organisation was desperate for funds. Without money, it simply could not wage a general election on a broad front. This fact Lloyd George knew only too well. It was the one card he had left to play.

However, more than simply an internal power game between Asquith and Lloyd George divided the two men in 1924. They were both divided (as was the party they led) on the tactics to be adopted towards Labour.

Asquith's position is easier to understand, because it remained more stable. Once Asquith had decided that Labour should be given its chance to govern, he seems to have hoped (with the condescension that so infuriated MacDonald) that before long it would make such a mess of affairs that MacDonald would resign, the King would send for Asquith and all would be right again with the world. In the meantime, the Liberals would support Labour, whilst repairing their own party machine.

Having decided on this general course, the early months of 1924 were characterised by a total lack of positive leadership by Asquith, whether in Parliament or the country. His attitude, once again, was that the best plan was to 'wait and see'. Before very long, his lack of leadership (made more noticeable by an illness in March) was producing widespread discontent within the Liberal ranks in the country.

Lloyd George, meanwhile, viewed the political scene very differently. In the very early days of December 1923 and January 1924 (if Lloyd George is to be believed, and if Scott's diary is a reliable testimony) Lloyd George hoped to see a period in which, in constructive partnership, the Labour Party, supported by the Liberals, would put a series of radical, reforming measures on the statute books. How long (given MacDonald's only too obviously hostile attitude) Lloyd George held to these views is unclear. By early February, however, other doubts had already begun to set in. The Abbey by-election (of March 1924) set Lloyd George's mind thinking in another direction: back to a revival of

Coalition.

Thus, the summer of 1924 arrived with relations between the Liberal and Labour parties at an embittered level (see pp. 99–100) and with no sign of any coming together of Asquith and Lloyd George.

The consequences of this divided leadership in the party were made worse by the attitude of those below Asquith and Lloyd George who might, by positive and constructive leads, have helped fill the vacuum. None was to succeed. Churchill, defeated in West Leicester in December 1923, and bitterly hostile to the decision to install Labour, had already deserted the Liberals. By March, with the Abbey by-election in Westminster, the break was final. Guest was occupied in trying to organise a right-wing breakaway. Simon, who might have filled such a vacuum, was bent on a negative anti-Socialist campaign, whilst Maclean and Gladstone were too busy fighting Lloyd George.

This failure of leadership, together with bitter personal divisions in their ranks, tended to obscure a more fundamental weakness in the party: its whole fundamental philosophy.

Given the political situation after the 1923 General Election, and the advent of a minority Labour Government, it was doubly important that the Liberal Party adopted a positive and constructive policy – and a distinctive one – that would set it aside from both Conservatives and Socialists in the eyes of the electorate. Without it, radical Liberals would increasingly feel that little separated them from moderate Labour, whilst the right-wing Liberals (to say nothing of those electors who had voted for Free Trade against Protection in 1923) would become increasingly tempted to rally to the Conservatives in the face of a Socialist (albeit moderate) Government.

The circumstances of the 1923 election – in particular the dominant role played by Free Trade in the campaign, had disguised the lack of distinctive policies held by the Liberals. Admittedly, Labour had attacked the Liberals on their lack of a social reform programme (and Conservatives had asked what Liberal policies would aid unemployment), but in general the campaign had been on favourable ground in 1923.

Now, all the factors in the equation had changed. The Conservatives – having buried Protection – were once again the party of the *status quo*. More than any other party, they could simply fight on a negative anti-Socialist policy. Labour had an equally straightforward task: Ramsay MacDonald's dual aim was to show the respectability of his party and prove that it could govern.

For the Liberals, their first basic objective lay still in deciding where they stood in relation to the Labour Party. In addition, on the major topics of the day – on economic policy, social reform, on industry and nationalisation – Liberal policy was equally unclear or non-existent. This was particularly true of economic policy, although this is not to say that the Liberals lacked economic thinkers. Such figures as Ramsay Muir, Keynes and Beveridge all found a home in the Liberal ranks. But the fruition of their ideas did not come until later.

As the months of 1924 progressed, this double Liberal failing – of leadership and policy – was exposed in a variety of ways. It was to be seen in the chaotic indiscipline of the party in the lobbies at Westminster; it was to be seen also in the disintegrating morale and organisation of the party in the constituencies; and it was to be witnessed in the important series of by-elections that occurred during the first Labour Government.

The total lack of unity in the Liberal ranks at Westminster rapidly degenerated towards a situation of farce. One section of the parliamentary party would support the Government; another section, often including Asquith and Lloyd George, would abstain; yet another group would consistently vote with the Conservatives.

Thus, a Conservative motion protesting against the Labour decision to discontinue the Singapore naval base, was defeated by 287 votes to 211 on 25 March. In the division, 118 Liberals voted with Labour, nine more paired, nine voted for the Conservative amendment while the rest abstained. A similar three-way split, with both Asquith and Lloyd George abstaining, occurred on the second reading of the Eviction Bill early in April. In this division, Labour was defeated by 221 votes to 212.

Against this background, morale in the constituencies rapidly began to decline. This was doubly ironic, for in several areas, most especially in the regions of Liberal revival in 1923 such as the Home Counties, East Anglia and the agricultural Midlands, Liberal Party organisation responded well to the stimulus of 1923.[5]

However, as 1924 progressed, even in such former strongholds as Wales, Scotland and the industrial North, the Liberals made little or no attempt either to adopt candidates, distribute propaganda, or improve organisation. Thus, in South Wales, as late as September 1924, the Liberals were without a single prospective candidate in Cardiff, Swansea, Newport and Merthyr. In industrial Scotland, the position was even worse. On the eve of the 1924 election, only one prospective Liberal candidate was in the field in Glasgow compared to 13 Conservatives.

Meanwhile, to add to the difficulties of the hard-pressed Liberal Party was the attack by Labour in the constituencies on sitting Liberal

[5] Chris Cook, *The Age of Alignment* (1975) p. 252.

MPs, whether radical or not. As early as April 1924, Vivian Phillipps was bitterly complaining that, despite Liberal help at Westminster, Labour's only response was to attack in the constituencies.

The net result of all these factors was a rapid disintegration of Liberal morale. Dreary reports came in of former Liberal candidates defecting to the Conservatives and of a general collapse of confidence.

Against this background, it was hardly surprising that the Liberals found themselves in a series of disastrous by-elections. Although only nine contested by-elections occurred during the lifetime of the first Labour Government, they provided clear evidence of the decline in Liberal fortunes. The Liberals not only lost their Oxford seat in June, but polled dismally in such constituencies as Kelvingrove and Westminster (Abbey).[6] The writing was already on the wall, and such Liberals as Lloyd George realised the party's plight. Indeed, in July, the rejection by Labour of any possibility of electoral reform decided Lloyd George that a showdown with MacDonald must now come. According to Scott, Lloyd George determined to force the issue over the question of unemployment. Lloyd George reasoned that, with Ramsay MacDonald personally closely involved at a delicate diplomatic juncture, he would not dare risk dissolution. However, Asquith and the other Liberal hierarchy refused to take the risk. The opportunity passed, with the Liberal Party more helpless than ever before.[7]

This disagreement in July between Asquith and Lloyd George was only one example of a far more fundamental difference between the two. The reunion in November 1923 had been, in many ways, a reunion in name only. Suspicion had remained, most particularly with such old Asquithians as Herbert Gladstone and Donald Maclean. Lloyd George, for his part, was determined to hold on to the one very tangible asset he possessed – the money in his Fund. This factor was crucial to Liberal fortunes, for with the Independent Liberals almost without resources after fighting two elections within two years the party was desperately short of finance. This factor, more than anything else, prevented the party rebuilding its organisation and adopting candidates. Throughout 1924, protracted negotiations took place to settle the financial question. But by the summer, despite repeated contacts, nothing had been achieved.[8]

By then, however, the political scene was also significantly changing, for an issue had arisen which was to end the life of the minority Labour

[6] See Chris Cook and John Ramsden (eds), *By-Elections in British Politics* (1973) pp. 44–71.

[7] T. Wilson (ed.), *The Political Dairies of C. P. Scott* (1973) entry dated 27 Nov. 1924.

[8] For the details of these discussions, see R. Douglas, op.cit., pp. 181–3.

Government: the question of relations with Soviet Russia. The issue of the Russian Treaty, however, was one on which Liberals again found themselves as divided as on most others – divisions reflected in the *Daily News* (sympathetic to MacDonald) and the *Daily Chronicle* (very much opposed to the Treaty, in line with Lloyd George's attitude). Lloyd George's antipathy to the treaty probably reflected the majority view of the party. Whilst a radical element, that included J. M. Kenworthy and J. M. Hogge, gave support to the treaty, most of the left-wing Liberals lined up with the right.[9]

The clamour against the treaty, led by Lloyd George, rapidly gained the support of Simon, Runciman, Grey, Mond, Maclean and C. F. Masterman. Possibly the Carmarthen by-election of 15 August also encouraged the Liberals to take a firmer line. On 3 September, the Liberal Party publication department produced a pamphlet entitled 'A Sham Treaty'. On 8 September, the *Daily Chronicle* followed up the attack with a series of articles entitled 'In Darkest Russia'.

Much, however, would depend in the last resort on Asquith's attitude. Asquith, who was ill at the time, gradually moved over towards the Lloyd George position. When Lloyd George saw Asquith early in September, he found him 'quite firm' in opposing the Treaty.[10] In a letter to *The Times* on 22 September, Asquith attacked the Russian Treaties as 'crude experiments in nursery diplomacy' and urged Parliament not to accept 'a loan of undefined amount, upon unspecified conditions'. However, at the same time, Asquith seemed to be urging the Liberals not to reject the Treaties totally but to amend them.

MacDonald, however, was determined to have no deal with the Liberals. At Derby, on 27 September, he left no doubt that he would fight an election rather than abandon his position. Four days later, as Parliament reassembled on 1 October, the Parliamentary Liberal Party supported a hard line. With only a handful of dissenters, the meeting passed a motion rejecting the idea of a guaranteed loan. It was notice on the Labour Government to quit.

Yet the Liberals were in an invidious position. If they stuck to their guns, a Labour defeat was inevitable. Yet was the issue of the Russian Treaty good ground on which to do battle? Kenworthy had warned the party meeting on 1 October that an election on this issue would be a disaster, a viewpoint shared by the *Manchester Guardian*.

<hr>

[9] T. Wilson, *The Downfall of the Liberal Party* (1966) p. 276.

[10] Fisher's diary, 16 Sept. 1923, *H. A. L. Fisher Papers*, quoted in T. Wilson, op.cit., p. 276.

The Russian Treaty had another tactical disadvantage for the Liberals. They occupied a dangerous middle ground; for whatever the party might think of a guaranteed loan, there was a considerable desire to improve relations with Russia.

The Liberals were, in fact, caught in their own trap. They could not compromise with Labour, because Labour would not compromise. They had to face an election, or abandon their posture that they were keeping Labour to a safe moderate course.

In fact, at this eleventh hour, the Liberal dilemma was unexpectedly resolved, for Labour chose to accept defeat, not on the issue of the Russian Treaties, but over the Campbell Case.

On 1 October, at the same meeting at which the Parliamentary Liberal Party decided to oppose the Russian Treaties, Asquith stated that his party would support a 'reasonable motion' on the Campbell affair. On 2 October, the Liberals put down an amendment to the Conservative motion of censure, calling for the establishment of a Select Committee to inquire into the matter. The fate of the Labour Government was effectively sealed when, at the end of the Campbell debate on 8 October, Baldwin announced that the Conservatives would vote for the Liberal amendment and not for their own motion. The Liberal amendment was subsequently carried by 364 votes to 199. Fourteen Liberals on the left wing of the party voted against the amendment proposed by their own party. They included Hogge, Kenworthy, Percy Harris and Jowitt.

After the defeat of the MacDonald Government on the Campbell Case, events moved swiftly. Parliament was dissolved on 9 October. The election itself was fixed for Wednesday 29 October. It was a horrific prospect for the Liberal Party, even though an event which they themselves had precipitated. For the advent of the general election in October 1924 found the Liberal Party totally and completely unprepared for the battle. At the dissolution, the party had only 280 candidates ready, whereas senior Liberals believed that 450 was the minimum necessary to wage an effective campaign.

The reason for this limited field of candidates was to be found in Lloyd George's unwillingness to provide money from his Fund. Eventually, with the election upon the party, Lloyd George agreed to contribute £50,000 – a hopelessly inadequate sum.

This financial handicap, however, was only one factor causing the massive reduction in Liberal candidates. In 1924, there was simply no will at constituency level to fight, even in constituencies where Liberals were within striking distance of victory.

Even more significant in reducing the numbers of Liberal candidates fielded was the arrangement of local anti-Socialist pacts by Liberals at constituency level. This, as much as any other factor, helped set the seal on the Liberal fate in the election.[11]

The overall result of Liberal lack of money, pacts with the Conservatives, a general disinclination to fight and problems in finding candidates was tremendous. The Liberals abandoned 136 seats fought in 1923 – no less than 96 in former three-cornered contests (55 in Conservative-held seats). At the close of nominations, whereas Labour fielded 514 candidates, an increase of 87 over December 1923, the Liberal total had slumped from 457 to 340.

The disastrous effect of fielding only 340 candidates was further compounded by an equally abysmal campaign. The Liberal Election Manifesto offered little new. Free Trade still figured prominently, whilst most other proposals could be found, in greater or lesser degree, in the Conservative and Labour manifestos. In the emotional and bitter campaign atmosphere of October 1924, the Liberals' lack of any real or distinctive Liberal policy was a calamity. Essentially, the 1924 election campaign was fought on three issues: Russia; the need for stable government; and the record of Labour in office, particularly in respect of housing and unemployment. All three were topics on which the Liberals had nothing to contribute. Or rather, the Liberals said nothing not being said already by Labour and Conservative. In the circumstances of 1924, Labour could thus launch a major attack on the Liberals – both for their lack of policy and their alliance with Conservatism.

Few Liberals had expected the party to fare well in the circumstances of October 1924. Few, however, envisaged quite the total annihilation that the party would suffer. The outcome of the election of October 1924 returned the Conservatives to power with 412 seats (46·8 per cent of the votes cast), Labour emerged with 151 seats (33·3 per cent of the total votes) and the Liberals with a mere 40 seats (17·8 per cent).

There were hardly any comforting factors for the party. Liberals lost no less than 105 seats to the Conservatives, who swept back to victory in the rural and middle-class constituencies lost in 1923. Virtually no area of the country escaped: in the English counties, the Liberals lost all but four of the 67 seats they were defending. In the South-East, Greater London and East Anglia not a single seat the Liberals were defending was retained. In South Wales, the only seat to return a Liberal was in Swansea West. In Scotland, although the Highland Liberal strongholds remained faithful (perhaps because three of the five seats here were uncontested), outside this Celtic fringe not a single other county constituency returned a Liberal.

[11] For these pacts, see Chris Cook, *The Age of Alignment* (1975) p. 294.

If the counties had deserted the Liberals, even worse was the almost total annihilation of the party in the boroughs. In the 139 constituencies in the 11 largest cities, the Liberals had elected only six members, while only Percy Harris, in South-West Bethnal Green, had faced Conservative opposition. Throughout the country, only seven Liberals managed to secure election in three-cornered contests. Even these only survived by the narrowest of margins: Lambeth North had a majority of only 29 and Bethnal Green South-West a majority of 212. Only a single Liberal took over 50 per cent of the poll in a three-cornered contest.

Of the 40 Liberals who survived the massacre, only perhaps 15 could be said to have won their seats unaided by Conservative or Labour votes. Of these, seven were in Wales and four in Scotland. To those Liberals who had voted with Labour over the Campbell affair, there could seem little justice in politics, for only two survived the election.

The size of the Liberal débâcle could not simply be measured in terms of seats lost. In many cases, sitting Liberal MPs found themselves suddenly at the foot of the poll. No less than 31 Liberal candidates defending Liberal-held seats finished third. They included such figures as W. R. M. Pringle (in Penistone) and Hogge in Edinburgh. In 26 seats the Liberal share of the vote fell by over 15 per cent. To make matters even worse, of the five unopposed Liberal seats in 1923 which were contested in 1924, only one was retained (at Wolverhampton East).

Hardly any Liberal leaders (except Lloyd George, Mond and Simon) escaped the massacre. Asquith lost his seat, and his fate was shared by Macnamara, W. R. M. Pringle, George Lambert (who had represented South Molton since 1891), Leif Jones, Geoffrey Howard and Isaac Foot.

In the wake of such an electoral disaster, the old historic Liberal party was finished. After the false dawn of 1923, the election of October 1924 had consigned the Liberal Party to virtual destruction.

What future was there for the Liberals? During the period from November 1924 to October 1926, the last phase when Asquith was leader of the party, the future looked bleak indeed. The old problems remained for the party – of finance, candidates, organisation and morale. For Asquith (now removed to the Upper House as Lord Oxford) the election results added a new problem. In 1923, the election returns had decimated the former Coalition Liberals and greatly increased the numbers of Asquith's followers. During 1924, the Parliamentary Liberal Party was overwhelmingly Asquithian. After October 1924, over half of the small band of Liberals were former Coalition Liberal MPs or candidates.

On 2 December Lloyd George secured his own election as Chairman of the Parliamentary Liberal Party, by 26 votes to seven, with seven abstentions. Meanwhile, a group of nine MPs who refused to acknowledge Lloyd George formed themselves into a 'Radical Group' under Runciman. Only weeks after a disastrous election, the Liberals were again an openly divided party. Not only was the party quite clearly deeply divided, it was more than apparent that, unless urgent action was taken, its grass-roots organisation would simply collapse.

Hence, immediately after the election, Asquith's first act was to appoint Maclean as head of committee to find out what was wrong with the Liberal Party – the first of many such inquests – and an attempt was made to put the finances of the party in order

It was not long before the attempt to restore the finances of the party (through the 'Million Fund' launched at a major Liberal Convention in January 1925) had also begun to collapse. By the end of 1925 the idea of restoring Liberal finances through an appeal to the ordinary supporter had foundered.[12]

At the same time, organisation was collapsing further as agents left and money was not forthcoming. As Lloyd George bitterly observed, whatever the decay of agriculture might have been, it was nothing to that which had fallen upon the Liberal organisations in a very large number of constituencies throughout the country.[13] Candidates were equally unobtainable.

Even in by-elections the tide went against the Liberals. In March 1926 the party lost a seat in the Combined English Universities to the Conservatives. The worst humiliation came on 29 November 1926 when Kenworthy, the Liberal M.P. for Hull Central, defected to Labour. In the ensuing by-election, Kenworthy was re-elected with 52·9 per cent of the poll, the Liberal taking a mere 9·5 per cent.

Meanwhile, relations between Asquith and Lloyd George deteriorated even further during 1925 and the first part of 1926. The perennial question of Lloyd George's contribution to the finances of the party continued to plague relations (most especially with the failure of the Million Fund). Lloyd George's radical plans for land and unemployment (see p. 107) further alienated Asquith – who was largely unconsulted about them. It only needed one more crisis to bring about the final rupture between Asquith and Lloyd George. It was to occur in May 1926 with the General Strike.

---

[12] T. Wilson, op. cit., p. 318.
[13] See Lloyd George's speech at the National Liberal Club, 5 Apr. 1927, quoted in T. Wilson, ibid., p. 315.

9 Lloyd George Again: 1926–1931

As with most other events, the advent of the General Strike exposed a further series of divisions in the Liberal ranks. Although there was much sympathy with the miners among many Liberals, the party recognised that the Strike was in effect directly challenging the Government. It was a challenge that few Liberals could support. The outstanding exception was Lloyd George.

The Liberal Shadow Cabinet made clear its position at the outset: all the resources of the Government should be used to achieve victory over the strike. As if to reinforce Liberal opinion that the strike must be crushed, Simon warned the trade union leaders that they stood liable at law to damages 'to the uttermost farthing' of their possessions – a highly dubious assertion. But whilst Simon was saying exactly the words that made music in the Conservative ears, Lloyd George was adopting a more radical position.

He wrote to Sir Godfrey Collins (the Liberal Chief Whip) declining to attend the Liberal Shadow Cabinet meeting fixed for 10 May. Lloyd George declared that he would not join in denouncing the strike unless the Government's handling of the situation and its refusal to negotiate were also denounced. Although Asquith seemed at first to react calmly, on 20 May he took issue with Lloyd George, denouncing him roundly to the delight of his followers.

The uneasy shadow war between the two antagonists was over: their last battle was under way. But it was a battle in which Asquith was to emerge the loser. A most acrimonious exchange of letters and views took place. On 1 June, twelve Shadow Cabinet Liberals wrote to Asquith, supporting his stand against Lloyd George. Its bitter language marked a new degree of acrimony in a struggle never lacking in vitriol.

Though Lloyd George had secured his position as Chairman by 26 votes to seven, it was unclear that he would win so easily if a vote of confidence was required. But, having assured his right-wing supporters that he had no intention of allying with Labour, Lloyd George won by 20 votes to ten. At this moment, Asquith suffered a stroke on 12 June, keeping him out of politics for three months. Five days later, the annual meeting of the National Liberal Federation began at Weston-super-Mare. Though recriminations were kept out, and a virtually unanimous resolution of support for Asquith was carried, these events were only shadow politics. In October, Asquith resigned the Leadership. He died on 15 February 1928.

In the circumstances of October 1926, the Liberals had to look to Lloyd George. Without him, the party was both leaderless and penniless. Knowing the strength of his position, now Asquith was removed from politics, Lloyd George laid down his terms. His price was nothing less than full control of the party machine, together with the departure or retirement of those Asquithians he so disliked. Lloyd George's offer of massive financial aid to the party meant the end for Phillipps, Gladstone and Hudson.[1]

Lloyd George was intent on a new broom. In place of the departed Asquithians, a new appointment of great importance for the future history of the party was made. The new head of the party organisation was Sir Herbert Samuel. It was an inspired choice, for Samuel was one of the few Liberals acceptable to all sections of the party, since during the bitter internal quarrels in the party he had been High Commissioner in Palestine.

The choice of Samuel to head the party machine was the first step towards revival. But Lloyd George's greatest contribution was in the field of policy. During 1925, with Asquith still leader of the party, Lloyd George had poured money and resources into devising and producing new Liberal policies – even though few Liberals except Lloyd George and his associates took much part in their formulation.

The first of the new policies – the land scheme – had already been published in October 1925. It had been greeted with mixed feelings. The report of the 'Land Inquiry Committee', published in book form as *'Land and the Nation'*, but popularly known as the Green Book, aroused criticism, both of its contents and of the way in which it appeared.[2]

Further opposition, from candidates and Liberal Associations, flared when it was announced that Lloyd George had founded a new organisation, the Land and Nation League, to campaign for the implementation of the Green Book. Despite opposition to both his methods and his proposals, Lloyd George had carried on regardless. His next major contribution was in the field of unemployment, where a 'Liberal Industrial Inquiry' had been set up in 1925. A remarkable team of politicians and economists, including E. D. Simon, W. T. Layton, J. M. Keynes, Ramsay Muir, Herbert Samuel, Philip Kerr,

[1] The intrigues and negotiations of these months are well detailed in both Douglas and Wilson. See R. Douglas, op.cit., pp. 188–97.

[2] Particular opposition was aroused by the proposal to end the private ownership of agricultural land by converting farmers into 'cultivating tenants' under the supervision of county committees.

Hubert Henderson and Lloyd George himself, had collaborated in this project. The fruit of their work was published as the first 'Yellow Book', *Britain's Industrial Future,* in February 1928. As Robert Skidelsky comments, the far-reaching proposals for government planning which it advocated were well in advance of anything else in existence at the time.[3]

Following the publication of the 'Yellow Book', a special committee headed by Lloyd George, Lord Lothian and Seebohm Rowntree was established to work out in detail the various schemes of national development. Its report, issued in March 1929 as *We Can Conquer Unemployment* provided the basis of the Liberal campaign in the 1929 general election.

The emergency programme outlined in *We Can Conquer Unemployment* gave priority to roadbuilding. A programme of roads, costing £145 million and employing 350,000 men for two years was envisaged. Housing was also given particular attention. In all, the programme constituted one of the boldest and most imaginative schemes yet put forward.

These sweeping policy proposals demonstrated that, once again, the return of Lloyd George, with his energy and dynamism, had brought a new sense of purpose to the party. And indeed, within six months of his return it seemed that at long last a real recovery was at hand. On 28 March 1927 the Liberals gained Southwark North from Labour. A series of by-election victories followed: Bosworth was won on 31 May 1927, Lancaster fell on 9 February 1928 and St Ives a month later. On 20 March 1929 Eddisbury fell to the Liberals, and the following day Holland-with-Boston was also gained. All these gains were from Conservatives and, with the partial exception of Bosworth, were in rural, agricultural areas. Had the Liberals been able to follow up their initial victories in Southwark North and Bosworth with a gain in the Westbury by-election of June 1927 (which the Conservatives retained by a mere 149 votes), the revival might have gathered even further momentum.

As it was, in the spring of 1928 optimism ran very high. Lord Rothermere wrote to Lloyd George on 10 April 1928: 'You are back to where the Liberal Party was at the election of 1923. . . . In my opinion, an election today would give you just about the same number of followers.' Rothermere went on: 'Continue as you are doing and I think you and I will agree . . . that there is almost a certainty that the Liberals will be the second party in the next House. This would give you the Premiership beyond any question.' While Rothermere's political

---

[3] R. Skidelsky, *Politicians and the Slump* (1967) p. 521.

judgement does not have to be taken too seriously, none the less the Liberals were doing undeniably well, as the following figures indicate.[4]

	No.	*Average*		
		Con. %	*Lab. %*	*Lib. %*
May 1926–end 1927	10	37·9	33·6	28·5
Jan.–Dec. 1928	15	39·8	30·5	29·7
1929–Gen. Elec.	5	33·6	44·6	21·8

However, even at the height of Liberal success in 1928, Lloyd George himself realised that Liberal by-election victories would not necessarily mean gains at a general election. He wrote to Garvin of the *Observer* in October 1928: 'I have followed your analysis of the by-election figures. I am convinced that 'the triangle' will enable Labour to sweep the industrial constituencies next time.' Lloyd George had written in similar vein to Philip Snowden: ' . . . owing to the fact that Liberal and Labour candidates are fighting each other, there are 170 seats which will go to the Conservatives which in straight fights would have been either Labour or Liberal.' Lloyd George's judgement was nearer the mark.

Labour was, indeed, the Achilles heel of the Liberal Party. Although the Liberals succeeded in winning a series of rural seats from the Conservatives, Labour was continuing to be the main beneficiary of the Government's unpopularity – capturing no less than twelve Conservative-held seats between 1924 and 1929.

Despite the strength of Labour, however, the coming of the 1929 election found the Liberals more confident and in better shape than for very many years. Armed with Lloyd George's sweeping proposals on unemployment, and with party organisation, as a result of Samuel's work, in a healthier state than at any time since before 1914, the Liberals entered the 1929 election making their last great effort of the inter-war period for power. As Trevor Wilson has written of the Liberal appeal in 1929,

> . . . It is unlikely that the British electorate has ever been paid the compliment of a more far-sighted and responsible party programme.[5]

Although the Liberals entered the 1929 election in confident mood, pouring out a mass of literature and propaganda, and although they fielded 513 candidates well supplied by the Lloyd George Fund, there were doubts on how well the party would really do. As Douglas has written, there were strange signs of doubting, even in the moment of

---

[4] D. E. Butler, *The Electoral System in Britain since 1918*, 2nd ed. (Oxford, 1963) p. 181.

[5] T. Wilson, *The Downfall of the Liberal Party*, p. 345.

battle.[6] With three-cornered contests in most constituencies, Liberals anxiously awaited the result as the nation polled on 30 May 1929.

The outcome of the general election was to prove a bitter disappointment for the Liberal Party.

It was, as the *Liberal Magazine* sadly admitted, 'a lost battle in view of our hopes and aims.'[7]

The result was as follows:

	Votes	%	Cands	MPs
Conservative	8,656,225	38·1	590	260
Liberal	5,308,738	23·6	513	59
Labour	8,370,417	37·1	569	287
Others	312,995	1·2	58	9
	22,648,375	100·0	1,730	615

Labour, for the first time in its history, had become the largest single party, but still without an overall majority. The Liberals finished with 59 seats. Although they had polled 5,308,738 votes (23·6 per cent of the total) they had won only 35 seats not captured in 1924 and lost 19. Of these 19 losses, 17 were to Labour. These figures demonstrated only too clearly Liberal inability to recapture industrial seats – indeed, the party lost further ground to Labour in the North-East, Yorkshire, Lancashire and the East End of London.

Virtually all of the 35 Liberal victories came in rural areas, including some such as Ashford, with no vestige of a Liberal tradition,[8] but mainly in the traditional areas of Liberal support – rural Scotland and Wales (where seven seats were captured), East Anglia (nine Liberal gains) and Cornwall (five Liberal gains). Apart from these traditional areas, no other part of the country returned a solid phalanx of Liberal MPs.

However, although 1929 was a battle lost in terms of seats won, in terms of votes cast the Liberals had achieved a remarkable result. In the 513 seats contested by Liberals, the party obtained 28 per cent of the votes cast. No less than 310 candidates (64 per cent of the total) polled between 14 per cent and 34 per cent of the votes – clear evidence of a more even spread of the Liberal vote throughout the country. In contrast, only 15 Liberals obtained more than 50 per cent of the total votes cast in their constituencies.

The best Liberal performance came, as we have seen, in the areas where the party was traditionally strong. The Liberals fared worst in Glasgow and Birmingham. Although not capturing any of Labour's

[6] R. Douglas, op. cit., p. 203.
[7] *Liberal Magazine*, Sept. 1929.
[8] T. Wilson, *The Downfall of the Liberal Party*, pp. 349–50.

strongholds in the mining areas, the Liberals polled well in the valleys of South Wales, coming second to Labour in Aberavon, Caerphilly, Gower, Neath, Ogmore and Pontypridd.

In the 103 constituencies which all three major parties contested in 1924 and 1929 the Liberal share of the poll increased from 24·8 per cent to 29·0 per cent. Yet, whichever way the Liberals argued, either in terms of seats or votes, they had lost the election. No change in the voting system would have given them a majority. They were now destined to the position of a third party, holding the uncomfortable middle ground in the politics of the second Labour Government. The high hopes engendered by the revival under Lloyd George had suffered a bitter disillusion.

The years between the formation of the second Labour Government in May 1929 and the general election of 1935 saw a transformation in British politics. The financial crash of 1931, the break-up of the Labour Government and the subsequent National Government all presented new problems and possibilities for the Liberals. During this period the Liberals experienced further dissension and serious decline, even though enjoying a taste of office that had not been theirs for a decade. By 1935, the Liberals had been reduced to the unimportant sidelines of British politics.

This disastrous period for the Liberals opened, as it had in January 1924, with the party once more supporting a minority Labour Government. Unlike 1924, however, Liberals did not need to give constant support to Labour in the division lobbies, since the government could survive even if Liberals abstained. This refinement, however, was of little consolation for the Liberals. They had fought for victory in 1929. The modest advance that had been achieved in fact only served to disguise a major disaster. The party had thrown everything into the battle. Its reserves of energy and purpose were gone. Leading Liberals were not long in recognising this. Hardly had the dust of the electoral battle settled before defections from the party began. William Jowitt (Liberal Member for Preston) accepted the post of Attorney-General in the Labour Government. Others, such as F. E. Guest, at last formally joined the Conservative Party.

For those who remained within the party, in Parliament and in the constituencies, the outlook was one of gloom. The most immediate problem facing the party organisation was finance. The 1927 agreement expired automatically three months after the election. Despite attempts by the Administrative Committee, Lloyd George obstinately refused to finance the party any longer. Eventually, under pressure, financial assistance continued until June 1930. Nothing was forthcoming after that date.

The consequence was not long delayed. Headquarters grants to the Federations ceased entirely. The Eastern Counties Federation reluctantly dismissed its last full-time officials. It was typical of other District Federations. Worse still, the party was forced to let by-elections go uncontested. In only a tiny number of the by-elections from 1929 to 1931 were Liberals brought forward. All fared disastrously. In the constituencies, candidates were simply not being adopted. Ramsay Muir estimated that at least £250,000 was required for improving organisation and supporting candidates.

Not surprisingly, Lloyd George's refusal to contribute further brought a renewal of bitter attacks. Old Asquithians, such as Vivian Phillipps, bitterly attacked the Fund as against the 'best traditions of our public life'. Less heated but quite definite attacks came from the *Manchester Guardian* and the *Daily News*.

It was against this background that the Parliamentary Liberal Party faced the position of once again holding the balance of power – a position with an unhappy precedent in 1924.

In 1929, the position was rather different. Baldwin had resigned straight after the election, so there was no question of the Liberals putting Labour into office. The first preoccupation of the Liberals, remembering their experience in 1924, was to present a united front. This feeling was strongly put forward at the first party meeting after the election in June 1929. Despite good intentions, this party unity lasted only a few months, destroyed by the basic and unanswered question – what should be the Liberal policy towards the Labour Government?

The publication of the Coal Bill in December 1929 brought this problem to a head. For whilst Liberals sympathised with many objectives of the Bill, in their view the many problems of the coal industry could be saved only by an imaginative policy imposed from above, including the amalgamation of pits into economic units. The Labour measure involved nothing so drastic. Liberals particularly objected to the Bill's proposed 'quota system' which would have tended to bolster inefficient pits. Despite attempts by William Graham, the President of the Board of Trade, to conciliate the Liberals, Lloyd George led the Liberal Party in voting against the second reading.

The result was the first of many Liberal splits. Two Liberals (Geoffrey Mander and Sir William Edge) voted with the Labour Government. Six others remained deliberately seated in the Commons. The outcome was a Labour majority of eight on 19 December. Two months later, in February 1930, on a crucial amendment to the Bill, four Liberals voted with the Government, whilst eight more abstained. On each occasion, three prominent Liberals helping to save the Coal Bill were

Runciman, Maclean and Leif Jones, all on the 'right' of the party and Liberal Council members. As in 1924, an incipient 'three-way split' was developing in the Liberal ranks at Westminster. The Chief Whip, Sir Robert Hutchinson, subsequently tendered his resignation. Although this was refused, the damage had already been done. Meanwhile, the Labour Party's inactivity on the unemployment front was being attacked by the Liberals. At the annual conference of the party in October 1929, Samuel attacked Thomas for having failed to rise to the level of the task ahead of him. More rudely, referring to Thomas's six-week trip to Canada, Sir Charles Hobhouse gibed that the government was rapidly becoming a subsidiary of Cook's Tourist Agency. In March 1930, Lloyd George had been widely expected to launch a major attack on the Government's handling of the unemployment question. The Liberal fiasco on the Coal Bill, however, initiated a dramatic change of policy on the part of Lloyd George. From March 1930 onwards Lloyd George adopted the policy of granting the Government general Liberal support – in particular in the two important areas of agriculture and unemployment. But Lloyd George's policy of Liberal – Labour co-operation had already been overtaken by events beyond his control.

During 1930, the unemployment question took a critical turn for the worse. So serious, in fact, that on 18 June MacDonald declared that the unemployment issue required the assistance and co-operation of all the parties. Although the Conservatives refused any co-operation, Lloyd George pledged that the Liberals would give assistance. A friendly, if unproductive, series of discussions then took place between Lloyd George, Lord Lothian, Seebohm Rowntree and the Labour leaders. These friendly discussions turned, on 18 September, to the wider question of future relations between Liberal and Labour. Lloyd George, making no secret of the fact that he would prefer to see a period of co-operation with Labour, made it clear that in return for such support Liberals would need the promise of electoral reform.

Such a dialogue between Lloyd George and the Labour Government was taking the party towards trouble. The rifts within the Liberal ranks over the degree of co-operation that should be extended to Labour were already wide. In November 1930, they cracked.

The occasion was precipated by the outcome of a vote on 3–4 November on a Conservative motion on the King's Speech. Despite the official Liberal instruction to abstain, five Liberals supported the Conservative amendment and four voted with the Labour Government. Among those voting with the Conservatives was the Liberal Chief Whip, Sir Robert Hutchinson. He subsequently resigned, and was replaced by Sir Archibald Sinclair.

At the same time as Hutchinson resigned, a further calamity hit the party. Sir John Simon, who had warned Lloyd George late in October that he could not support Labour on a vote of confidence, made public his letter in the press. The Liberals were at war with one another once again. Simon, by declaring that he wished to ally with the Conservatives to bring down the Labour Government at the earliest opportunity, had effectively destroyed the unity and credibility of the party. As Roy Douglas has written: 'It was no longer a question of isolated rebels opposing Lloyd George on isolated measures; rather Simon had publicly declared war on Lloyd George's whole policy towards the Labour Government.'

Simon, whatever many Liberals thought of his action, was in many ways only telling the unpalatable truth: namely, that the Liberals were only maintaining a Labour Government for fear of the electoral consequences. Meanwhile, the fortunes of the Liberal Party went from bad to worse. In March 1931 Sir Archibald Sinclair (Hutchinson's successor as Chief Whip) resigned after a particularly hopeless example of Liberal cross-voting. The outcome of the crisis was a party meeting to lay down future policy. This meeting passed a weak resolution affirming the independence of the party, outlining the principles of Liberal policy and agreeing to support this or any government which would help put this policy into effect.

Even this tepid resolution failed to produce a united front. Only 33 voted for the motion, with 17 against. Of these, seven were Simonites, the rest, led by Ernest Brown, argued against the Liberals providing even 'general' support to the Labour Government.

The net result of this division and disunity, together with the growing support for Protection in the country, left the Liberal Party in a parlous condition in mid-1931. To add to its difficulties, the Liberal Press was becoming a rapidly depleted force. Two important dailies, the *Westminster Gazette* and the *Daily Chronicle* both passed out of existence.

On the electoral front, the Liberal by-election record proved equally dispiriting. In the first contests after the 1929 General Election, the Liberal vote was uniformly so, with particularly poor results at Twickenham (August 1929) Nottingham Central (May 1930) and Bromley (September 1930). Although the party did well at Shipley (November 1930) and Whitechapel (December 1930), during 1931 the outlook grew bleaker. In every contested by-election (except for Scarborough, where no Labour candidate stood) the Liberal share of the poll had fallen, in many cases disastrously. Other seats simply went uncontested. To complete the misery being heaped on the party, Simon's breakaway came to a head when he, together with Ernest Brown and

Hutchinson, resigned the Liberal whip on 26 June 1931, thus provok-
ing a fresh crisis in the party. A month later, on 27 July, just before
Parliament rose for the summer recess, another blow hit the party:
Lloyd George became very seriously ill. The effective management of
the party passed to Sir Herbert Samuel, the Deputy Leader of the
Parliamentary Liberal Party. With Lloyd George out of action, the
party split, taunts from the Conservatives, and persistent humiliation
at the hands of Labour, the Liberal Party faced a bleak future when
Parliament adjourned on 31 July 1931.

This situation was transformed in August 1931 when the Labour
Government collapsed. On 23 August, MacDonald went to see the
King. The King subsequently saw both Samuel, who supported the
case for a National Government, and Baldwin, who also argued a
similar case. On Monday 24 August, after the resignation of the
Labour Cabinet, MacDonald became Prime Minister of a new
National Government. Samuel, after consulting Lloyd George (who
was still seriously ill) suggested various Liberal names to serve in the
new Government. In the event, the new Cabinet included four Labour
ministers, four Conservative and two Liberal. Sir Herbert Samuel
became Home Secretary; and the Marquis of Reading Foreign Secretary. Other senior Liberals to take office included Sir Donald Maclean
(President of the Board of Education), Sir Archibald Sinclair (Secretary of State for Scotland) and the Marquis of Crewe (Secretary for
War).

Not surprisingly, a meeting of Liberal MPs, peers and candidates
gave warm support to the decision to enter the National Government.
The decision was similarly widely approved at constituency level, with
the Liberals showing a rare degree of unanimity.

The reason was clear to see. MacDonald, though splitting his own
party, offered a way of salvation for the Liberals. The hard-pressed
party had been offered an alternative to the election they so feared
which gave them the chance to co-operate with a government and,
indeed, to take office in it.

It was only later that the trap into which the Liberals had fallen was
revealed. The Conservatives had welcomed the National Government
in that it meant the end of a Labour government, but they were
also determined to have an election. Pressure to this end mounted
during September, despite dogged Liberal resistance.

On 23 September, a meeting of Liberal MPs instructed Samuel to
convey to MacDonald their determined opposition to a general election. The Liberals, however, had no effective way of preventing an
election. MacDonald, with only the support of a tiny breakaway
Labour group, himself could provide no barrier to add to the Liberal

argument. The Simonites, secure in the knowledge that they would not face Conservative opposition, were not slow to discomfort Samuel by agreeing with the Conservative clamour for an election.

On 4 October, Samuel saw Lloyd George, who argued vehemently against an early election. On the evening of 5 October, despite the opposition of Samuel and Reading, the Cabinet decided on an appeal to the country. On 6 October, MacDonald formally saw the King. Polling day was fixed for 27 October.

Despite their opposition to an election, neither Samuel nor Reading resigned from the Government. Meanwhile Lloyd George fumed at the decision that had been taken; and two of his family resigned junior posts in the Government. The Liberal decision to fight the election as part of the Coalition did not only alienate Lloyd George. The Conservatives were far from pleased fighting alongside a party they were hoping to discredit. Not surprisingly, Liberal-Conservative relations became considerably strained during the campaign.

The Liberals, in fact, entered the 1931 election in a hopeless position. With Lloyd George hostile to the election, no funds were forthcoming from his Fund. In consequence, only a mere 112 candidates were fielded by the Samuelites, leaving many of the promising seats fought in 1929 uncontested. Money, however, was not the only factor. Few Liberals in 1931 evinced much fighting spirit. The will to win had vanished. For, in everything but name, the Liberals fought the election as prisoners of a Conservative-dominated Coalition.

The Liberals thus entered the 1931 election with few illusions on the likely result. As Ramsay Muir admitted, the dice were loaded against the party. On every side, the prospects for the party were bleak. The Liberals has simply no independent policy to put forward – except support for National candidates who were in most cases Protectionist. Meanwhile, the fact that the Liberals supported the National Government, and were represented in it, did not stop Conservatives attacking sitting Liberals. Although Samuel himself was supported by Baldwin, no less than five Liberal Ministers were opposed by Conservatives, whereas all 30 Conservative Ministers were unopposed by Liberals. No less than 81 clashes took place between Samuelite Liberals and Conservatives.

By way of contrast, the Simon Liberals enjoyed a much happier position. Not only, by and large, were their constituencies more safely Liberal, but by agreeing to support the Government's tariff proposals, they enjoyed far more Conservative goodwill. No less than 35 of the 54 Conservative candidates withdrawn in 1931 were to support Liberal Nationals (as the Simonite Liberals became known). Only one solitary straight fight occurred between a Conservative and a Liberal National, whereas 26 occurred between Conservatives and Samuelite Liberals, and only four constituencies saw a clash of Simonite and Conservative candidates.[9] Thus although the Simonite Liberals fielded only 41 candidates, their electoral prospects were immeasurably brighter. With Lloyd George opposed to Samuel's policy, and encouraging Liberals to vote Labour in the absence of Liberal candidates, the hapless Liberal Party entered the election attempting to travel in three directions simultaneously. The Simonites had adopted a semi-Conservative position, the Samuelite official party adopted a non-Conservative, anti-Labour stance and finally there was Lloyd George's attempt to revive a Liberal–Labour alliance.

In the circumstances of 1931, a victory for the National Government was almost inevitable. The Conservatives were returned with no less than 473 seats, Labour secured only 52 while the Liberals returned 72. Of these 72 Liberals, 35 were Liberal Nationals, 33 were followers of Samuel and there were the four Independent Liberals, all members of Lloyd George's family group.

On the surface, the Liberals had increased their representation by 13. This, however, was an increase in numbers without real substance. Its seats gained were won from Labour in the absence of Conservatives, whereas in 1929 its seats had been won by its own merit. Only ten of the 72 elected Liberals had been faced with Conservative opponents, six of these in Wales or Scotland. The Liberals held 46 of the seats won in 1929, losing 13 (all to Conservatives) and taking 26 – again all from Labour. Thus in Durham, Liberals captured such normally solid Labour seats as Consett and Bishop Auckland in the absence of Conservative candidates. Although Samuel retained his seat at Darwen with a 4000 majority, Donald Maclean only narrowly held North Cornwall. Two Liberal Ministers, Milner Gray in Mid-Bedfordshire and E. D. Simon in Penryn, were both defeated.

It was in terms of votes cast, however, that the Liberal reverse was most noticeable. Compared to 1929, the combined Liberal vote had fallen by over three million, the Labour vote by only 1¾ million. From virtually every side, the Liberals had lost ground. In the 51 seats contested in 1929 and 1931 by all three parties, the Liberal vote slumped. Only where no Conservative candidate was in the field were Liberals able to benefit from the swing to the National Government. Once again, as the party looked at the debris of the 1931 battle, the old truth again became apparent. Without Lloyd George, the Liberal Party did indeed seem doomed.

[9] These four clashes were in Ashford, East Dorset, Nuneaton and the Western Isles.

10 Dissension and Decline: 1931–1945

The outcome of the 1931 general election was a disaster for the party. The reconstruction of the Cabinet which followed the election reflected the greatly diminished importance of the Liberals in the new Parliament. Both Reading and Crewe retired from the Government; no Liberals replaced them, thus reducing the Liberals to an even smaller voice in the Cabinet. The Liberal Nationals, in contrast, were well rewarded. Simon was offered the Foreign Secretaryship, whilst Runciman became President of the Board of Trade.

The 1931 election had not merely been a severe defeat in electoral terms. The outcome left the party totally lacking in any sense of direction or purpose. This was particularly noticeable over the key question of the party's participation in the National Government.

As 1932 progressed, Liberal discontent at the National Government mounted. In March 1932, the National Government's decision to introduce the Import Duties Bill provoked a rebellion by the Samuelite Liberals. Although the Free Trade Cabinet Ministers were persuaded not to resign (through the agreement to differ), some 31 Liberals voted against the Bill's Second Reading. The growing hostility of both backbenchers and constituency opinion to the National Government was much in evidence at the annual conference of the party at Clacton in April 1932. At local level, this increasing hostility was soon evident in by-elections in such seats as Henley and North Cornwall, where Liberals waged virtually open war on Government candidates.

Meanwhile, as the National Government continued, the gulf between the Liberals and Liberal Nationals widened. In July 1932, the Liberal Nationals had set up a 'Liberal National Council'. The new organisation, with Hutchinson as chairman of its Executive Committee, set about co-ordinating Liberal National relations with the Conservatives and acted as a general propaganda and fund-raising machine.

This growing separation of Liberals and Liberal Nationals was brought to a head by the Ottawa Imperial Economic Conference. The agreements reached at Ottawa culminated in the resignation on 28 September of Samuel and the other Liberal Ministers (with the exception of Runciman) from the Government.

Samuel, although resigning from the Government, attempted a peculiar compromise. The Liberals took up seats on the Government backbenches, as critics but not as outright opponents of the Government. Although Samuel's curious compromise was approved by the Liberal Council and the National Liberal Federation, it was to prove an unworkable formula.

Samuel's decision to leave the National Government marked yet another divide with the Liberal Nationals. By October 1932, the gap between the two wings was virtually unbridgeable. Simon and the Liberal Nationals tightened their links with the Conservatives, whilst Samuel was left to work out what the role of the Liberals should be on the Government backbenches.

Both in Parliament and in the constituencies, Liberal difficulties mounted throughout 1933. In Parliament Liberal backbench opposition to National Government measures increased. In March, Liberals opposed the Agricultural Marketing Bill, in May Liberals voted against the Rent Restrictions Bill, and in June the Government's proposals for a World Economic Conference were denounced. By July, the Liberal position on the Government backbenches was becoming ludicrous. Within the party, it was clear to such figures as Sir Archibald Sinclair that the party would have to move into outright opposition. Sinclair, in fact, echoed the voice of the party at the grassroots. In May 1933, the party's annual assembly carried a motion calling for a move into opposition. A similar motion was passed at the Scottish Liberal Federation's annual meeting. Both assemblies carried a variety of motions strongly critical of the Government's unemployment and fiscal policies.

There was, perhaps, an unspoken reason why the party needed to move into opposition. The very identity of the party, and its morale, was visibly disintegrating. The party was virtually bankrupt; its by-election record was hardly encouraging; constituency organisation was in chaos. On 18 October, Samuel returned to England from an overseas visit. After sounding out the party, Samuel at last decided to bring the party into opposition. On 13 November, Samuel finally crossed the floor.

Even this decision, however, prompted further defection. Four of the 33 Liberals who had previously supported Samuel refused to follow him.[1] To offset this, Samuel's decision was warmly welcomed by the National Liberal Federation and all the area organisations.

The move into opposition, however, made little effective change in the fortunes of the party.

---

[1] R. H. Bernays, J. A. Leckie, W. McKeog, J. P. Maclay. As a compensation one former Liberal National (A. C. Curry) came over with Samuel.

Indeed, with the completion of Samuel's move to the opposition benches, as Liberals took stock of their position, the outlook looked dismal beyond measure. By 1933 the Liberals seemed really to have come to the point of no return. The party went on because it could go nowhere else.

The electorate seemed to share this view. In a disastrous by-election at Manchester Rusholme on 21 November the party polled a mere 9 per cent, compared to 33 per cent in 1931. A by-election at Harborough on 29 November confirmed that Liberal fortunes were fast declining. At the same time, the death in October of Lord Cowdray removed one of the party's chief benefactors.

Despite the move into opposition, the party found itself still unable to offer a very clear alternative to the National Government or Labour opposition. *Vis-à-vis* Labour, Liberals found themselves in particular difficulties, for although the party was opposed to nationalisation, on such issues as disarmament, support for the League of Nations, Free Trade, opposition to the cuts in unemployment pay and in plans for housing and social reform, Liberal policy was almost identical with Labour's.

Equally, *vis-à-vis* the National Government, Liberals found themselves as much at a loss to put forward a distinctly separate image. Over India, Liberals were in agreement; tariffs were proclaimed as a temporary expedient only; Baldwin claimed to support the League of Nations; and cuts in unemployment pay were restored in the budget of 1934. On many major issues, the National Government occupied the middle ground in British politics towards which Samuel aspired, and try as he might he could not dislodge it.

Thus the Liberal move into opposition, far from restoring the fortunes of the party, only served to make them worse. The by-elections of 1934 were even more disastrous than in 1933. On 8 February, the Liberals polled a mere 7 per cent at Cambridge, a seat where they had picked up 25 per cent of the votes in 1931. Only five of the twelve by-elections between April and December 1934 were fought by the party, with disastrous results in Weston-super-Mare, Rushcliffe and North Lambeth.

Against such a background, a distinct air of defeatism pervaded the party. Both the *News Chronicle* and the Liberal and Radical Candidates Association supported a revival of 'Lib–Labism'. Some Liberals abandoned the party altogether – the most important defector being H. L. Nathan, Liberal M.P. for Bethnal Green North-East, who joined Labour in July 1934. Lower down the scale, the number of prospective candidates deserting the party increased. All these defections, and rumours of defections, did nothing to increase Samuel's stature in the party.

It was hardly surprising that, once again, many Liberals turned their thoughts towards their one-time leader Lloyd George. In February 1934, the North Wales Liberal Federation called on Lloyd George to lead a great revival campaign throughout the country. In May, the National League of Young Liberals added their voice to the call. But Samuel was not willing to approach Lloyd George, whilst Lloyd George himself was still determined to pursue his own highly individualistic path, intervening in several by-elections not contested by Liberals to support Labour candidates, as at Swindon (in support of Christopher Addison) and Putney (in support of Edith Summerskill).

Consequently, the Liberal Party entered 1935 still lacking firm leadership or any stiffening of morale. Even more than hitherto, lack of finance and lack of enthusiasm in the constituencies resulted in by-elections being left uncontested. No by-election in 1935 was fought until May, when in a disastrous contest at Edinburgh West the party's share of the vote slumped. The previous month, to add to Samuel's problems, control of the Scottish Liberal Federation was temporarily lost to the Liberal Nationals. Whilst the Samuel Liberals were suffering these additional setbacks, and whilst the party drifted aimlessly on, Lloyd George returned to the political limelight.

On 17 January 1935, in a much-publicised speech at Bangor, Lloyd George launched his 'New Deal' campaign. The campaign, aimed at uniting under one banner all those opposed to the National Government, was essentially designed to ensure that as many 'progressive' MPs as possible were returned at the next election. Lloyd George's 'New Deal', however, did nothing to restore the Liberals. The coming of the 1935 general election found the Liberal Party disheartened, disorganised and in disarray.

Hopelessly short of finance, the Liberals fielded only 159 candidates, 41 more than in 1931 but 354 fewer than in 1929. With Liberal advocacy of Free Trade appearing almost unrealistic in the midst of world recession, and with the Abyssinia crisis forcing Liberals both to condemn and support the National Government simultaneously, the campaign hardly augured well for the Liberals. Gloomy predictions of a Liberal disaster by such figures as Ramsay Muir proved to be only too accurate.

The outcome of the election was yet another disaster for the Liberals; the party could win only half the seats won in the débâcle of 1924. With a mere 21 seats, the Liberals had been reduced to almost total impotence.

No significant area returned any number of Liberals: a few agricultural seats, such as the party's victory in Cumberland North, together with the isolated urban strongholds such as East Wolverhampton and East Birkenhead, were all that the party had left. The Liberals also lost their best men: Herbert Samuel was out at Darwen, Isaac Foot lost Bodmin and Walter Rea was ousted at Dewsbury. Only six Liberals returned had been opposed by both Labour and National Government candidates – three of these in rural Wales. The party's share of the national vote had fallen to a mere 6·4 per cent, even lower than the 7·2 per cent achieved in 1931. On average, each candidate obtained only 13 per cent of the votes cast. Even worse, many of the party's best seats went uncontested in 1935 because of the collapse of local organisation. In the 30 seats contested by all three major parties in 1931 and 1935, the Liberal share of the vote fell by 4 per cent. Whether in terms of votes or seats, whichever way Liberals attempted to analyse the results, there was only gloom to be seen.

On the surface, the Liberal Nationals, with 33 members, seemed to have done well. But their seeming strength was illusory; all were dependent on Conservative votes in their constituencies – indeed, no Liberal National was opposed by a Conservative. Curiously only in Denbigh and Oldham were Liberal Nationals opposed even by Liberals.

One consequence of the election, following the defeat of Sir Herbert Samuel by 1,157 votes in a contest in Darwen, was the election of a new leader. On Lloyd George's suggestion (the results of 1935 had partly healed the breach with the Lloyd George family group), Sir Archibald Sinclair, M.P. for Caithness and Sutherland, and Liberal Chief Whip in 1930–1, was elected. Sinclair appointed Percy Harris (M.P. for Bethnal Green South-West and the only Liberal to be returned in London) as Chief Whip.

The results of the 1935 election were additional proof, not only of the fading popular support for the Liberals, but of the almost total decay into which constituency organisation had fallen. Between 1931 and 1935 such Liberal Associations as had survived until then began to fall apart. The few organisations still active had either defected to the Liberal Nationals or were in a state of suspended animation, waiting for a lead that never came.

The disastrous results of 1935 were followed almost immediately by a by-election humiliation in Ross and Cromarty. In a Highland seat with a strong Liberal tradition, the party could only poll 4 per cent of the votes cast.

These shattering election results had a curious sequel. They revealed not only that the party was in complete decline but that it might disappear altogether. Even the blindest of Liberals could see the peril facing the party – a peril made even more imminent now that the

Liberal Nationals were Conservatives in everything but name.

Thus the sequel of the 1935 election was the appointment of the Liberal Reorganisation Commission (under Lord Meston) to reconsider the whole structure of party organisation. Its task was nothing less than to consider how to rebuild the party, and how to reshape the confused and unco-ordinated bodies that dated back to before 1914 – the National Liberal Federation, the Liberal Central Association and the variety of other autonomous bodies.

The proposals of the Meston Report were discussed at a party convention in London in June 1936. The essential central feature of this Report was the creation of the Liberal Party Organisation in place of the old National Liberal Federation. But the change was one of name rather than structure. Although aiming to provide a single policy-making body for the party, this new body left effective authority still in fact divided between the Annual Assembly, the party council, the executive and the leader. One longer-term effect of the Meston Report was to give considerably extra power to the Parliamentary Party and the Whips. The most immediately obvious weak feature of the report was its failure to pay much attention to the constituencies – the weakest part of the party. Meston's report had concentrated on rebuilding the party from the top, not from the foundation.

The essential fact of the Liberal Party in the late 1930s was that it lacked any very definite image. Sinclair, undoubtedly, saw his party as the non-Socialist alternative to Baldwin and Chamberlain. It was hardly realistic. Others, such as the Duke of Montrose, a recent convert from the Conservatives, saw the Liberals as the 'Centre Party'. Finally, the young radicals, rather foreshadowing developments thirty years later, wanted Liberalism to pursue a course away from the sterility and conservatism (as they saw it) of both the major parties. It was against this background that the idea of a 'United Front' gained much attention.

This idea was not absolutely rejected by the Liberals, although a fairly firm dismissal of the proposal was given by the Executive Committee of the Liberal Party in February 1937. The reasons for this rejection were set out in a letter from Milner Gray, the chairman of the Executive, to Aldous Huxley. Gray emphasised that, if the Labour Party was willing to co-operate on an agreed programme of reform, and if proportional representation could be introduced, then it would be possible for the two parties to fight on a united front at the polls and subsequently to co-operate in Parliament.

In fact, this possibility was never really on. As Lord Lothian remarked in April 1937, for the Liberals co-operation with Labour was never possible as long as Labour retained nationalisation at the forefront of its programme. Even had this barrier been overcome, it was clear that the great majority of the Labour Party were against any such 'United Front' proposal. The Labour Annual Conference at Edinburgh in 1936 had rejected the 'Popular Front' idea. By the end of 1937 the proposal had completely faded.

Relations with Labour were one problem for Liberals. Equally, the party's position *vis-à-vis* the Liberal Nationals was still in the balance. On both sides, hopes of a reconciliation still remained – during 1937 prolonged discussions between the two sides took place. But the issue of Free Trade remained a crucial stumbling-block. In January 1938 the talks finally broke down.

Despite the recommendations of the Meston Report, there was no obvious sign of a noticeable Liberal recovery, either in by-elections or in municipal elections. In the first twelve by-elections following the party's disaster in Ross and Cromarty, no Liberal candidates appeared. But from mid-1937 the by-election scene appeared a little more cheerful; Liberals did well, although not well enough for victory, in St Ives (30 June 1937) and in Dorset North (13 July 1937). During 1938, however, only two candidates came forward in 18 by-elections. Meanwhile Liberals suffered two further defections to the Liberal Nationals. In municipal elections, the two trends which had dominated municipal Liberal politics in the decade from 1918 to 1929 continued after 1930: a slow but persistent fall in the number of candidates brought forward, and an equally uninterrupted and persistent net loss of seats each November.

The percentage of Liberal candidates, which had stood at 18 per cent in 1922, had fallen to 12½ per cent by 1929. By 1931, the total had fallen below 10 per cent, by 1935 it was down to 7·9 per cent and by 1938 to a mere 5·6 per cent. The reduction in the number of Liberal municipal candidates, in itself a symptom of the malaise afflicting the party, was mirrored in the net loss of seats suffered each November. In every year (apart from the anti-Labour landslide of 1931) Liberals suffered a net loss of seats. Perhaps a better indication than this was to be found in the *share* of seats won by Liberals each November. The percentage of council seats won by Liberals fell from 14 per cent in 1931 to 10 per cent in 1935 and a mere 7·2 per cent by 1938.

These overall figures of gains and losses to a certain extent disguised a significant change in the *type* of seats won by Liberals during the 1930s. During this period Liberals lost steadily and persistently to Labour in a variety of Midland and Northern industrial districts, whilst themselves picking up isolated gains from the Conservatives in a few seaside and middle-class resorts.

Throughout the 1930s, the temptation of hard-pressed Liberal councillors to join forces with the Conservatives in an anti-Socialist 'municipal alliance' continued to increase. Each November, it was possible to detect another borough where the anti-Socialist forces had joined ranks. Thus, in 1932, it was the turn of Plymouth; in 1934 of Doncaster and Ipswich.

In the late 1920s, these anti-Socialist pacts had often provoked division and dissent within the Liberal ranks, especially from the more radical Young Liberals. During the 1930s, few such revolts occurred. Indeed, one of the most consistent features of municipal Liberalism in the 1930s was the absolute lack of any attempt to provide an independent Liberal challenge.

The domestic problems of the Liberal Party, however, were increasingly overshadowed by the growing threat of war. The Munich settlement itself provoked a division in the parliamentary party – 14 Liberals voting with Labour, four with the Government. Similar cleavages developed with the introduction of conscription in 1939, six Liberals supporting the measure, seven voting against. With the outbreak of war, however, the party lined up unanimously in support of the war. No senior Liberal spoke out against the declaration of hostilities.

With the outbreak of war against Nazi Germany in September 1939, it was agreed to suspend party electoral activity. Accordingly, the Whips of the three parties signed an agreement under which the general election (due in 1940) would be suspended for the duration of hostilities, the three parties would cease from political activities and that, when by-elections occurred, the party which had last gained the vacant seat would be allowed an unopposed return.

Whilst, quite obviously, wartime conditions demanded some form of electoral truce, none the less the actual signing of this agreement came as a surprise to the Liberal Party, whose Council had met only in June 1939 to make plans for a possible autumn general election. In fact, the electoral truce occasioned not only surprise but considerable resentment. This was perhaps natural in the Liberal ranks, for the party stood to lose more than Conservative or Labour from an indefinite cessation of political activity.

Although no important Liberal voice was raised against the declaration of war, many Liberals shared a total lack of confidence in Neville Chamberlain as war leader. In his last memorable speech to Parliament, in May 1940, when Norway had fallen, Lloyd George urged Chamberlain to make his own sacrifice to the war effort by laying down the seals of office. Other Liberals, most particularly Clement Davies, urged the removal of Chamberlain and his replacement by Churchill.

Chamberlain in fact resigned on 10 May 1940. The same day, Churchill formed a Government. The Liberals, like Labour, agreed to serve.

And, although no Liberal was included in the five-man 'Inner War Cabinet', Sir Archibald Sinclair was appointed Secretary of State for Air. Other Liberals accepted less senior positions.

With Sinclair fully occupied at the Air Ministry, the task of marshalling the Parliamentary Liberal Party devolved upon Percy Harris. Before long, the task had become a most difficult one as the party at the grass-roots became increasingly restive over the electoral truce. This discontent found focus with the birth in 1941 of the Liberal Action Group.

The originators of the Liberal Action Group, later known as Radical Action, included Lancelot Spicer (Chairman of the Group), Honor Balfour and Everett Jones. The group rapidly grew in size and influence. By February 1943 it was claimed that over 23 prospective candidates and as many members of the Council belonged to it. By the autumn of 1944, its supporters included five MPs and 34 prospective candidates.

Although not committed particularly to any distinctive 'line', most members of the group opposed the Parliamentary truce. As protests and complaints on the truce mounted, the Party Council was faced (on 17 June 1942) with a resolution urging the party to reconsider its position over the matter. This motion was withdrawn when a compromise was reached that it would be presented to the Leader, but none the less a variety of Independent Liberals began contesting by-elections.

The first such by-election occurred in Chippenham in August 1943. Dr Donald Johnson, a prominent member of the Council of the Liberal Party, resigned his position to contest the division as an Independent Liberal. The result was highly significant. In a safe, rural Conservative seat, which had been won with a majority of 5,421 in 1935, the Conservative scraped home with a tiny majority of only 195.

Further embarrassment for the Liberal Party came when, in November 1943, a prominent member of the Liberal Action Group, Miss Honor Balfour, similarly resigned her offices in the party to fight the Darwen by-election. Admittedly, the constituency had returned Herbert Samuel as a Liberal until 1935, but none the less Honor Balfour's performance in coming within 70 votes of victory, despite a letter from Archibald Sinclair supporting the official government candidate, was impressive.

The advent of 1944 only saw the split and discomfiture within the Liberal ranks widen. In February, Honor Balfour wrote a spirited article in *Liberal Forward* entitled 'I Challenge the Electoral Truce'. Shortly afterwards, the chairman of the Women's Liberal Federation resigned her offices to contest the by-election in Bury St Edmunds. Her candidature was endorsed by the Radical Action Group and the result was again close.

At the same time that Radical Action was embarrassing the party, further defections occurred. Sir Richard Acland, the Liberal M.P. for Barnstaple, formed an organisation known as Forward March which later became Common Wealth. Acland resigned from the party in September 1942.

These defections from the Liberal ranks were partly compensated for by very clear signs of disintegration within the Liberal National ranks. When Churchill had formed his coalition in May 1940, with Sir John Simon taking a peerage to become Lord Chancellor, the Liberal Nationals were henceforth led by Ernest Brown. His leadership was hardly a happy time. In February 1942, three MPs resigned from the party – Edgar Granville eventually joined Labour in 1945 and Hore-Belisha the Conservatives.

During the war an abortive attempt was made to fuse the Liberals and Liberal Nationals. This stemmed from an offer by Ernest Brown for discussions in July 1943 which Sinclair clearly welcomed. The stumbling block, however, was that Brown wanted the National Government to continue after the war. Both to Sinclair and to grass-roots Liberal opinion, such an attitude was impossible. The talks finally collapsed in November 1944. To compensate for these problems, the war saw one major recruit to the party – Sir William Beveridge. He was subsequently to play a prominent part in the 1945 election campaign.

In May 1945, with victory over Germany achieved, the Labour Party withdrew from the Churchill Government. In the subsequent 'Caretaker' government which preceded the general election, the Liberals did not continue in office.[2]

Thus, after the six-year electoral truce, party politics resumed in earnest in the summer of 1945. However, the Liberal Party machine was totally unprepared for an election. Despite this unpreparedness, and despite its parliamentary strength of only 18, the party had certain grounds for optimism. They rightly believed that the electorate would reject the Conservatives, despite the prestige of Churchill; more mistakenly, the Liberals believed the country would reject Socialism, and turn instead to the Liberal social reform programme.

In this respect, the party placed great hopes on Beveridge. Beveridge himself had become a Liberal Party member in July 1944; and in October 1944 he had succeeded George Gray as Liberal M.P. for Berwick-on-Tweed. For the 1945 election, Beveridge provided the Lib-

---

[2] With the exception of Gwilym Lloyd George, who remained as Minister of Fuel and Power.

eral Party with his report, *Full Employment in a Free Society*. It was the most important policy contribution the Liberals had offered since Lloyd George's 'We Can Conquer Unemployment' in the 1929 election.

Beveridge was the party's greatest hope, but far from their only one. The leader of the party, Archibald Sinclair, had an impressive record as head of the wartime Air Ministry. Lady Violet Bonham-Carter was a forceful platform campaigner. In addition, the Liberal ranks were fairly united – in itself an achievement. Moreover, there was some evidence that the party was appealing to a younger generation – 87 per cent of the Liberal candidates in 1945 were fighting their first Parliamentary election.

Any hopes that the Liberals would field over 500 candidates for the general election were rapidly doused when the election was called for July. Only 307 Liberal candidates were nominated – an insufficient total, even if all had been elected, for the party to have formed a government.

For the election, the Liberals put forward a radical manifesto that was propounded with great energy by Beveridge, the campaign chairman. These efforts, however, brought the party an almost nil return when the votes were counted. The election proved yet another disaster for the Liberals. The Conservatives, together with their National Liberal allies, polled 9,988,000 votes. Labour swept to power with nearly twelve million, whilst the Liberals could manage only 2,252,430, a mere 9 per cent of the total votes cast.

The Liberal Party in Westminster was decimated. Its total fell from 18 to 12. All the party leadership suffered defeat. Sinclair was out by 62 votes in Caithness and Sutherland; the Chief Whip, Sir Percy Harris, was defeated in Bethnal Green South-West; Beveridge himself failed at Berwick-on-Tweed – one of seven sitting Liberals to lose their seats.

Of the twelve Liberals who survived, one, Gwilym Lloyd George, ought really to be classed as a Conservative. He never attended meetings of the Liberal Parliamentary Party; he had remained a member of Churchill's caretaker Government after the Liberal Party had withdrawn, and his candidature in Pembrokeshire had the full support of the Conservatives. Only two Liberals could really be said to possess safe seats, Clement Davies in Montgomeryshire and Roderick Bowen in Cardiganshire.

Apart from the twelve elected Liberals, only eleven other candidates had come within striking distance of victory. In percentage terms, Rasmussen has calculated that only 8·8 per cent of Liberals secured second place, whilst 84·9 per cent came third.[3]

[3] J. S. Rasmussen, *The Liberal Party: A Study of Retrenchment and Revival* (1965).

There were other equally dismal features in 1945. Liberal-held seats at the dissolution (such as Bristol North) were not even contested; the average percentage vote achieved by each Liberal candidate fell to 18 per cent. After the disasters and dissensions of the inter-war years, the post-war period had brought the party to its lowest-ever level. It was, perhaps, a fitting comment on the fate of the party that the most traditionally Liberal of all seats – Lloyd George's old constituency of Caernarvon Boroughs – should desert to the Conservatives.[4]

---

[4] Lloyd George himself died in March 1945, having previously been elevated to the House of Lords as Earl Lloyd-George of Dwyfor.

11 A Party in the Wilderness: 1945–1956

In the general election of 1945, the Parliamentary Liberal Party had come near to extinction. In the years that followed, the party came very close to disappearing altogether. In the municipal elections, the story was the same. By 1938, except in an occasional stronghold in Yorkshire and Lancashire, the party had almost ceased to be represented on many borough councils. The municipal elections of November 1945, with their sweeping Labour gains, finally ended what remained of the old Liberal Party. A mere 92 Liberals (4.2 per cent), from a tiny field of 360 candidates, were successful, compared to 1,372 Labour and 384 Conservatives. Labour's tally of gains amounted to a massive 972 seats.

Such sweeping gains removed the last Liberal councillors in a variety of centres. In Wolverhampton, the elections left the town without a single Liberal councillor. In Birmingham the last three Liberals were swept away, in most cases in total humiliation. In Leeds, only a solitary Liberal was left on a council of 104.

The provincial boroughs where Liberals now retained a separate and strong identity had virtually all vanished. In none of the eighty largest county boroughs were Liberals in overall control. Only in Huddersfield did the Liberals just remain the largest single party. They were not even the second largest except in three towns – Burnley, Halifax and Keighley.

Elsewhere, Liberals had temporarily survived either by amalgamation with the Conservatives (as in the 'Citizens' Party' in Bristol, or the 'Progressives' in Sheffield) or by fighting as 'non-party' independents. In parliamentary by-elections, the party suffered the same fate. In the 52 by-elections during the Labour Government, Liberals fought only fourteen. Indeed, only in contests in the City of London and Bermondsey Rotherhithe could they obtain over 20 per cent of the votes polled. Elsewhere, they forfeited nine deposits from 14 candidates.[1]

With the party in such dire straits, only one course was open to it; a complete reconstruction and reconsideration of the whole organisation and machinery of the party. This the Liberals lost no time in doing. An

[1] See Chris Cook and John Ramsden, *By-Elections in British Politics* (1973) pp. 191–2.

eight-man Committee on Party Reconstruction was appointed, whose report duly appeared as *Coats off for the Future*. This was submitted to the Liberal Party annual assembly in the spring of 1946. At the same time, the party began turning its attention towards the problem of finance.

Throughout the inter-war period, the party had relied for financial help on the Lloyd George Fund, on rich candidates, and on such wealthy supporters as Lord Cowdray. By 1945, these sources of revenue were increasingly insufficient. The Lloyd George Fund was no longer there: radical candidates who could also pay their election bills had become increasingly rare. And yet the party had relied heavily on such candidates in 1945. The defeated Liberal Chief Whip wrote after the 1945 election:

> . . . to have found the number of candidates we did was no mean achievement. We had no large Headquarters fund to finance candidates and they had to depend, first on contributions out of their own pockets and secondly on monies raised locally.[2]

Such dependence on candidates who were financially well-off was hardly healthy. Hence, at the end of 1945, a committee was set up to examine the financial question.

The result was the launching of a 'Foundation Fund' in May 1946, designed to raise £125,000 over a five-year period. It started well, and after eight months of operation pledges of over £58,000 had been received. The annual official report to the assembly of March 1949 was able to state that the party's accounts were in the black.

Likewise, the organisation of the party in the constituencies improved. By 1947, according to Philip Fothergill, the chairman of the party executive, over 500 active local associations existed, compared to 200 only eight months earlier.

Although the financial position was improving, and to a certain extent morale was reviving, the recruitment of suitable prospective candidates remained a major problem. It was a problem partly of the Liberals' own making, for the party had no organised, systematic policy to recruit candidates. Chronic lack of funds left this matter largely in the hands of the secretary of the Liberal Central Association with the result that, in practice, much of the responsibility for securing candidates rested with the local associations.

To some extent, a corollary of the difficulty of attracting candidates was a fall in candidate standards. In 1946, the party established a

---

[2] *Westminster Newsletter*, Aug. 1945, quoted in J. S. Rasmussen, *The Liberal Party: A Study of Retrenchment and Revival* (1965) p. 209.

five-man Prospective Candidates Committee whose main function came to be the quality of adopted candidates, but in the rush to adopt candidates in 1950, this standard was virtually abandoned as 'vetting' of candidates lapsed. The result was a flood of inexperienced candidates who seriously weakened the party's image.

An even more fundamental problem than finance or candidates also faced the Liberals after 1945: to what degree, if any, should the party assist or co-operate with either the Conservatives or the Liberal National group which had severed itself from the main body in 1931?

Attempts had been made during the war, as we have seen, and had failed, to restore unity between the Liberal Party and the Liberal National Party. After 1945, the latter (which changed its name to National Liberal Party in 1948) moved closer into the Conservative ranks. In May 1947, an agreement was arrived at between Lord Woolton, the chairman of the Conservative Party, and Lord Teviot of the National Liberals. This provided for the establishment of joint Conservative–Liberal Associations in those constituencies where both parties were already in existence. In constituencies where only one of the parties was organised, it was agreed to offer membership to all those who supported joint action against the Socialists, and to rename the Association accordingly.

The Woolton–Teviot agreement found a quick response in the independent Liberal ranks, who called on their members to stand firm against this insidious Conservative overture. At the time, however, there was speculation whether the Liberal Party, as well as the National Liberal Party, might succumb to the Conservative embrace. In November 1946, the Liberal headquarters issued a statement denying rumours of a Liberal–Conservative pact.

Such statements eventually ended these rumours; but much valuable time for reconstruction was lost by these debates within the party on relations with the Conservatives and National Liberals. The vital consequence was that, with the advent of the 1950 general election, the revitalisation of the party had still a long way to go.

Whether the Liberal leadership really expected that 1950 would see the long-awaited revival is open to doubt. True, the party fielded 475 candidates, but at the same time the party insured itself with Lloyds for all deposits lost after the first 50 up to 250. It was a wise move, for the result of the 1950 election was an unrelieved débâcle. The loss of 319 deposits literally reduced the party to a music-hall joke.

The Liberals had, it is true, increased their vote to 2,621,487 – but with 169 more candidates than in 1945 this was hardly an achievement. Turnout, in any case, rose from 72·7 to 84·0 per cent, so the Liberal percentage of the total vote had merely remained stable at 9·1 per cent.

The results of the 1950 election were as follows:

	Votes	%	MPs
Conservative	12,490,507	43·4	299
Labour	13,267,466	46·1	315
Liberal	2,621,487	9·1	9
Communist	91,812	0·3	–
Others	301,043	1·1	2
	28,772,317	100·0	625

Nor had any particular region showed any major Liberal revival. The Liberal vote was in fact fairly evenly distributed throughout Britain. In only three areas – the South-West, North-East Scotland and rural North Wales – did the party obtain more than 20 per cent of the vote. In the whole country, only in three urban constituencies, all of them geographically dispersed, were Liberals able to achieve 20 per cent. By 1950, the party had been reduced almost without exception to the agricultural backwaters – though even here, in such areas as Gloucestershire and Southern Scotland, Labour had become the alternative to the Conservatives. Nor did the middle-class constituencies – the backbone of the Liberal revival after 1962 – offer any signs of encouragement.

Yet, if the party thought the position could hardly be worse after 1950, it was mistaken. To recover from the disaster of 1950, the Liberal Party desperately needed time to rebuild. Such a period of recuperation was not allowed the party. The second Attlee administration, weakened by death and dissension, ended with the calling of an election. Parliament was dissolved on 5 October 1951, and polling day fixed for 25 October 1951. A combination of factors left the Liberals able to field only 109 candidates. Morale was low, funds scarce, but above all candidates were virtually unobtainable. Even experienced Liberal candidates held back. These factors, together with the patent disunity of the parliamentary party in the lobbies in the 1950–1 period, ensured that 1951 was to be another disastrous election.

It proved to be more than this. It marked the nadir of the electoral fortunes of the party.

The full results of the 1951 election were:

	Votes	%	MPs
Conservative	13,718,199	48·0	321
Labour	13,935,917	48·7	295
Liberal	743,512	2·6	6
Others	198,966	0·7	3
	28,596,594	100·0	625

The total Liberal vote had fallen to 743,512, a mere 2·6 per cent of the total poll. Although six MPs were returned, 66 of the 109 candidates forfeited their deposits. In all, 92 of the 109 had suffered either massive defeat or total rout; only eight came near to joining the six elected members.

The party lost four seats, including Anglesey, which Lady Megan Lloyd George had represented. Only one seat was gained, Bolton West. This, though ostensibly a gain, was really the result of a local Conservative–Liberal pact. No Conservative opposed the Liberal, Arthur Holt, in Bolton West, while the Liberals gave the Conservatives a free run in Bolton East. In fact, with the solitary exception of Jo Grimond in Orkney and Shetland, no Liberal member was returned in the face of Conservative opposition.

The party thus faced the first peacetime Churchill Government with a parliamentary force of six, a demoralised party in the constituencies, and with no conceivable prospect in the near future of revival.

It was in this position that, immediately after 1951, Churchill offered Clement Davies, the Liberal leader, the tempting proposition of a position in the new Government and a Conservative–Liberal coalition in the Commons. Since the Conservatives had a perfectly workable majority of 17, the offer was presumably one of genuine goodwill to the Liberals.

Whatever the motives, Churchill and Davies met at Chartwell on 28 October 1951. Davies then consulted leading Liberals before making public his refusal to join the Conservative Administration. The Liberals had decided to soldier on alone.

It was a brave decision in the face of mounting evidence of the party's lack of morale. In by-elections, the record of the party was abysmal, whilst in municipal elections, the Liberals fared equally disastrously. Only 2·2 per cent of the borough councillors elected in 1950 were Liberals; by 1955 this total had fallen even further (to 1·5 per cent) as the table below shows:

	Con. and Con.-supported Ind.	Ind. without Con. support	Labour	Liberal	Total
1950	1,610	510	1,132	72	3,324
1951	1,893	548	883	79	3,403
1952	1,138	488	1,718	53	3,397
1953	1,571	447	1,448	60	3,526
1954	1,498	511	1,438	74	3,521
1955	1,604	514	1,470	56	3,644

No significant council remained in Liberal control during this period, whilst such major cities as Liverpool and Birmingham, later to see a municipal Liberal revival, had no Liberal representation.

However, in all this darkness there appeared one beacon. In a by-election in Inverness in December 1954 a Liberal who had not even contested the seat in 1951 took 36 per cent of the poll, sweeping Labour into third place. Admittedly, turnout was very low, but the by-election heralded, a decade in advance, the breakthrough the Scottish Liberals were to make in the Highlands in 1964 and 1966.

It was against this background that the Liberals faced the 1955 General Election. The outcome was once again depressing. Of the 110 candidates fielded by the party (one more than in 1951) no less than 60 lost their deposit. The total poll of the party was a mere 722,402 – even less than 1951, although turnout was down. Many of the Liberal campaigns were efforts wasted – only 32 of the 110 candidates had professional agents. The party failed to gain any seats although it retained all six it was defending – itself a remarkable feat. Overall, the party had marginally improved its position – the average share of the vote for each candidate rose from 14·7 per cent to 15·1 per cent.

Although 1955 was the first election since 1929 in which the party had made any improvement on its previous election performance, the ground for optimism was hardly very great. As in 1950, it was the agricultural seats which held out most hope. Sixteen of the 18 seats in which Liberals won more than 20 per cent of the poll were primarily rural, whilst the other two constituencies (Bolton West and Huddersfield West) were both the subject of local Conservative–Liberal pacts.

Despite these minor improvements, the 1955 election had again demonstrated two major shortcomings in the party. First, leadership at the top was lacking: Clement Davies, though much respected, had no longer the force necessary to revitalise the party. Secondly, the party lacked real political direction or discretion – thus, for example, Lord Moynihan and Lord Salter were urging Liberals to vote Conservative where no Liberal was standing, at the same time as Lady Megan Lloyd George was urging them to vote Labour. In 1955, the party still had not decided which road it was to travel.

However, immediately the election was over the first move taken by the party was the establishment of a committee to lay plans for the next general election. Under Sir Andrew McFadyean, the committee included such future Liberal notables as Jeremy Thorpe, then prospective candidate for North Devon, John Baker, Edwin Malindine and Roy Douglas, then chairman of the National League of Young Liberals.

The establishment of this committee was important as a psychological reassurance that the party, though as much in the wilderness as ever, did still mean business. A second lift in morale came with the Torquay by-election of 15 December 1955, when the party took 23·8 per cent of the poll, compared to 14·2 per cent in the general election. In February 1956, the Hereford by-election provided further ground for optimism. Frank Owen, the Liberal, forced Labour into third place, taking 36·4 per cent of the poll.

At the same time as the party was slowly lifting itself from the electoral trough of 1951 and 1955, there were further defections, the most notable being Dingle Foot, formerly Liberal M.P. for Dundee, who joined the Labour Party. Contrariwise, the party lost Lord Moynihan and Edward Martell to the Right.

Though these defections, particularly in the case of Dingle Foot, were serious, in the end they benefited the party. It was an inevitable part of the process of transition.

But transition to what? This was unclear so long as Clement Davies remained leader. Despite many hints that Davies ought to make way for a younger man, the old leader at first displayed no sign of departure. But a change was not to be long delayed. Clement Davies resigned the Liberal leadership on 29 September 1956, choosing the Folkestone Assembly to make the announcement.

12   The Sound of Gunfire: 1956–1967

Clement Davies was succeeded as leader of the party by Jo Grimond. The day before the announcement of Clement Davies' retirement, Grimond had addressed the assembly with a powerful speech which left little doubt that the challenge of the Liberal leadership would fall in his direction. It was a challenge which Grimond took up with vigour and enthusiasm. And his leadership was to have a lasting impact, not only on the Liberal Party, but on the course of British politics.

Grimond rapidly proved to be the most attractive and popular leader the party had secured in its recent history. At a comparatively youthful 43, with an excellent academic and war background, Grimond soon showed that he was also a forceful and attractive speaker. His personal popularity was evident in his constituency of Orkney and Shetland, which he had won in 1950 and converted into a Liberal stronghold.

Under Grimond's leadership, the party enjoyed a revival that had seemed impossible in the dark days of 1951. But the first years of Grimond's leadership proved far from easy. An immediate test of Grimond's skill arose over the Suez crisis. The Liberals, like the Conservative and Labour parties, split over the issue. With only a small Parliamentary force, this Liberal division was more obvious. On 30 October 1956, three Liberals, Davies, Arthur Holt and Donald Wade, voted in support of the Conservative Government's ultimatum to Egypt. Then, only two days later, the Liberals present in Parliament voted for a Labour motion deploring the Egyptian action.

On the one side were those Liberals, such as Holt, supported by others such as Howard Fry, Peter Cadbury and John MacCallum Scott, who gave support to the Conservative line. At the other extreme were the radicals, totally opposed to military action by the British Government.

This initial division was remedied on 2 November 1956, when the Liberal Party organisation issued a forthright condemnation of the Conservative Suez policy. Four days later, the Liberal parliamentary party endorsed this policy. This Liberal condemnation was, to a degree, a dangerous policy. In the 1955 election, all the Liberals except

Grimond had been elected without Conservative opposition. What would happen if, by attacking so vigorously over Suez, the Liberals forfeited this Conservative restraint?

This problem was soon answered with the occasion of a by-election in Carmarthen, the seat formerly held by Sir Rhys Hopkin Morris for the Liberals. In the event, the Liberals defended the seat with a pro-Suez candidate who was without a Conservative opponent. These tactics failed to help the Liberals. In the by-election held on February 1957, Labour took the seat from the Liberals. To add the final touch of humiliation, the victorious Labour candidate was none other than Lady Megan Lloyd George. With the loss of Carmarthen, Liberal representation in the Commons was down to a mere five, the lowest-ever total in the long and uninterrupted decline of the party. It was an inauspicious opening for Jo Grimond's tenure of the leadership.

Yet there was consolation for the Liberals. Carmarthen was not typical of the general trend of by-election results as 1957 progressed. Rather, the main feature was the growing disenchantment with the Conservative Government. It was evidenced mainly in a series of marked swings to Labour in successive by-elections. But it was noticeable also in a variety of good by-election results for Liberals. The party began to achieve some impressive results during 1957, taking over 20 per cent of the vote at Edinburgh South (20 May 1957) and over 36 per cent of the vote in North Dorset (27 June). Further impressive results followed at Gloucester (12 September) and Ipswich (24 October).

The Liberals began 1958 in even happier fashion with a remarkable by-election result at Rochdale. For the by-election, in a seat which had seen a straight fight in 1955, the Liberals chose Ludovic Kennedy, a well-known television personality, as their candidate. His spirited and energetic campaign produced a Conservative humiliation and a near-triumph for the Liberals. Labour won the seat with 22,138 votes (44·7 per cent); the Liberals finished in second place, only 4,500 votes short of victory, with 35·5 per cent of the poll; the Conservatives managed a mere 19·8 per cent.

Two weeks later the Liberals achieved the by-election breakthrough that had eluded them for a generation, when they won Torrington from the Conservatives. Without detracting from Mark Bonham-Carter's individual triumph, the by-election was not quite the dawn of the promised era that many Liberals imagined. The seat had been held by George Lambert, sitting as a Conservative and National Liberal. No independent Liberal had fought in 1955, and clearly much of the traditional Liberal vote in this constituency had either abstained (turnout rose by 11·4 per cent to 80·6 per cent in the by-election) or found a temporary home in the Conservative ranks. As it was, the Liberals gained Torrington by the narrow margin of 658 votes – only to lose the seat again in 1959.

Torrington failed to inspire any similar Liberal breakthrough, although the party polled some impressive performances in a variety of residential and agricultural seats: 24·5 per cent at Weston-super-Mare and 27·5 per cent in Argyll (both on 12 June 1958), 24·3 per cent in East Aberdeenshire (20 November 1958), 24·2 per cent at Southend West (29 January 1959) and 25·7 per cent in Galloway (9 April 1959).

The revival represented by Torrington was noticeable in other ways. The number of affiliated constituencies, which had risen to over 330 in both 1956 and 1957 rose to over 360 in 1958. Even the perennial financial problem facing the party eased; by the end of 1957, Liberal accounts had balanced at over £24,000. The success at Torrington, and other by-election results, had acted as a much-needed tonic to the party.

When Harold Macmillan called an election for October 1959, the Liberals were able to field 216 candidates. The result was a modest but important improvement in the Liberal position:

	Votes	*%*	*Seats*
Conservative	13,750,935	49·4	365
Labour	12,216,166	43·8	258
Liberal	1,640,761	5·9	6
Others	254,846	0·9	1
	27,862,708	100·0	630

Although the party had returned only six members, failing to hold Torrington or regain Carmarthen, the Liberals had polled 1,640,761 votes, over twice their percentage share in 1955. Only 56 of the 215 candidates had forfeited their deposits, whilst the average vote in contested seats rose from 15·1 per cent in 1955 to 16·9 per cent in 1959.[1]

However, there were many unhappy features about the Liberal results. Although Jeremy Thorpe gained the rural North Devon constituency, there had been no other breakthrough. Indeed, the party fared worst where its electoral prospects were strongest. The Liberal vote fell in eight of the thirteen seats in which the party had received over 30 per cent of the votes in 1955. Significantly for the future, by and large the party was unable to hold its position in the seats in which it had done well in by-elections.

Despite these qualifications, however, the Liberals could comfort themselves with the fact that, at a time when the Labour Party had

---

[1] David Butler and Richard Rose, *The British General Election of 1959* (1960) p. 233.

suffered its third consecutive electoral defeat, the party was making discernible, if slow progress. When the Conservatives captured the highly marginal Brighouse and Spenborough constituency from Labour in March 1960, it began to seem that the Labour Party would soon tear itself to pieces.

But before Liberals could benefit from this Labour split, they had to overcome internal problems of their own. A bitter row developed over the role the Liberal Campaign Committee (established with Frank Byers as chairman to organise the 1959 campaign) should play in the running of the party once the election was out of the way. The Campaign Committee rapidly assumed powers which it had never been expected to exercise. The affair concluded with the resignation of H. P. F. Harris, the General Director of the party. The editor of *Liberal News*, Reginald Smith, resigned in protest at the treatment Harris had received. Byers had triumphed; but the consequences of the bitter argument lingered.

The second problem to arise dated from the dark days the party had faced in 1951. In that year, the Bolton Liberals had created a local arrangement with the Conservatives, in which the latter were not opposed by Liberals in East Bolton, whilst Arthur Holt was returned as a Liberal M.P. in West Bolton with Conservative support. The net result had been to deny both seats to Labour. In 1960, a by-election vacancy arose in Conservative-held East Bolton. What policy should Liberals adopt?

It was arguable that, if the Liberals allowed the by-election to go uncontested in an industrial Northern constituency with a Liberal tradition, the Liberal claim to be the alternative to Labour would be very open to ridicule. For whatever reasons, the decision was made to contest. In the event, a leading Liberal figure, Frank Byers, was adopted. He finished in third place, polling 10,173 votes and 24·8 per cent of the poll. It was a highly creditable result, and it proved to be a harbinger of the beginnings of a Liberal awakening.

The first real indication – in parliamentary terms – of the Liberal revival came with the by-election in April 1961 at Paisley (Asquith's old constituency). A spirited campaign by John Bannerman brought the Liberals within 2,000 votes of victory.

In the space of the next ten months, the Liberals managed to secure second place in eight by-elections in constituencies in which the party had been third in 1959. Similarly, in the municipal elections, the party improved its base in May 1960 (130 Liberals elected) and in May 1961 (196 Liberals elected). By the autumn of 1961, the increase in Liberal support had gathered momentum, and by the spring of 1962 a Liberal tide was undoubtedly flowing.

The climax of the Liberal revival came in March 1962. On 14 March, a Liberal candidate came within 973 votes of victory in the rock-solid Conservative seaside resort of Blackpool North. The following day, when polling took place in Orpington, a middle-class Kent commuter suburb, a Conservative majority of 14,760 was overturned into a Liberal majority of 7,855. The Conservative share of the poll had fallen by 22 per cent to give Eric Lubbock a resounding victory. There was little doubt that Orpington had proved to be the most sensational by-election since East Fulham in October 1933.

For the Liberals, after a generation in the wilderness, the promised land seemed at last to have arrived. Indeed, for a fleeting moment, the *Daily Mail* National Opinion Poll (published on 28 March 1962) showed the Liberals to be the most popular party in the country (the figures were: Liberals 30 per cent, Labour 29·9 per cent, Conservatives 29·2 per cent). Meanwhile, on the same day as Orpington, the Liberals forced the Conservatives into third place at Middlesbrough East. Other by-elections, though not repeating the Orpington victory, indicated the force behind the Liberal revival. The party took 27 per cent of the poll at Stockton-on-Tees (April 1962), 25 per cent in Derby North (also in April), whilst in the Montgomeryshire by-election following the death of Clement Davies this Liberal stronghold was easily retained. In West Derbyshire, the party missed victory by a mere 1,220 votes, whilst on 12 July in North-East Leicester the excellent Liberal vote, coupled with a humiliating Tory performance, prompted Macmillan's drastic Cabinet reshuffle. It was this event which brought about Thorpe's scathing remark against Macmillan: 'greater love hath no man than this, that he lays down his friends for his life.'

In addition to these by-elections, the most impressive evidence of the Liberal advance was to be seen in the May 1962 municipal elections. The size of the Liberal advance could not be disguised. In such safe home counties territory as Aldershot, Finchley, Kingston and Maidenhead, the Conservatives lost every seat they were defending. In a variety of seaside and spa towns (such as Southend, Blackpool and Harrogate) the Liberals made equally impressive gains.

Outside this type of middle-class and suburban area, however, Liberal progress was markedly less. Thus in the Midlands and North (except for such towns as Leicester and Bolton) their gains were very much smaller.

However, much the most disquieting aspect of the Liberal upsurge was that virtually no gains had been made at the expense of Labour. Even in the commuter suburbs, the Liberals secured very few seats in the Labour-controlled boroughs – none at all in Acton, Watford or

Mitcham. The Labour strongholds emerged unscathed from the Liberal attack.

The result of these election triumphs was predictable. The party achieved a publicity it had not known for a generation. Even the finances improved and the party treasurer, Colonel Gardner-Thorpe, was able to raise the target for income for 1962 from £100,000 to £150,000. New recruits such as Sir Frank Medlicott (former National Liberal MP for Norfolk Central) joined the party. But this Indian Summer was soon to be over.

It was evident by the autumn of 1962 that the Liberal tide had begun to recede. By October those intending to vote Liberal had dropped below 20 per cent in the opinion polls; thereafter, the decline in support was steady and uninterrupted.

Although the May 1963 local elections rather disguised the fact (since the Liberals were contesting seats last fought in 1960), Liberal support in the boroughs was ebbing fast. Further evidence of the rapid Liberal decline came from the by-elections. At Luton (November 1963) the Liberal failed to save his deposit. The following month (in Sudbury and Woodbridge) the party actually polled a worse percentage than at the preceding general election.

The polarisation towards the two main parties continued during 1964 – as the date of the general election approached. In May, in the last three by-elections fought by Liberals under the Conservative Government, the results proved depressing. By June 1964, support for the Liberals in the National Opinion Poll was down to 9 per cent. Meanwhile, Labour's lead over the Conservatives in the Gallup Poll fell from 8 per cent on 3 July to 6 per cent on 7 August and to 5 per cent on 13 September.

Before the election campaign proper was under way, Grimond delivered a keynote speech (on 20 June 1964) on the theme 'Charter for New Men'. It was a major appeal for a classless, dynamic society, emphasising greater promotion opportunities for the young technologists and executives, a reduction of the burden of income tax on earned incomes and a ceiling on mortgage rates. This appeal provided the basis of the 1964 Liberal Manifesto, 'Think for Yourself, Vote Liberal'.

Although sadly short of money, the party fought a vigorous and enthusiastic campaign in October 1964. With 365 candidates in the field (an increase of 149 over 1959) the party was challenging on a wide front. Grimond's successful television appearances further encouraged Liberal optimism. And yet, when the results came in, the Liberals had little tangible comfort. The outcome of the 1964 election was a bitter disappointment. The full result was:

	Vote	%	*Seats*
Conservative	12,002,906	43·4	303
Labour	12,205,779	44·1	318
Liberal	3,101,103	11·2	9
Others	367,094	1·3	–
	27,676,882	100·0	630

The Liberals had gained only four seats: Bodmin in Cornwall, and Inverness, Caithness and Sutherland, and Ross and Cromarty in Scotland. They lost Bolton West and Huddersfield West, where Conservatives fielded candidates for the first time since 1950.

At least, the Liberals had the consolation in 1964 that all their nine MPs had been elected in three-cornered fights, whilst the marginal victory won in North Devon by Jeremy Thorpe in 1959 was now secure with a 5,136 majority.

The real Liberal success in 1964, however, was not in seats won but in votes polled. The party, with 365 candidates in the field, polled 3,101,103 votes and forfeited only 53 deposits. The Liberal share of the poll was 11·2 per cent compared to 5·9 per cent in 1959. In the seats contested by Liberals, each candidate polled on average 18·4 per cent and in the seats contested in both 1959 and 1964 this percentage rose to 20·6 per cent. Whilst the seats won had been in the 'Celtic fringe' the party polled well in many parts of Britain. In the South-East area, in addition to Orpington, which was retained with a reduced majority in the face of a massive Conservative challenge, the Liberals took over 25 per cent of the poll in a variety of Home Counties seats. Similarly, in the North-West, the party polled well in such Manchester commuter suburbs as Cheadle (which recorded the highest Liberal vote in the country). In all, there were sixty-eight seats in which the percentage gap between the Liberals and the winning party was less than 25 per cent. However, the irony of the 1964 election was that, in the best performance by the party since 1929, the Liberals returned only nine MPs – all of whom, with the solitary exception of Eric Lubbock, were elected in the 'Celtic fringe'.

As in 1959, however, the real significance of the election lay not in how well the Liberals had done, but in the cardinal fact that, by however small a margin, Labour had narrowly snatched victory from the Conservatives. Nor could the size of the Labour victory have been more harmful to the Liberals – because, whilst the party never actually held the balance of power, it had come as near as made no difference. In the tightrope parliamentary situation between the general elections of 1964 and 1966 very few things went right for the Liberals. Almost the only exception was the victory of David Steel in the Roxburgh by-election of

March 1965. Even this victory, however, though giving a boost in morale to committed Liberals, had little wider impact. Except in the earlier by-election in East Grinstead (February 1965), where the party pushed up its percentage of the poll to 31·5 per cent, the by-elections told a depressing story. In three-cornered contests in the seven other by-elections fought by Liberals up to the summer of 1965, the percentages were: Leyton, 13·9; Nuneaton, 16·2; Altrincham and Sale, 19·4; Salisbury, 12·9; Saffron Walden, 11·9; Birmingham Hall Green, 16·4; and Hove, 16·7.

Behind these uninspiring by-election results lay more fundamental troubles. The narrow Labour victory in 1964 had effectively destroyed the cherished Liberal hope of replacing Labour as the alternative to the Conservatives. The Liberal Party, after 1964, had lost both its sense of purpose and its sense of direction. The Liberal dilemma took a new twist when Grimond gave an interview to the *Guardian* in which he quite clearly indicated that he would be prepared to contemplate coming to terms with Labour if the parties could agree on long-term policies and aims. Whatever Grimond intended to produce by these remarks, he must have been considerably pained by the instant hostility aroused in the party. The idea was shelved, but the future role the party should play remained as undecided as ever. Such divisions within the Liberal hierarchy did nothing to improve the image of the party.

The by-elections in Erith and Crayford and the Cities of London and Westminster in November 1965, in which the Liberal polled 7·2 per cent and 6·3 per cent of the poll respectively, were further evidence of the slump in Liberal fortunes. In both seats, the result was a worse performance than even the 1950 General Election.

This pattern of a 'squeeze' on Liberals in third place was repeated in the crucial Hull North by-election in January 1966. The Liberals could poll only 6·3 per cent in the by-election, compared with 15·9 per cent in the preceding general election. As one correspondent wrote, the party had been ground to fine powder beneath the upper and nether millstones of government and alternative government.

The result in Hull North, with its tonic for Labour morale of a 4·5 per cent swing in their favour, was widely interpreted to herald an early election. The speculation was soon proved correct.

Facing a second election within two years was not a happy prospect for the Liberal Party. By late February, the Liberals had only 251 prospective candidates ready – significantly, 175 of these in Conservative-held seats and only 72 attacking Labour constituencies.

Not only was the party relatively short of candidates. It entered the election against a triple disadvantage: there was a clear 'squeeze' on the party in every constituency in which it was not the 'alternative' party;

the 1964–6 Parliament had ensured a quite distinct loss of identity for the party, which was almost inevitable in the tightrope parliamentary situation after October 1964 – only in the debate on steel nationalisation had the Liberals really made a distinctive, constructive contribution. Finally, and linked to these factors, was the definite loss of unity at the top that had accompanied the decline in fortunes – in particular, criticism of Grimond's leadership had mounted after an episode in which he had openly discussed his future as leader.

It was against this background that the party entered the 1966 election. The party manifesto, 'For all the People', emphasised the moderating role which, it claimed, the Liberals had played; and committed the party to major defence cuts, entry into Europe and a new approach to industrial relations.

When nominations closed, the party fielded 311 candidates, 54 fewer than in 1964. This reduction, however, disguised the fact that the party entered the fray in 33 constituencies which had not been contested in 1964, but withdrew from 87 seats fought at the previous election.

Compared with 1964, the results of the election were as follows:

	1964			1966	
	Vote	*Seats*		*Vote*	*Seats*
Labour	12,205,779	318	Labour	13,064,951	363
Conservative	12,002,906	303	Conservative	11,418,433	253
Liberal	3,101,103	9	Liberal	2,327,533	12
Others	347,094	–	Others	452,689	2
	26,676,882	630		27,263,606	630

Although, with a reduced field of candidates, the Liberal vote had fallen by more than 750,000, the party had emerged with its representation increased to twelve. On the 'Celtic fringe' the party lost two seats (Cardiganshire, unsuccessfully defended by Roderic Bowen, and Caithness and Sutherland, involving the defeat of George Mackie) but gained North Cornwall and West Aberdeenshire. The most encouraging gains were Cheadle, a Manchester residential commuter seat, won by Michael Winstanley, and Colne Valley, won by Richard Wainwright.

It was ironic, however, that the election which produced the largest Liberal contingent for over twenty years also marked the end of the road for 'Orpington-style' Liberalism. Whichever way the position of the party was reviewed, the underlying fact was that the hopes of the Orpington era had been finally shattered.

This was particularly true of the seats in which the Liberals had been the major challengers in 1964. Then, the party had finished second in fifty-five constituencies: by 1966, this total had fallen to twenty-nine.

Even these twenty-nine seats (largely confined to safe Conservative suburban or remote agricultural seats and equally safe Labour-held industrial backwaters) were hardly promising territory. In only eight constituencies throughout Britain were the Liberals within 5,000 votes of victory. There were other equally depressing aspects of the election for the Liberals. Whilst the party had won Colne Valley (by virtually eliminating the Conservative vote), in the former Liberal strongholds of Bolton and Huddersfield the party's vote had rarely been weaker. John Vincent was to write of the results in *New Society*:

> Even where you would have expected results there are none. In every seat round Orpington (Chislehurst, Bromley, Dartford, Sevenoaks, Reigate), the Liberals ran third, behind Labour, in 1966. There is no general 'Orpington syndrome' in suburban areas. Drawing-room constituencies like Wokingham, Poujadist landlady seats like Southend, Brighton, Blackpool, Bournemouth and Southport, areas of intense local activity like Finchley and Maidenhead, all failed to return a Liberal in second place.[2]

To this extent, the hopes engendered by Orpington were indeed dead. The Liberals had proved they had considerable support as the middle-class, suburban alternative in Tory-held seats. But they had totally failed in the assault on Labour's natural areas of strength. The 1966 election marked the end of the road in another sense also. For it was followed, not very long afterwards, by the resignation of Jo Grimond as Leader of the party. Although Grimond stated that his resignation was timed to give the new leader time to prepare for the next battle, in terms of 'real politic' the resignation seemed to confirm the failure of the dreams of the radical alternative. At least, so it appeared to contemporary opinion. Writing in *New Society* on the leadership change, John Vincent declared:

> . . . It alters nothing. It introduces no new factor. It stresses, if it needed stressing, that the hopes of the Grimond era are as dead as the liberal conservatism of the Macmillan era.

And Vincent concluded:

> For ten years it has lived in a dream that was never probable and is now probably impossible.

---

[2] 'What Kind of Third Party', *New Society*, 26 Jan. 1967.

13 The Thorpe Leadership: 1967–1976

Jo Grimond was succeeded as Leader of the party by Jeremy Thorpe. Although Thorpe was probably the best known of the Liberal MPs, he was by no means the obvious successor. When the Parliamentary Liberal Party first voted on the leadership, Jeremy Thorpe received six votes, whilst his two rivals, Emlyn Hooson and Eric Lubbock, each received three. Both Hooson and Lubbock then withdrew from the election, leaving Thorpe to be elected unanimously. Born in 1929, Thorpe was 38 when elected leader of the party. Educated at Eton and Oxford, he had subsequently made a distinguished legal career. He had first been elected for North Devon in 1959 (which he had won by a mere 362 votes) but had since held the seat continuously. He was a brilliant speaker, with a gift for mimicry which led some critics to see him as essentially a political lightweight, and his experience in Liberal politics had included the Treasurership of the party since 1965.

Thorpe became leader at a difficult and frustrating period for Liberals. The election of 31 March 1966 had returned Wilson to power with a massive majority. For the first time in British history, an outgoing Labour Government had been returned to power with an increased majority. Within a very short period, however, public opinion shifted violently against the government. In a variety of by-elections, Labour fared disastrously. Normally safe Labour seats fell to Conservative candidates, whilst in Scotland the Nationalists also gathered a large protest vote. But the Liberals made almost no electoral impact. The early years of Thorpe's leadership thus proved an unhappy time for the party. Morale in the constituencies was low. There was a sharp decline in the number of really active associations. The numbers of delegates at the Party Assembly went down from 1,400 at Brighton in September 1966 to 900 at Brighton three years later. By April 1970, the party had only seventeen constituencies with full-time agents. The performance of the party in by-elections was equally unencouraging. In twelve of the twenty-eight seats contested the party lost its deposit.

Faced with a swing to the Right at by-elections, and with Parliament preoccupied with the economic crisis, Liberals found it increasingly difficult to identify the party on many issues or to present a clear image to the electorate – a problem compounded by the recurrence of the party's perennial financial problems. Ironically, the issues on which the party was most active (such as its vigorous opposition to the Immigration Bill) were hardly issues likely to win the middle-class seats in which Liberals were in second place.

Among Thorpe's many difficulties within the party, the growing radical militancy of the Young Liberals was perhaps the most pronounced. The leftward trend in the Young Liberals had, by the time Thorpe became leader, already gone a very long way. By 1966, the radical Young Liberals were demanding the withdrawal of all American troops from Vietnam; workers' control of nationalised industries; non-alignment in the Cold War; Britain's withdrawal from NATO; opposition to the wage freeze; unconditional support for the 1965 seamen's strike; majority rule for Rhodesia; massive reductions in armaments; and entry into a Europe that would include the Communist bloc states of Eastern Europe.

These policies, adopted at the 1966 Young Liberal Conference at Colwyn Bay, seemed to older Liberals more representative of the Young Socialists (or indeed Maoists) than of the party of the middle-class suburbs. Not surprisingly, when the Young Liberals attempted to convert the party's annual conference at Brighton in 1966 to the new ideology, bitter clashes developed.

Young Liberals attacked the party leadership for being over-cautious, for being too worried about defending their constituencies rather than launching a crusade in the country. The party establishment attacked the Young Liberals as Marxists and disruptive militants. From 1966 onwards, the Young Liberals and the party hierarchy grew increasingly further apart. Virtual civil war in the party occurred in 1970 when Louis Eaks (the chairman of the Young Liberals) seemed to be claiming responsibility for the sabotage of county cricket grounds that had been done by those hoping to stop the South African cricket tour. Thorpe, with the support of his Parliamentary colleagues, denounced these tactics as 'hooliganism'.

On 25 January 1970 the National League of Young Liberals disclaimed responsibility for the cricket 'sabotage' and reaffirmed their belief in non-violent opposition to the tour. They nevertheless carried a vote of confidence in Eaks, who promptly proceeded to provoke a new storm by attacking Israel, declaring that Zionist apartheid was no more acceptable than South African apartheid. Renewed demands for his dismissal and even expulsion from the party followed.

On 31 January the Party's national executive hit back officially. A vote of censure was passed by a large majority which 'requested' the Young Liberals to dismiss Eaks. This only drew a rebuke from the Young Liberal wing for 'interfering' and it soon became obvious that many Young Liberals were rallying behind their leader. To some extent the tension eased when, at the Skegness Young Liberal Conference in March 1970, Eaks was succeeded as chairman by Tony Greaves, albeit by the narrow margin of 222 votes to 199.

Greaves's victory was symbolic of another development within the party during these years that was to see its fulfilment after 1970: the rise of 'community politics'. The roots of this new 'community politics' lay in student and radical disillusion with the Labour Government after 1964. Experience in direct action campaigns and demonstrations convinced many young activists – particularly in the YLs – that the only way to secure effective change was at a grass-roots, community level. In particular, this idea had been developed since 1968 by two radical Young Liberals, Gordon Lishman (the vice-chairman of the Young Liberals) and L. Freedman (then chairman of the Liberal Students). The background model for 'community politics' was neither particularly Liberal nor indeed British.

The most direct model was the kind of community work project organised by the civil rights movement in America. This was mirrored in Britain by grass-roots activists like George Clark, who left the Campaign for Nuclear Disarmament to live and work in Notting Hill.

The technique of 'community politics' was soon perfected by Liberals. Ordinary people in a given area would be encouraged to fight for local improvements. Such groups were not Liberal, but their success in local battles with the town hall tended naturally to breed support for the Liberals who encouraged and guided them. From then onwards, using local newsletters and every form of propaganda, Liberals rapidly built up a strong council base. Thus, after 1966, Liberals succeeded in building up local election successes in Liverpool, parts of Leeds but most of all in Birmingham, where Wallace Lawler had proved himself a highly successful exponent of these tactics.

The luck of a by-election in the Ladywood division of Birmingham, almost at the heart of the Lawler empire, provided a critical test for the new 'community politics'. Ladywood hardly seemed likely Liberal territory. It was a rock-solid Labour stronghold, with much slum housing; it was also the most depopulated constituency in Britain, in a city that had not sent a Liberal to Westminster since 1886. Yet the outcome was a triumph for Wallace Lawler. On 26 June 1969, he gained the seat from Labour with a comfortable majority.

The Ladywood result was a spectacular success, not merely for Wallace Lawler but for the 'community politics' Liberalism which he represented. Yet as the realists in the party knew, Ladywood was not representative of the party nationally. Other by-elections showed disappointing Liberal results, whilst the party's financial problems together with the Young Liberal rebellion left the party with poor press publicity.

Meanwhile, the party devoted itself at the 1969 Annual Conference to the discussion (in private session) of a new constitution prepared by a Constitutional Committee under the chairmanship of Baroness Seear.

The new constitution authorised the Liberal MPs to elect the party leader (as they had in effect done in the past), but only after the Chief Whip had called a meeting of a new national committee of the party to sound opinion. A controversial plan to switch the authority of the annual assembly to a series of quarterly conferences, which would clearly be dominated not by delegates but by candidates and MPs, was defeated. The policy resolutions accepted by the Assembly included proposals for a fifteen-year education plan, a £50 million community works scheme, a Bill of Rights, a floating rate of exchange and widespread co-partnership in industry.

These somewhat grandiose and ambitious plans contrasted rather starkly with the electoral prospects of the party. When an election was called for 18 June 1970, the party was hardly optimistic: the last by-elections had been very bad for the party: the 1970 municipal elections produced the worst results for a decade. Nor was the party particularly well prepared, with only 282 prospective candidates when the dissolution was announced.

However, large donations during the campaign (amounting to nearly £200,000) eased the party's financial position, whilst the number of candidates in the field rose to 332. The candidates, in fact, provide an interesting comment on the types of person the Liberals were attracting. Over 56 per cent of the candidates were fighting their first election. Only 23 were women. Over 55 per cent of the candidates had been to university, nearly one in four to Oxbridge. Even more overwhelming was the preponderance of middle-class candidates – the Liberal tally included 37 lecturers, 55 company directors, 32 solicitors and barristers, 57 business executives and consultants and a strong contingent of journalists, writers and white-collar workers. In marked contrast, only five manual workers were in the lists of Liberal candidates.

Although the Liberals had entered the election without any great hopes, the actual result was worse than any Liberal had supposed. The party secured 2,117,638 votes, compared to 2,327,533 in 1966. Its share of the total vote fell from 8·5 per cent to 7·5 per cent. No fewer than 182 of the 332 Liberal candidates forfeited their deposits. Even worse, Liberals lost no fewer than seven seats – Ladywood and the Colne Valley to Labour; Orpington, Cheadle, Bodmin, West Aberdeenshire and Ross and Cromarty to the Conservatives. Thorpe retained North Devon by a mere 369 votes; David Steel was in at Roxburgh by only 550.

Even more disastrous than the seats lost by the Liberals was the fact that only in a few seats was the party able to poll over 20 per cent of the vote.

Not only had the number of seats in which the Liberal challenge had brought the party near to victory declined alarmingly, but the party was back to its position of really only putting up a challenge in very safe Tory-held seats. With six MPs, and not a really safe seat amongst them, the party had come full circle to its parliamentary representation of 1959.

The June 1970 election seemed to set the seal on the revival that had followed in the wake of Orpington. Indeed, it had seemed to mark the end of the road for Nationalists as well as Liberals. On separate occasions, each of the three smaller parties had seemed set to achieve a major political breakthrough – the Liberals at Orpington in March 1962, Plaid Cymru with the triumph of Gwynfor Evans at Carmarthen in July 1966, and the Scottish National Party when it swept to victory in the hitherto Socialist citadel of Hamilton in November 1967. The results of the 1970 election hardly seemed to indicate that the forthcoming Parliament would be one where both Liberals and Nationalists would secure their greatest triumphs so far. But so it proved to be. After 18 June 1970, public disillusion with the Conservative Government and Labour Opposition reached new heights.

In the immediate wake of June 1970, however, very little went right for the Liberals. The Liberal by-election record produced some of the most depressing results the party had ever suffered, and Jeremy Thorpe suffered a personal tragedy with the death of his wife in a car accident.

It was at this nadir of the party's fortunes that the first signs of the new 'community politics' became evident. At the 1970 party conference, at which most delegates were sunk in gloom at the party's prospects, conference accepted a radical Young Liberal resolution which proposed that the party should start campaigning and working on a community level.

These new advocates of 'community politics' had often little time for Jeremy Thorpe or other party leaders. Peter Hain, the former Young Liberal Chairman, stated: 'The party leadership does not understand what community politics is all about, and if they did they wouldn't like it'. The new radicals constituted almost a separate entity within the party. The 'Radical Bulletin' group (as they called themselves) held their own seminars, published their own journal and helped secure election to key posts in the party. The group was to produce the famous Liberal names of the 1972–3 revival; thus David Austick, the by-election victor at Ripon, was a founder member; Graham Tope, the victor of Sutton, was equally prominent.

In a variety of cities, the new radicals began work; but above all Cyril Carr and Trevor Jones ('Jones the Vote') in Liverpool were the pioneers.

In the 1971 local elections, the first gains became apparent. Significantly, the Scarborough Assembly in 1971 was notable for the deep hostility between the mass of the party and the new radicals. But the radicals went on undismayed, making spectacular progress in local elections in Liverpool, a city in which in May 1968 Liberals had only one councillor, compared to 79 Conservatives and 34 Labour. By 1973, Liberals had become the largest single party. All this in a town where the Liberals had not won a Parliamentary seat since the Free Trade election of December 1923.

By autumn 1972, 'community politics' was to score its second major victory. At the Margate Assembly, Trevor Jones, the radicals' new standard-bearer, was elected President of the Party, defeating the leadership's candidate. Meanwhile, the advocates of 'community politics' moved from purely municipal successes to by-election triumphs.

The first breakthrough for Liberals came with a by-election in Rochdale (one of the very few constituencies in the country where Liberals were the main challengers to Labour). Cyril Smith won a decisive (if no doubt partly personal) victory, taking the seat with a 5,093 majority on 26 October 1972.

Critics of the Liberal revival were able to dismiss Rochdale relatively easily. The sensational result in the Sutton and Cheam by-election of 7 December 1972 could not be dismissed so easily. In a rock-solid true blue Conservative commuter suburb, an able and youthful Liberal candidate, preaching (and indeed practising) the gospel of community politics, swept to a landslide victory.

The understandable Liberal euphoria at overturning a Conservative majority of 7,417 on a greater turnover of votes than even Orpington had witnessed was soon sharply lessened by the result of the Uxbridge by-election which (on the same day as Sutton in a constituency not so very far distant) produced a Liberal lost deposit.

Meanwhile, partly as a result of a growing shift to the Left in the Labour Party, coupled with poor by-election performances by Labour, the winter of 1972 began to produce much comment on the possible desire of the voters for a 'Centre Party' and a realignment of British politics.

It was against this background that three by-elections were held on 1 March 1973 – at Lincoln, Chester-le-Street, and Dundee. The results were sensational: at Lincoln, the outcome was a victory for Dick Taverne with a majority of 13,191, a result which was widely interpreted as evidence of a growing desire for a 'Centre Party'. Meanwhile the very strong Liberal poll in Chester-le-Street, part of the Labour stronghold of the industrial North-East (an area of virtual Labour one-party rule for a generation), also seemed to support this argument, whilst in Dundee East the Nationalist challenge brought the party to within 1,141 votes of victory. Dundee, coming after very strong Nationalist votes in Merthyr Tydfil (13 April 1972) and in Stirling and Falkirk Burghs (16 September 1971) provided yet more evidence that party loyalties were more than ever in flux and that a political realignment was a distinct possibility.

After the by-election sensations of March, the Liberals continued to attract attention with an assault on the Labour city-centre stronghold of Manchester Exchange. Michael Steed, the Liberal candidate, took 36 per cent of the vote leaving the Conservative with a humiliating 7·1 per cent.

Meanwhile, the 1973 round of local elections provided the Liberals with plenty of jubilation. In addition to a striking breakthrough in Liverpool the party not only swept to outright control in Eastbourne but became the largest party in five other authorities. In a further 20 councils Liberals succeeded in becoming either the main opposition group or the second largest party. Among the district councils where Liberals were now the largest party were Maidstone, Newbury, Pendle (Lancs.) and two authorities in Sussex.

Perhaps even more pleasing to the party was the toehold Liberals were able to establish in such hitherto barren areas as Bristol (where the party won a ward that had not returned a Liberal since before the war), Stoke and Harlow (an authority where Liberals now provided the only opposition to a solid Labour phalanx). The string of Liberal successes in local elections in 1973 (culminating on 7 June when 36 per cent of all Liberal candidates were elected) was not, however, quite as impressive in many of the larger industrial areas where Labour's strength was concentrated.

In the elections to the GLC and the new metropolitan and county councils, Liberals won only 178 of the 2,514 seats at stake. Even these 178 seats were heavily concentrated. Liberals won only six seats out of 308 in the metropolitan areas of South Yorkshire, Tyne and Wear and the West Midlands. Outside Merseyside (where Liberals picked up 19 of 99 seats at stake), the Liberals polled well, albeit unevenly, in Greater Manchester (13 out of 106) and West Yorkshire (11 out of 88). Even these figures disguised the extent to which many industrial towns, especially in South Yorkshire and the West Midlands, were still utterly barren Liberal territory.

These qualifications about the Liberal municipal revival, however, tended to be overlooked as, in parliamentary by-elections, the Liberal upsurge reached its climax. On 26 July polling took place in two of the safest Conservative strongholds in the country – Ripon and the Isle of Ely. At Ripon David Austick, the Liberal candidate, fought a community politics campaign centred on suburban Lower Wharfedale (three-fifths of the constituency), where he had won a metropolitan county seat. All the tactics of a Liberal 'community politics' campaign were once again to be seen, with *Focus* newsletters (airing local grievances) using the techniques of tabloid journalism to sound out local grievances.

Austick achieved a remarkable victory, taking the seat with 43 per cent of the vote and a 946 majority. Meanwhile, an equally sensational victory was achieved by Clement Freud in the Isle of Ely. Freud won by 1,470 votes, taking 38·3 per cent of the poll. It was the first occasion in living memory that the Liberals had won two by-elections on the same day. Two further by-elections completed the triumph of the Liberal and Nationalist bandwagon: Berwick-on-Tweed fell to Alan Beith and the Scottish Nationalists won Glasgow Govan.

Even when every excuse was made to try to explain the Liberal success, its dimensions could not be played down altogether. It was a revival greater in degree and scale than anything seen for a generation. During this period of revival, the main lines of Liberal policy remained largely unchanged, although there was a more marked emphasis on the need to redistribute wealth and tackle inflation. At the 1973 Liberal Assembly, motions were passed calling for a guaranteed minimum wage, higher pensions and a tax credit system. Motions calling for major industrial reform, including worker directors, also received much attention.

Against this background of by-election triumph, striking successes in local government elections and a revitalised radical policy, Liberals were understandably buoyant. As the winter of 1973 approached, Liberal support in the opinion polls was now at a high level and gathering increasing momentum.

How far this Liberal bandwagon might have continued to progress has to be conjecture. For, faced with an intractable miners strike, and with the country in the throes of a three day week, Heath chose to call an election to seek a renewed mandate for his government. Polling day was fixed for 28 February. It provided the Liberals with an opportunity that few had expected to come so soon to appeal to the electorate. Never before had the Liberals faced an election when riding so high in the opinion polls. Never had the opportunity to transform a by-election revival into a general election breakthrough seemed so possible. An immediate consequence of this Liberal optimism was to be seen in the nominations. When nominations closed, the Liberals had fielded 517 candidates, the highest total the party had ever fielded (exceeding the 513 brought forward in 1929 and the 475 who contested the 1950 election). The Liberal standard-bearers in the February 1974 election provided interesting evidence on the type of person attracted to the 'New Liberalism'. The Liberal candidates were overwhelmingly middle-class, predominantly young with a pronounced radical slant. The professions accounted for no less than 279 candidates, mainly teachers, academics, lawyers, journalists and white-collar workers. The average age of the Liberal candidates was only 37. There were again very few women candidates and almost no manual workers.[1]

With the largest ever Liberal contingent, with Plaid Cymru fighting every seat in Wales, and with SNP candidates fighting all but one of the seats in Scotland (Jo Grimond's in Orkney and Shetland), no one could deny that the British electorate had their opportunity to vote for a third force.

The main lines of the Liberal manifesto followed the resolutions adopted at the 1973 Annual Conference. The party manifesto laid much emphasis on a permanent prices and incomes policy backed by penalties on those whose actions caused inflation. Among other proposals put forward by the party were: a statutory minimum earnings level; profit-sharing in industry; a credit income tax to replace means tests and existing allowances; pensions of two-thirds of average industrial earnings for married couples; a Bill of Rights, the replacement of the Housing Finance Act and a permanent Royal Commission to advise Parliament on energy policy.

For Liberals, armed with a wide-ranging policy programme having a strong radical flavour, as well as with a massive force of candidates, the outcome of the election was doubly disappointing. Having entered the contest with their highest hopes for a generation, they came out of the battle with a staggering six million votes, but a mere 14 seats. The only Liberal gains were Cardiganshire and Colne Valley (from Labour), Bodmin and the Isle of Wight from the Conservatives and the new seat of Hazel Grove, won by the former Liberal MP for Cheadle, Michael Winstanley. Perhaps the greatest individual triumph was the victory of Stephen Ross in the Isle of Wight, where he increased the Liberal share of the poll from 22·2 per cent to 50·2 per cent. The Liberal leaders also achieved outstanding personal results – thus Jeremy Thorpe obtained an 11,072 majority, David Steel was in by 9,017 votes, John Pardoe by 8,729 and Clement Freud by 8,347 in the Isle of Ely.

However, the greatest Liberal achievement in February 1974 was not

[1] Hugo Young, 'The Liberal Candidates', *Sunday Times*, Feb. 1974.

in seats won, or even in the remarkable personal triumphs of leading Liberals, but in votes polled. Seats like Petersfield, Wrexham, Shrewsbury, Devizes, Taunton, Burnley and Chorley saw a near trebling of the vote, while in others – such as Bedford and Hereford – the vote was more than trebled. But in only a few of these seats was the Liberal total good enough to run the winners close – mostly in Conservative-held seats. In only 14 Conservative-held seats were Liberals within 4,000 votes of victory, whilst the Labour citadels had hardly suffered at all from the Liberal advance.

Lack of seats won in 1974, and lack of inroads into Labour strongholds (such as the North East, where Liberals had entertained high hopes), were only two out of many disappointments for the Liberals. Even the Liberal share of the vote was only 19 per cent, not the 22–3 per cent predicted by the polls, nor the 25–30 per cent they needed for their 'take-off'. The greatest Liberal disappointment was in those seats in which the party had polled well in 1970 and might have seemed in sight of victory in 1974. In a long list of these seats which they hoped to win, they seemed to run up against a ceiling which kept the prize from them; places like Eastbourne, St Ives, Dorset North, Liverpool Wavertree, Southport and Oswestry.

The Liberals also suffered a different disappointment in that they had hoped to gain seats not only in areas of past strength but also in the territory where they had recently had such local government successes. But in London they lost Sutton and failed to take Richmond from the Conservatives or Enfield from Labour. In Liverpool, the magic of 'Jones the Vote' worked so ineffectually that they were nowhere near success in Edge Hill and not even second in Trevor Jones's own constituency of Toxteth. In areas outside Liverpool where Liberals had built up a local power base, such as Nelson and Colne (Liberals nearly gained control of Pendle District Council in 1973), local government success again failed to transform itself into seats at Westminster.

Despite these disappointments, however, in certain areas of the country – especially in the South-East, the Home Counties and the West Country – Liberals had made amazing progress. The peak of the Liberal revival came in the fenland seats around the Isle of Ely by-election breakthrough. Elsewhere the Liberal impact varied, not only by region, but by the type of seat contested. In Conservative marginals, where the pressure to vote for one of the big two parties was strongest, the Liberals were getting about 21 per cent of the vote. In Conservative strongholds, where Labour had no chance of winning, the Liberal vote was on average 31 per cent. In many of the Conservative 'strongholds' the Labour vote almost collapsed and the Liberals – strengthened by these extra votes – surged ahead, as happened in Berwick, the Isle of

Ely and the Isle of Wight. In each case former Labour votes helped to win them for the Liberals.

Overall, however, the 'squeezing' of Labour votes in safe Conservative seats could not disguise the essential fact that the Liberals had failed to make their expected breakthrough. What, then, had really gone wrong for the Liberals?

Their failure was centred round two factors: the Liberals did not poll quite as well as they (and many others) had expected in the final days of the campaign: and they underestimated the extent to which the electoral system discriminated against them.

The election results confirmed that the composition of the Parliamentary Liberal Party would stay markedly to the Right of the Liberal activists in the country – particularly of Trevor Jones and the Young Liberal radicals. However, although the party might be to the right in terms of internal Liberal politics, there was little possibility that the offer made by Heath for Thorpe to support a Conservative administration would ever succeed. Heath's attempt to thwart a Labour Government duly failed.[2] However, the brief but stormy furore in the Liberal ranks when the proposal was made had only served to emphasise that the party could easily indulge in fratricidal warfare if talk of coalition was not handled very carefully.

As it was, Thorpe faced a difficult task after the February election. With a minority Labour Goverment, and with a general election widely forecast for the autumn, it was essential to keep the Liberal Party in top gear and in the public view. Although Liberal support in the opinion polls held relatively steady during 1974, the absence of by-election contests prevented the Liberals from getting any renewed momentum going.

As substitutes for by-election victories, the Liberals found two alternative weapons: the launching of a coalition campaign and the defection of Christopher Mayhew from Labour. The Liberal 'coalition campaign' was launched in a party political broadcast on 25 June by David Steel, the party's Chief Whip. The broadcast, with its appeal for a 'Government of National Unity', stated that Liberals would be 'ready and willing to participate in such a government if at the next election you give us the power to do so'. In an ITV interview the same evening Thorpe stated that such a Government of National Unity 'reflects the views of millions of people'.

Thorpe may have been right. But within the Liberal Party the coalition plan was not received with total approval. Ruth Addison, the Young Liberal chairman, attacked the scheme as ludicrous. Radical .

---

[2] For a detailed discussion of this period, see D. Butler and D. Kavanagh, *The British General Election of October 1974* (London, 1975) pp. 49–50.

candidates, who needed Labour votes to win Tory-held county seats, were equally sceptical. The fact that any Government of National Unity would almost certainly not include any significant part of the Labour Party also tended to diminish the whole political realism of the scheme.

In July, however, Liberal attempts to foster a realignment in politics achieved a marked step forward with the defection of Christopher Mayhew, a former Labour Minister and M.P. for Woolwich East, to the Liberal ranks. His defection increased the number of Liberal MPs from 14 to 15 and was accompanied by very wide press coverage. But those who expected further defections from sitting Labour members were to be disappointed. Meanwhile, the Liberals began frenetic activity to revitalise derelict constituency associations so that the party could fight virtually every constituency in the coming election. By the late summer of 1974, both Liberals and Nationalists were prepared for the largest-ever assault on the two-party system. When nominations duly closed for polling day, no less than 619 Liberal candidates had come forward, a rise of 102 on the February total – and an all-time record for the party. Every seat in England and Wales (except for Lincoln) was contested by a Liberal. In Scotland only Argyll, Glasgow Provan and Fife Central were not.

The Liberal election manifesto (*Why Britain Needs Liberal Government*) pledged the party to break the two-party system, to break what Thorpe attacked as the party of management alternating with the party of trade unionism. The twin pillars of the Liberal manifesto were social reform, together with the introduction of a statutory prices and incomes policy. Among the social reform proposals advocated were reform of family welfare provisions, higher pensions, the introduction of flexible mortgage schemes and a complete overhaul of the social security system. Other proposals included self-government for Scotland and Wales, greater autonomy in the regions, reform of the voting system, teachers' salaries to be paid by the Exchequer, the introduction of worker-participation in management, reform of company law and a major attack on monopolies.

To some extent, however, Liberal policy mattered less than the overriding question of which party Liberals would support in the event of a deadlock election. Labour's repudiation of any 'Government of National Unity' effectively meant that, if Liberals entered a Coalition, it would be a Conservative-dominated Government. For Liberals seeking Labour votes to unseat Tories in rural-suburban seats, this was hardly a good vote-winning line. In the event, despite widespread predictions that Labour would win with a fairly massive majority, the result proved to be yet another cliff-hanger. As more and more

Conservative-held marginal seats stubbornly defied the swing to Labour, computer forecasts of Labour's eventual overall majority came lower and lower. In the event, Labour won 319 seats, the Conservatives 277, Liberals 13, the Scottish National Party 11 and the Welsh Nationalists 3.

Once again, Liberal dreams had been rudely shattered. The party had entered the October election with their largest-ever field of candidates and with high hopes that the six million votes secured in February would prove a springboard for parliamentary success. They came out of the battle with fewer votes, a reduction in seats and with morale having suffered a severe setback.

The Liberals managed only a solitary gain in October 1974, at Truro, where David Penhaligon, an able Liberal who had been widely tipped to secure the seat, was in by 464 votes. Meanwhile two seats went down to the Conservatives, Hazel Grove and Bodmin, lost by Michael Winstanley and Paul Tyler. Not one of the many hoped-for Liberal gains materialised. Bath defied Christopher Mayhew's assault, whilst Leominster, Newbury, Skipton and Hereford all survived a strong Liberal attack.

Meanwhile the total Liberal vote had fallen from the 6,063,470 (19·3 per cent) cast in February to 5,346,800 (18·3 per cent) in October. This decrease tended to disguise the fact that, with 102 more candidates than in February, their vote in most constituencies had fallen quite considerably. In 93 per cent of constituencies contested by Liberals on both occasions, the Liberal share of the vote declined. Nor did the Liberal leaders fare as well as they had in February. With the exception of Richard Wainright in Colne Valley and Jo Grimond in Orkney and Shetland, all the sitting Liberals had their majority cut – by 6 per cent in the case of Jeremy Thorpe and 11·5 per cent for Cyril Smith at Rochdale. As a result only four Liberals possessed majorities over their nearest rivals of more than 10 per cent.

As a result of the October election, the areas of relative Liberal strength and weakness also saw some changes. The South-West (and most particularly Devon and Cornwall) remained the best area for the Liberals, followed by the suburban metropolitan areas, whilst East Anglia lost much of the February upsurge.

The change in areas of traditional Liberal strength can perhaps best be seen in comparison with the 1970 results.

	% 1970	% October 1974
Devon and Cornwall	20·6	31·5
Rural Wales	15·0	20·5
Rural Scotland	13·1	13·7
South-East (Outer)	12·7	23·3
Outer Metropolitan Area	11·0	23·2
South-West (exc. Devon and Cornwall)	11·0	25·3

In 1970, Liberals were strongest in Devon and Cornwall; their two next best areas were both their traditional Celtic fringe strongholds, rural Wales and rural Scotland. By 1974, whilst Liberal strength in the South-West had firmed greatly, and Liberal strength in the Home Counties had doubled or even more than doubled, rural Scotland has hardly changed in percentage terms. To this extent, the SNP upsurge has achieved what may well be the end of Liberalism as the party of the Celtic fringe.

Meanwhile, the areas of greatest Liberal weakness have seen less change. Industrial Scotland remains barren Liberal territory (and rural Scotland is now nearly as bad), whilst the West Midland conurbation and South Yorkshire remain equally desolate. Merseyside, once the great hope of the 'New Liberalism', slipped back in October 1974 to become one of the Party's weakest areas.

Although the increased number of Liberal candidates produced more lost deposits than in February (some 125 deposits were lost), on average the party polled a respectable 15 per cent in seats not fought in February (indeed, in Houghton le Spring Liberals took second place with 21 per cent of the vote in a seat not fought since 1929). The worst Liberal area remained Glasgow and industrial West Scotland, where in such Glasgow seats as Govan, Cathcart and Shettleston Liberals polled under 3 per cent of the votes cast. In those seats in which Liberals intervened it seems that Liberals took a bigger share of votes from the Conservatives in Labour seats, and from Labour in Conservative seats. It is also interesting that the fall in turnout was considerably less in seats where Liberals 'intervened', indicating that there are clearly many voters who will deliberately abstain in the absence of a Liberal candidate. Although, in seats fought in both elections, the Liberal vote dropped, only in ten seats was this percentage fall greater than 6 per cent. The worst collapse of Liberal support, ironically, was at Eastbourne (13·2 per cent), the one local council with an overall Liberal majority. Of the other drops of over 10 per cent, two were in Liverpool and one was at Nelson and Colne (part of Pendle, where the Liberals were the largest party on the council). In Liverpool, despite a local power base, there were lost deposits in six out of eight seats; the average Liberal vote, at 12·7 per cent was lower than in any other English or Welsh city.

Outside these areas in which Liberals had entertained high hopes, the Liberal decline tended to be most marked in the key marginal seats, where the Liberal vote had been effectively squeezed.

One of the greatest single disappointments for the Liberals in October 1974 was the almost complete absence of 'tactical voting', whereby supporters of a party in a hopeless position would vote Liberal to unseat the sitting Conservative or Labour Member. In such seats as Bath, Chippenham, Hereford and Newbury Liberals had entertained high hopes that the Labour vote would go over to their camp. As the first results came in on election night it became clear that this was not happening. In one or two seats (such as Truro) a very limited amount of tactical voting occurred (and in Colne Valley and Cardiganshire Tories seem to have voted Liberal to keep Labour out) but such examples were rare in the extreme. The number of Labour lost deposits dropped from 28 in February to only 13 in October, thus reflecting the rise in the Labour vote even in the most hopeless of constituencies. Indeed, far from losing votes to the Liberals in strong Liberal areas, Labour appear to have recaptured votes lost in February. The election of October 1974 had thus seemed to set the seal on the high hopes of the 1973 revival. The party, despite its ability to poll a very large number of votes, had seemed to have come full circle to the situation of 1966. But there were some optimistic features of the results. In 27 seats, the party still managed to increase its share of the vote. The Liberals still remained in second place in some 102 constituencies, 92 of these held by Conservatives and 10 by Labour.

The disappointing outcome of October 1974 was continued in a series of relatively poor by-election results. With Thorpe having already led the party for seven years, speculation began to mount over whether he would lead the party into the next election. Very shortly the leadership issue was to be at the forefront of Liberal politics. A luckless association with a collapsed secondary bank (London and County Securities) did nothing to help Thorpe, but it was the Scott affair that precipitated his downfall. Scott, a former male model, alleged that Thorpe had had a homosexual relationship with him. Thorpe denied the allegation, but the affair refused to die. Indeed, the allegations grew ever more lurid. Events moved swiftly. On 4 March the Liberals narrowly lost their deposit in a by-election in Coventry North-West. On 8 March Pardoe made it clear that he was a contender for the Leadership. Cyril Smith rather less clearly, seemed to be about to resign.[3] At the same time the party had published its proposed new scheme for electing its future leaders, a plan based on a complex system involving the establishment of an electoral college based on constituency associations. On 11 March polling took place in The Wirral and Carshalton by-elections. In The Wirral the party fared disastrously, losing its deposit for the first time since 1950. Steel urged that the leadership issue be settled. Thorpe countered by offering to fight a leadership election when the new procedures had been agreed. He again categorically denied the Scott allegations. It seemed

[3] Cyril Smith subsequently did resign, on the ground of ill health, after the immediate crisis had subsided. He was succeeded by Alan Beith, the MP for Berwick-on-Tweed.

the crisis was over. In May however more rumours over the Scott affair surfaced. The local election results were dismal. Against this background Thorpe took his decision to resign the Liberal leadership. On 10 May, in a letter to the acting Chief Whip, David Steel, Thorpe resigned his position as leader which he had held since January 1967. In the unseemliest possible way the Thorpe era had come to an end.

Thorpe's unhappy exit left the party in a turmoil. with its proposed new electoral college not yet approved by the party, the Liberals in fact devised a welcome escape from their dilemma. Almost unanimously the Liberal Parliamentary Party invited Jo Grimond to return as Leader on an interregnum basis. On 12 May Grimond accepted this invitation. Shortly afterwards, at a specially called Assembly, the party accepted the new proposals for electing its Leader. The new system required a vote by all constituency party members for the leadership candidate. Each candidate, in order to be validly nominated, had to be backed by one-quarter of the Liberal MPs. This was a pioneering democratic initiative in the constitution of a British political party. Paradoxically, in the political realities of 1976, it limited the actual number of contestants to two – John Pardoe and David Steel. Both men were different in style rather than content. Pardoe was pugnacious and ebullient; Steel, more orthodox, less flamboyant but by far the more skilful campaigner. After a not terrribly dignified contest, on 7 July Steel was declared victorious by 12,541 votes to 7,032.

14 Pacts and Alliances: 1976–1984

The election of David Steel in July 1976 brought to an end the unhappy final saga of the Thorpe era. But it did not change the fundamental problems facing the party, in particular its strategy to avoid being relegated again to the sidelines of British politics. When Steel made his first conference speech as party leader he effectively also launched his own beliefs in Liberal strategy – namely the politics of co-operation. Not that, in many ways the leadership battle had been one of strategies; rather it was one of style marked as the *Annual Register* noted, by unedifying personal exchanges. The victor, Steel, had been the youngest MP in the House when returned for Roxburgh, Selkirk and Peebles in the 1965 by-election. By profession a journalist and broadcaster, in political terms he was firmly in the left of centre Grimond mould. He was equally convinced that the Liberal Party could only lever its way to power by working with politicians of other parties in order to achieve a breakthrough on to the political stage. In fact David Steel's enthusiasm to take the Liberal Party into a co-operation strategy with other politicians was to be tested at an earlier moment than could have been expected. By early 1977 the Callaghan Administration was in dire straits. On 23 March an opposition motion of non-confidence was due for debate. Weakened both by by-election losses (Workington and Walsall had been lost to the Conservatives in November 1976) and by defections (two Labour MPs had formed the breakaway Scottish Labour Party) Callaghan's position was perilous. Defeat was possible, even probable, with an immediate general election to follow. In these circumstances Callaghan looked urgently to negotiations with the Liberals. On the Liberal side the climate was favourable. Few Liberals wanted an early election with Margaret Thatcher returning on a landslide to Westminster. Hence within the party there was a natural anti-Conservative element that welcomed the discussions that led to the Steel–Callaghan deal – the 'Lib–Lab Pact' as it became dubbed.

On 23 March, the day of the crucial debate, a joint statement by Callaghan and Steel outlined the agreement they had reached. A joint consultative committee was established (chaired by Michael Foot) to examine governmental policies prior to their presentation to Parliament; there were to be regular meetings between Callaghan and Steel and between the Chancellor and the Liberals' chief economic spokesman. The Cabinet agreed to introduce a Bill for direct elections to the European Parliament, and to 'take account' of Liberal desires for these elections to be conducted on a proportional representation system. The Government also agreed to proceed toward devolution in consultation with the Liberals and to provide time for the Housing (Homeless Persons) Bill which the Liberals strongly favoured. It was announced also that the pact was to last until the end of the current parliamentary session. Margaret Thatcher denounced the agreement as 'shabby, devious manipulations', but Labour was saved. The Government won the no-confidence debate by 322 votes to 288. Although David Steel claimed the pact had 'stopped socialism', it was less obvious what benefits grassroots Liberals had gained from the pact.

Indeed, Liberal criticism of the pact was vocal. Liberal activists had wanted tangible gains – in, for example, electoral reform – whereas Steel himself seemed more interested in the *concept* of an agreement. These criticisms, led by such figures as Cyril Smith, centred on the argument that, for having saved the life of the Government, more favourable terms could have been obtained. These criticisms mounted, and the pact almost succumbed to an early death over the direct elections to the European Parliament due to be held for the first time in June 1979. By an Act of the Community each member state was to be allowed to adopt its own electoral system and procedures for these elections. At the conclusion of the Lib–Lab Pact in March 1977, the Steel–Callaghan talks had included undertakings on this subject. Callaghan committed his Government to introduce the necessary legislation for the elections to be held (it was official Labour Party policy to oppose direct elections and many Labour anti-Europeans wished to boycott them). The European Assembly Elections Bill was duly published on 24 June and included in its provisions a regional list system of proportional representation. Although the Bill passed its second reading on 7 July by 394 votes to 147, no fewer than 126 Labour MPs, including 6 Cabinet Ministers and 26 junior ministers voted against direct elections.

It was against this background that, on 28 July 1977, the pact was renewed for the coming session, with the Liberals insisting that the Government adhere rigidly to its pay policy objectives. The ever vocal Cyril Smith opposed the renewal of the pact.[1] Jo Grimond, the party's elder statesman warned that continued collaboration would make it more difficult to present a separate identity to the electors. The party assembly supported Steel (despite the Association of Liberal Councillors' warning that the party was bleeding to death), but on condition that

[1] After the party assembly vote supporting the renewal of the pact, Cyril Smith resigned as Liberal spokesman on employment.

the Cabinet and a majority of Labour MPs vote for proportional representation in elections to Europe. This was naïve politics. The vote on the second reading had already demonstrated the extent of anti-Europe hostility in Labour ranks. The crunch came in November 1977. Only 147 out of 308 Labour MPs voted for the Bill with its provisions for a regional list system of proportional representation. Electoral reform for the European elections was lost. Many Liberals felt bitter and cheated. A special party conference was called for January to discuss the future of the pact. In the event, despite a sizeable and vocal minority against continuing the arrangement, at the special Assembly held on 21 January 1978, the Lib–Lab Pact was endorsed by 1727 votes to 520, a majority of 1207. In electoral terms, critics of the pact continued to point to a sharp and continuing decline in the party's fortunes in both local elections and parliamentary by-elections. In the ten by-elections between the formation of the pact and its termination, the Liberal share of the vote dropped by an average 9.5 per cent.[2] Liberals reckoned that the 1977 county council elections were the worst results for the party in the ten years from 1972 to 1981, while in the Birmingham Ladywood and Stechford by-elections the party finished a disastrous fourth place behind the National Front. As David Steel was later to remark, it was the failure and unpopularity of the Labour Government that had rubbed off on the Liberals. Indeed Labour lost such hitherto impregnable strongholds as Stechford and Ashfield in the aftermath of the pact. This unpopularity of Labour intensified when Callaghan, to the amazement of most political commentators, continued to soldier on until 1979. The 'winter of discontent' played into the hands of the Conservative Party. Eventually the whole lamentable Labour Government collapsed when the referenda on devolution in Scotland and Wales (held on 1 March 1979) proved an embarrassing fiasco. Faced with an opposition vote of no-confidence, with the Liberal pact having ended and the Nationalists embittered and furious, this time Labour had no means of escape. On 28 March 1979, for the first time since 1924, the Government fell in a vote in the House of Commons. In these circumstances, the Liberals therefore entered the 1979 election very much on the defensive. The Conservatives could attack the Liberals for propping up an increasingly unpopular Labour Administration, whilst the Liberals could see little evidence in by-elections or opinion polls of any electoral upsurge in their favour. Indeed, only in two by-elections between October 1974 and 1979 had the Liberals achieved good results. Both were in extremely unrepresentative seats. The first was at Newcastle Central on 4 November 1976; the second, on the very eve of the general election was at Liverpool Edge Hill on 29 March 1979. In the first, the Liberals achieved a remarkably good

[2] V. Bogdanor (ed.), *Liberal Party Politics* (1983) p. 94.

result in a city centre working-class area of Newcastle. The Liberal candidate, a local councillor and active community politics advocate, transferred a lost deposit to a good second place with 29 per cent of the vote. In Liverpool Edge Hill the outcome was even more dramatic. An able Liberal candidate, David Alton, scored a sensational victory, raising the Liberal vote from 27 per cent to a commanding 64 per cent with Labour collapsing from 52 per cent to 24 per cent and the Conservative losing his deposit. Although both results demonstrated the efficacy of community politics in inner-city areas, neither had any very wider significance. Otherwise, the Liberal by-election record presaged the set-back that was to occur in May 1979.

The Liberal manifesto, like that of the Conservatives, had been geared for a 1978 election. Indeed, as early as March 1978 the Liberals had decided on the four main issues on which it proposed to campaign: political reform, industrial and economic reform, tax reform and ecological issues. Among specific political reform proposals in the manifesto (entitled *The Real Fight is for Britain*) were electoral reform, a Freedom of Information Bill, a new Second Chamber to replace the House of Lords, a Bill of Rights and devolution for the English regions as well as for Scotland and Wales. Among the party's other proposals were energy conservation (the ecology movement was catching public attention at this time), a switch from direct to indirect taxation, encouragement of employee share ownership, the abolition of the domestic rating system and a permanent statutory prices and incomes policy.

The campaign itself (despite the fillip of the Edge Hill by-election triumph) was a difficult one. The Conservatives started very much as favourites with Labour an easy target and the Lib-Lab pact an equally easy weapon with which to fight the Liberals. Steel conducted a skilful campaign and the fact that the Liberals did not suffer even more serious reverses owed much to his leadership.

In the event the Liberals returned 11 MPs, compared to the 14 with which they entered the election. The three Liberal losses were Emlyn Hooson in Montgomeryshire (a seat previously held by Liberals at every election this century), Jeremy Thorpe in North Devon and John Pardoe in North Cornwall.

The outcome was

Party	Votes	%	MPs
Conservative	13,697,923	43.9	339
Labour	11,523,218	37.0	269
Liberal	4,313,804	13.8	11
Nationalists	636,890	2.0	4
Others	1,060,613	3.3	12

Although the Liberal share of the vote had fallen from 18.3 per cent to 13.8 per cent, with the loss of a million votes, there were some encouraging features. Indeed, in 62 constituencies the Liberals increased their vote, mainly in seats where they were already strong and credible contenders. But overall the set-back was clear. In the 531 constituencies comparable to 1974 in England and Wales, the Liberal vote fell by 5.1 per cent. The fall was fairly even, with local factors accounting for deviations from this pattern. Thus the adverse publicity surrounding Jeremy Thorpe (and also another former Liberal, Peter Bessell) probably accounted for the disaster in the Liberal heartland of Devon and Cornwall. In five contiguous seats in this area the Liberal vote plummeted 9.4 per cent. The two best areas for the Liberals were in Liverpool (where David Alton held the Edge Hill constituency gained in the by-election) and the Anglo-Scottish border country (the strongholds of David Steel in Roxburgh and Alan Beith, the Chief Whip, in adjacent Berwick).

The convincing victory of Margaret Thatcher in the 1979 election seemed to point to an end to the volatile and uncertain politics of the 1974 to 1979 period. In fact, precisely the opposite was to happen. With Labour's internal feuds reaching a new level of bitterness, an upheaval was about to happen in British politics. In November 1979 Roy Jenkins, in his Dimbleby Lecture, called for a realignment in British political life. In effect it was the signal to launch the Social Democratic Party. Jenkins had previously cultivated the ground assiduously before making such a move. In fact, the antecedents of what was to become the Social Democratic Party stretched back many years. Thus, back in March 1973 Dick Taverne had forced a by-election (and been successfully returned) in his Lincoln constituency as a Democratic Labour supporter in protest at the growing activities of the Left in the party. The Liberals had welcomed Christopher Mayhew, the Labour MP for Woolwich East, as a defector to their ranks in July 1974. But these had been isolated examples. The 1979 Labour defeat opened the floodgate as more and more of Labour's Right found Conference decisions on such issues as unilateral nuclear disarmament and withdrawal from the EEC impossible to tolerate. The Special Labour Conference at Wembley in January 1981 (which reaffirmed the decision to establish an electoral college for future leaders, with a strong weighting towards the trade unions) marked the breaking-point. The four leaders of the new movement (Shirley Williams, David Owen, William Rodgers and Jenkins himself – popularly known as the 'Gang of Four'–moved swiftly. A week after the Wembley Conference the Gang of Four published the Limehouse Declaration, announcing the establishment of a Council for Social Democracy. Initially this was not a separate party, simply a pressure group round which potential support would gather. On 2 March, however, 12 Labour MPs (including David Owen and William Rodgers) resigned the party whip and announced that they would not seek re-election as Labour MPs. On 26 March 1981 the new Social Democratic Party was formally launched, consisting initially of 14 MPs. (13 Labour and a lone Conservative, Brocklebank-Fowler, MP for Norfolk North-West). A new Party had been launched in British politics, aided by the largest defection of Labour MPs since the days of MacDonald in the 1930s. But it was not only a new party. One of the SDP's first decisions was to start to negotiate an electoral arrangement with the Liberals. A new Alliance had been born, the product of the lengthy series of negotiations between David Steel and Roy Jenkins.

In the opinion polls the Alliance got off to a heady start. This was a welcome turnaround for the Liberals. Indeed, the first test for the Liberals after the 1979 elections had come with the first direct elections to the EEC. Held in June 1979 the elections engendered a turnout of only 32 per cent in Great Britain. The result was a disaster for the Liberals in terms of representation. The results are set out below for Great Britain.

Party	Seats won	Votes	%
Conservative	60	6,509,000	51
Labour	17	4,253,000	33
Liberal	–	1,691,000	13
SNP	1	219,000	2
Plaid Cymru	–	83,000	1
Others	–	88,000	1

With 1,691,000 votes, 13 per cent of those cast, the Liberals had emerged without a single representative in the European Parliament. Only in the north of Scotland had the Liberals even come within striking distance of victory.[3] Nor had the by-elections prior to the birth of the Alliance brought any great encouragement. The local elections of May 1981, in the wake of the advent of the SDP, brought the Liberals a welcome net gain of 250 seats. Although a few individuals fought under the SDP banner, the party had declared that it would not fight as a national party.

On 16 June the SDP and Liberals issued an important policy statement, *A Fresh Start for Britain*. There were no surprises in its main proposals. These included parliamentary reform and proportional representation, a Freedom of Information Act, devolution, industrial partnership, support for NATO and continued EEC membership. These proposals formed the core of the party's 1983 manifesto policies.

[3] The Liberals were 3882 votes behind the Scottish Nationalists in the Highlands and Islands constituency and 13414 behind the Conservatives in the North-East Scotland seat.

Critics noted it was less precise over economic matters (such as incomes policy) and defence issues (especially the nuclear deterrent).

Although the SDP was riding high in the opinion polls, it had yet to fight its first real electoral battle. This came on 16 July 1981 with the Warrington by-election. Warrington was a safe industrial Labour seat in Cheshire. Although a Liberal candidate was already in the field, it was widely expected that a leading SDP figure would seek to fight the seat. After a nasty dose of the dithers, Shirley Williams declined. Roy Jenkins took on the challenge. In a seat in which the Liberals had polled less than 3,000 votes in 1979, Jenkins achieved a major moral victory. The outcome was Labour (14,280), SDP (12,521) and Conservative (2,102). Although it was the first election battle Jenkins had ever lost, he described it as 'by far the greatest victory in which I have participated'.

Prior to the autumn party assemblies the SDP continued to strengthen its organisation. The Llandudno Liberal Conference marked an important stage forward. The previously unratified alliance with the SDP was overwhelmingly supported at the Conference, only 112 out of 1,600 delegates voting against. The Liberal Conference also voted in favour of a statutory incomes policy, but defied the leadership by voting for unilateral British nuclear disarmament. The following month the SDP held its first ever Conference, beginning on 10 October in Perth before moving on to Bradford and London. The Alliance with the Liberals was endorsed by enthusiastic acclamation. Meanwhile, the SDP (their ranks now swollen to 21 by further defecting Labour MPs) faced the problem of the by-election in Croydon North-West. The Conservative-held suburban marginal seat had fallen vacant in July. This time, backed by David Steel, Shirley Williams eagerly indicated that she would run. The local Liberals, equally eagerly, insisted on readopting their own candidate. Since the Alliance involved Liberals and Social Democrats alternating in fighting by-elections, the Liberals got their way. On 22 October William Pitt, the Liberal candidate, swept to a remarkable victory, with 13,800 votes compared to 10,546 for the Conservatives and 8,967 for Labour. Although the seat was near to Sutton (won in a famous 1973 by-election) it was the first time ever in modern times that Liberals had won a Tory–Labour marginal.

If Croydon North-West was a remarkable victory, the Crosby by-election produced a political sensation. Crosby, a middle-class Merseyside constituency, had been a rock safe seat for the Conservatives since its creation. In May 1979 the Conservative majority had exceeded 18,000. It was a daunting majority which, when the local Liberals withdrew in her favour, Shirley Williams decided to tackle.

The result was a dramatic triumph for Shirley Williams, who captured the seat with 28,118 votes compared to the 22,829 of the

Conservative. A left-wing Labour candidate lost his deposit. Thus Shirley Williams became the first elected SDP MP, having captured one of the safest Conservative seats anywhere in the country. This trio of Liberal–SDP by-election gains was mirrored in local authority by-elections. Of 214 contests from July to December 1981 the Alliance made 100 gains. Meanwhile, on 13 October, the Alliance leaders announced their electoral pact for the next general election. Each party would field candidates in half the constituencies. The arrangements concerning the allocation of individual seats would be worked out at regional level.

With Shirley Williams returned to Westminster, only Roy Jenkins of the 'Gang of Four' was without a seat. The by-election at Glasgow Hillhead provided the opportunity. On 25 March 1982 Jenkins won a remarkable victory, taking the seat with 10,106 votes to 8,068 Conservative and 7,846 Labour.

The capture of Hillhead, however, was the prelude to a dramatic change in the political mood of Britain. On 2 March 1982 Argentina invaded the Falkland Islands. Thatcher reacted by sending a naval task force to retake the islands. The British public responded with a wave of patriotic enthusiasm. A month after the recapture of Port Stanley, the opinion polls gave the Conservatives 46 per cent, with the Alliance third with 24 per cent. In March the Alliance and Labour had shared first place with 33 per cent. The 'Falklands factor' had arrived. Its effect was to be seen in the first *national* test of public support for the Alliance which came with the May 1982 local elections. In the wake of the victorious Falklands task force, the results showed a 9 per cent swing from Labour to Conservative since the previous year. For the Alliance a close analysis revealed some very worrying factors. Overall, the Alliance polled an average 28 per cent of votes cast (almost exactly in line with the opinion polls), but the number of seats won came nowhere near to this level of support. The SDP actually lost more seats than it gained (mainly the result of defecting Labour councillors being soundly defeated). And, as *The Economist* noted,[4] the different performance of the two Alliance partners was dramatic: the Liberals won nearly five times as many seats as the SDP. The significance of individual results was also very noticeable. In Mitcham and Morden (where a parliamentary by-election was to be held on 3 June) the Alliance vote was only 20.1 per cent, a poor third. And in Croydon North-West, scene of the by-election victory, the Alliance vote was only half of the Conservatives. The lesson for a general election was clear. Without an increased level of support the Alliance would garner a huge tally of votes, but win only a handful of seats.

[4] *The Economist*, 15 May 1982.

The parliamentary by-elections after the May elections repeated this pattern. The Alliance lost Mitcham and Morden on 3 June 1982, came a deposit-losing fourth in Coatbridge and, even with Dick Taverne as candidate, came nowhere near to winning Peckham. The only further by-election victory of the Alliance came in the exceptional circumstances of the Bermondsey contest. Here, a left-wing Labour candidate, Peter Tatchell, was opposed by a rebel Labour candidate who was supported by the former Labour MP. The by-election was one of the dirtiest in recent history. The Liberal, Simon Hughes, fought an excellent campaign, capturing the docklands seat with 58 per cent of the vote.

Bermondsey was an exceptional contest. All the opinion polls showed a commanding Conservative lead. By May 1983 the pressure was on the Conservatives to take advantage of this and call an early election. On 9 May it was announced that polling would take place on 9 June. The time had come to see if the Alliance could indeed break the mould. Despite some rival Alliance candidates (notably in Liverpool Broadgreen and Hackney South and Shoreditch) the Alliance campaign went well. The Alliance manifesto (the first to be published) offered a firm commitment to a programme of economic expansion aimed at reducing unemployment by 1 million within two years. Among the other proposals were the imposition of compulsory secret ballots for union elections, reform of the social security system, an incomes policy, continued membership of the Common Market and multilateral disarmament. The Alliance also called for proportional representation and for devolution of power to Scotland, Wales and the regions. With their opinion-poll support increasing, Alliance hopes ran high as the campaign closed. The result, in terms of seats, came as a bitter disappointment.

The outcome was

	Votes	%	*MPs*
Conservative	13,010,782	42.4	397
Labour	8,456,504	27.6	209
Liberal/SDP			
Alliance	7,781,764	25.4	23
Nationalists	457,284	1.5	4
Others	962,940	3.1	17

Only 23 Alliance MPs had been returned. Although the Liberals had gained 5 seats, most were in their traditional areas of strength. The gains were Yeovil, Montgomery, Gordon, the new constituency of Roxburgh and Berwickshire and Leeds West – the only Liberal gain from Labour in the election. Although the Liberals retained Southwark and Bermondsey, the Croydon North-West by-election was lost. The Alliance seats are set out in table A.

TABLE A

Liberals (17)

Constituency	Majority	Party second
Berwick-on-Tweed	8215	Cons.
Cambridgeshire North-East	5195	Cons.
Ceredigion and Pembroke North	5639	Cons.
Colne Valley	3148	Cons.
Gordon	850	Cons.
Inverness, Nairn and Lochaber	7298	Cons.
Isle of Wight	3503	Cons.
Leeds West	2048	Lab.
Liverpool Mossley Hill	4195	Cons.
Montgomery	668	Cons.
Orkney and Shetland	4150	Cons.
Rochdale	7587	Lab.
Roxburgh and Berwickshire	3396	Cons.
Southwark and Bermondsey	5164	Lab.
Truro	10,480	Cons.
Tweeddale, Ettrick and Lauderdale	8539	Cons.
Yeovil	3406	Cons.

SDP (6)

Constituency	Majority	Party second
Caithness and Sutherland	6843	Cons.
Glasgow Hillhead	1164	Lab.
Plymouth Devonport	4936	Cons.
Ross, Cromarty and Skye	1704	Cons.
Stockton South	102	Cons.
Woolwich	2725	Lab.

For the SDP the outcome was a disaster. Only 5 of their sitting MPs escaped defeat. Two of the 'Gang of Four' (Shirley Williams and William Rodgers) were among the casualties. Not a single seat was gained from Labour, the solitary SDP gain being in the Ross, Cromarty and Skye constituency – an area of Liberal strength in any case. For the Liberals in particular the election was a frustrating one. Nearly all the seats they had hoped to win (such as Chelmsford and Richmond) eluded their grasp.

The real achievement of the Alliance in June 1983 was in terms of votes cast. The 25.4 per cent polled exceeded with ease the 19.3 per cent achieved by the Liberals alone in February 1974 and even exceeded the 23.6 per cent achieved in the Lloyd George revival of 1929. It was the best result since the 1923 'Free Trade' election, when Liberals had polled 29.7 per cent of votes cast. Moreover, the Liberal vote was evenly spread. As the polls had forecast, support was highest in the shire counties of the south and Midlands (28.6 per cent), followed by the northern shires (24.9 per cent) but weakest in the metropolitan areas (23.8 per cent). The figures for Scotland (24.5 per cent) and Wales (23.2 per cent) are less comparable because of the presence of Nationalist candidates. Very significantly only 11 Alliance candidates forfeited their deposit, compared to 119 Labour.

This geographical spread of support was mirrored in the appeal of the Alliance to different sections of the population. According to a MORI poll in the *New Statesman* (17 June 1983) Alliance support was high in class ABC1 (upper and middle) at 28 per cent, the same figure in C2 (skilled working class) but less in DE (semi and unskilled working class) at 24 per cent. According to MORI, 29 per cent of trade unionists voted for the Alliance. Among age groups of the electorate, support was 22 per cent (18–24 band), 29 per cent (25–34 band), 27 per cent (35–54 band) and 24 per cent (55 and over). Approximately the same proportion of men (25 per cent) and women (27 per cent) voted for the Alliance.

As a result of the 1983 election, the areas of best Alliance support showed some interesting differences compared to the historic Liberal heartlands (see p. 159 for 1974 comparisons).

TABLE B

Areas of Highest Alliance Votes: June 1983

Area		Alliance %	Seats	Alliance seats
1	Scottish Borders	54.2	2	2
2	Isle of Wight	51.0	1	1
3	{ Highlands and Islands	40.8	5	4
	{ Cornwall	40.8	5	1
5	Somerset	37.0	5	1
6	Northumberland	36.3	4	1
7	Devon	35.4	11	1

Table B demonstrates how Liberals (with 6 of the 7 seats at stake) have captured the two extremities of Scotland: the border area in the South and the Highlands and Islands of the far north. It also shows the relative decline of Devon – the Alliance polled a greater percentage of votes in Northumberland and Somerset than in Devon.

The tragedy for the Alliance in 1983 was not in votes cast but seats won. With 23 per cent of the vote in 1929, Liberals had won 59 seats; with 29 per cent of the votes cast in 1923, 158 seats. In 1983 the Alliance had a mere 23. As Table C shows, even on a 5 per cent swing to the Alliance, only another 27 seats would fall.

TABLE C

The Alliance Near Misses, June 1983

1   The Liberal Hopefuls (14)

Constituency	Won by	Votes Majority	% Votes Majority
Richmond and Barnes	Cons.	74	0.2
Chelmsford	Cons.	378	0.6
Edinburgh West	Cons.	489	1.1
Sheffield Hillsborough	Lab.	1546	2.8
Hazel Grove	Cons.	2022	4.1
Hereford	Cons.	2277	4.7
Fife North-East	Cons.	2185	5.9
Strathkelvin and Bearsden	Cons.	3700	7.7
Cardiff Central	Cons.	3452	8.9
Cornwall North	Cons.	5059	9.4
Cheltenham	Cons.	5518	9.6
Twickenham	Cons.	4792	9.6
Pudsey	Cons.	5314	9.9
Southport	Cons.	5039	9.9

2   The SDP Hopefuls (13)

	Won by	Votes Majority	% Votes Majority
Islington South*	Lab.	363	1.0
Erith and Crayford*	Cons.	920	2.2
Renfrew West and Inverclyde*	Cons.	1322	3.2
Stevenage	Cons.	1755	3.3
Clwyd South-West*	Cons.	1551	3.6
Durham City	Lab.	1973	4.0
Crosby*	Cons.	3401	5.3
Norfolk North-West*	Cons.	3147	5.9
Blyth Valley	Lab.	3243	7.7
Edinburgh South	Cons.	3655	8.2
East Kilbride	Lab.	4336	9.2
Edinburgh and Pentlands	Cons.	4309	9.9
Southampton Itchen*	Cons.	5290	10.0

* Seat formerly held by SDP MP.

Significantly, of the 14 seats which would fall to a Liberal swing of 5 per cent, all but 1 (Sheffield Hillsborough) are Conservative-held suburban or rural seats. Of the 13 SDP hopefuls, only 4 are Labour-held. The Alliance is still very far from threatening anything but an isolated handful of Labour-held industrial constituencies. Moreover, of the 13 SDP best results, 7 were in seats defended by sitting SDP Members. These seats must look less winnable than the statistics suggest. Moreover, the Alliance knows that several of its own seats are held on a fragile majority. Three of the 23 Alliance seats have majorities under

1,000,[5] 12 would fall on a 5 per cent swing against the Alliance. The frustrations of the electoral system for the Alliance were repeated in the first by-election of the new Parliament. In July 1983 in the Penrith and the Border contest (made necessary by Whitelaw's elevation to the Lords), the Liberals came within 552 votes of victory in a seat which had returned Whitelaw with a 15,421 majority a month earlier.

In the wake of the 1983 election the future for the Alliance is uncertain. The autumn party assemblies demonstrated not only the control that both David Owen (who was elected unopposed when Jenkins stepped down in June 1983) and David Steel have over their parties, but also that the Alliance would continue much as before. Although with stronger public support than previous Liberal revivals, the Alliance faces the same problems as the Liberals have encountered in previous elections. Their fortunes will vary with the appeal of the Conservative and Labour Parties (the Kinnock–Hattersley leadership of Labour could herald a revival in that party). Their progress will always be held back by the electoral system. The party still lacks a secure geographical base. There are also problems of the party's philosophy and place in the political spectrum. The party faces other handicaps. It has no large source of income; it lacks the numbers of agents needed to turn winnable seats into strongholds. The party also lacks a secure outlet in the media (there are many Liberal journalists, but no Liberal mass-circulation daily papers). In the long term these problems may be overcome. In the short term, as the Liberals seek to weaken further a humbled Labour Party, the immediate beneficiaries can only be the Conservatives. The similar period of realignment from 1918 to 1929 had exactly this consequence. But, despite these problems, one fact is certain. The Liberals have come back after a generation in the political wilderness. But they have yet to enter the promised land.

[5] Stockton South (102): Montgomery (668): Gordon (850).

Appendix I

Major holders of Party Office, 1900–84[1]

Party Leaders[2]

February   1899 Sir Henry Campbell-Bannerman
April   1908 Herbert Henry Asquith[3]
October   1926 David Lloyd George
November   1931 Sir Herbert Samuel
November   1935 Sir Archibald Sinclair
August   1945 Clement Davies
November   1956 Joseph Grimond
January   1967 Jeremy Thorpe[4]
July   1976 David Steel

Leaders in the House of Lords

1900	Earl of Kimberley	1931	M. of Reading
1902	Earl Spencer	1936	M. of Crewe
1905	M. of Ripon	1944	Vt. Samuel
1908	E. (M) of Crewe	1955	Ld. Rea
1923	Vt. Grey	1967	Ld. Byers
1924	Earl Beauchamp		

[1] Source: D. E. Butler and A. Sloman, *British Political Facts, 1900–1979* (1980).
[2] All were Liberal 'Leaders in the House of Commons'. Sir H. Campbell-Bannerman from 1899 to 1908 and H. Asquith from 1908 to 1926 were the only 'Leaders of the Liberal Party'.
[3] After Asquith's defeat at the 1918 General Election, Sir Donald Maclean was elected leader of the Parliamentary Party but resigned this post on Asquith's return to the Commons in March 1920.
[4] Jeremy Thorpe resigned on 10 May 1976. Jo Grimond became caretaker Leader until July.

Chief Whips in the House of Commons

1900	H. Gladstone	1931	G. Owen
1905	G. Whiteley	1932	W. Rea
1908	J. Pease	1935	Sir P. Harris
1910	Master of Elibank	1945	T. Horabin
1912	P. Illingworth	1946	F. Byers
1915	J. Gulland	1950	J. Grimond
1919	G. Thorne	1956	D. Wade
1923	V. Phillipps	1963	E. Lubbock
1924	Sir G. Collins	1970	D. Steel
1926	Sir R. Hutchinson	1976	C. Smith
1930	Sir A. Sinclair	1977	A. Beith

Chief Whips in the House of Lords

1896	Ld. Ribblesdale	1949	M. of Willingdon
1907	Ld. Denman	1950	Ld. Moynihan
1911–22	Ld. Colebrooke	1950	Ld. Rea
1919	Ld. Denman	1955	Ld. Amulree
1924	Ld. Stanmore	1977	Ld. Wigoder
1944	Vt. Mersey		

NATIONAL LIBERAL FEDERATION, 1900–36

Chairman of Committee

1900	(Sir) E. Evans
1918	Sir G. Lunn
1920	A. Brampton
1931	R. Muir
1933	R. Walker
1934	M. Gray

Secretary

1893	(Sir) R. Hudson
1922	F. Barter
1925	H Oldman
1930	H. Oldman and W. Davies
1931	W. Davies

Treasurer

1901	W. Hart
1903	J. Massie
1907	R. Bird
1910	F. Wright
1923	Sir R. Hudson
1927	Sir F. Layland-Barratt
1934	P. Heffer

LIBERAL PARTY ORGANISATION, 1936–77

Head

1936	W. Davies (Secretary)		
1952	H. Harris (General Director)		
1960	D. Robinson (Directing Secretary)		
1961	P. Kemmis (Secretary)		
1965	T. Beaumont (Head of Liberal Party Organisation)		
1966	P. Chitnis (Head of Liberal Party Organisation)		
1970	E. Wheeler (Head of Liberal Party Organisation)		
1977	H. Jones (Secretary-General)		

Chairman of Executive Committee

1936	M. Gray
1946	P. Fothergill
1949	Ld. Moynihan
1950	F. Byers
1952	P. Fothergill
1954	G. Acland
1957	D. Abel
1959	L. Behrens
1961	D. Banks
1963	B. Wigoder
1965	G. Evans
1968–69[1]	J. Baker

Treasurer

1937–50	Sir A. McFadyean
1937–41	P. Heffer
1941–47	Ld. Rea
1942–47	H. Worsley
1947–53	Ld. Moynihan
1950–58	W. Grey
1950–52	Vt. Wimborne
1953–62	Sir A. Suenson-Taylor (Ld. Grantchester)

1955–59	P. Fothergill
1959–62	Miss H. Harvey
1959–60	P. Lort-Phillips
1961–62	J. McLaughlin
1962–65	R. Gardner-Thorpe
1962–66	Sir A. Murray
1963–65	T. Beaumont
1966–67	J. Thorpe
1967–68	L. Smith
1968–69	J. Pardoe
1969–72	Sir F. Medlicott
1972–77	P. Watkins
1977–	Ld. Lloyd of Kilgerran
1977	M. Palmer

Chairman

1966	Ld. Byers
1967	T. Beaumont (Ld.)
1968	Ld. Henley
1969	D. Banks
1970	R. Wainwright
1972	C. Carr
1973	K. Vaus
1976	G. Tordoff

[1] In 1969 this post was combined with the Chairmanship of the party.

Appendix II[1]

THE LIBERAL VOTE: 1918–84[2]

Election	Candidates	Unopposed returns	MPs elected	Forfeited deposits	Total votes	% of UK total
1918	421	27	163	44	2,785,374	25·6
1922	477	10	115	31	4,080,915	28·3
1923	457	11	158	8	4,301,481	29·7
1924	340	6	40	30	2,931,380	17·8
1929	513	0	59	25	5,308,738	23·6
1931	118	5	37	6	1,506,630	7·2
1935	161	0	21	40	1,443,093	6·8
1945	306	0	12	76	2,252,430	9·0
1950	475	0	9	319	2,621,487	9·1
1951	109	0	6	66	743,512	2·6
1955	110	0	6	60	722,402	2·7
1959	216	0	6	55	1,640,761	5·9
1964	365	0	9	52	3,101,103	11·2
1966	311	0	12	104	2,327,533	8·5
1970	332	0	6	184	2,117,638	7·5
1974 (Feb)	517	0	14	23	6,063,470	19·3
1974 (Oct)	619	0	13	125	5,346,800	18·3
1979	577	0	11	284	4,313,804	13·8
1983[3]	633	0	23	11	7,781,764	25·4

THE NATIONAL LIBERAL VOTE 1931–66

Election	Candidates	Unopposed returns	MPs elected	Forfeited deposits	Total votes	% of UK total
1931	41	7	35	0	809,302	3·7
1935	44	3	33	0	866,354	3·7
1945	49	0	11	0	737,732	2·8
1950	55	0	16	0	985,343	3·4
1951	55	0	19	0	1,058,138	3·7
1955	45	0	21	0	842,113	3·1
1959	39	0	20	0	765,794	2·7
1964	19	0	6	0	326,130	1·2
1966	9	0.	3	0	149,779	0·5

[1] Source: F. W. S. Craig, *British Parliamentary Election Statistics* (Glasgow, 1968).
[2] Including both Liberal and National Liberal candidates in 1922, and Independent Liberals in 1931.
[3] Includes the Social Democrat wing of the Alliance.

Bibliographical Note

There is no authoritative comprehensive history of the Liberal Party from the Victorian period to the present day. There are, however, a mass of monographs and detailed studies of particular periods and particular themes. It is hoped this list will point the student to some of the more important articles and studies. In addition to the books mentioned below, two works of reference are of particular relevance. These are C. Cook and B. Keith, *British Historical Facts, 1830–1900* and D. Butler and A. Sloman, *British Political Facts, 1900–1979*. Both books contain a mass of biographical, electoral and statistical material.

For the Victorian Liberal Party, the basic and essential starting-point is J. Vincent, *The Formation of the Liberal Party, 1857–1868* (London, 1966). For the general background of Liberalism, there is R. B. McCallum, *The Liberal Party from Earl Grey to Asquith* (London, 1963) and also J. L. Hammond and M. R. D. Foot, *Gladstone and Liberalism* (London, 1959). The most recent study of Gladstone (by E. J. Feuchtwanger) is an excellent introduction for students.

The 1867 Reform Act is covered by M. Cowling, *Disraeli, Gladstone and Revolution* (Cambridge, 1967). A useful specialist article on the 1868 election is A. F. Thompson, 'Gladstone, the Whips and the General Election of 1868', *English Historical Review*, LXIII (1948). There is much useful material in D. Southgate, *The Passing of the Whigs, 1832–1886* (London, 1962).

For the period after 1874, there is much relevant material in D. A. Hamer, *Liberal Politics in the Age of Gladstone and Rosebery* (Oxford, 1975). The origins and development of the National Liberal Federation are covered by B. McGill, 'Francis Schnadhorst and Liberal Party Organisation', *Journal of Modern History*, Mar. 1962. The old account by R. Spence Watson of the National Liberal Federation is still of value, as is M. Ostrogorski, *Democracy and the Organisation of Political Parties* (London, 1902).

A detailed account of the Midlothian campaign has been written by R. Kelly, 'Midlothian: A Study in Politics and Ideals', *Victorian Studies*, IV, No. 2 (1960). The crucial period of the Home Rule crisis is superbly covered by A. B. Cooke and J. Vincent, *The Governing Passion: Cabinet Government and Party Politics in Britain, 1885–1886* (Brighton, 1974). The problem of Liberal Reunion is covered by M. Hurst, *Joseph Chamberlain and Liberal Reunion: The Round Table Conference of 1887* (Newton Abbot, 1967). For Joseph Chamberlain's career, see P. Fraser, *Joseph Chamberlain; Radicalism and Empire* (London, 1966). Liberal strength and weakness in General Elections can be clearly followed in M. Kinnear, *The British Voter: An Atlas and Survey since 1885* (London, 1968). This book is of value for every election from 1885 to 1966.

Among the detailed specialist studies of Gladstone during this later period, there are R. T. Shannon, *Gladstone and the Bulgarian Agitation, 1876* (London, 1963), M. Barker, *Gladstone and Radicalism: The Reconstruction of Liberal Policy in*

Britain (Brighton, 1975) and D. M. Schreuder, *Gladstone and Kruger: Liberal Government and Colonial Home Rule* (London, 1969). On the Irish question, there is J. L. Hammond's 1938 classic *Gladstone and the Irish Nation*, new ed.; (1964). A useful specialist article is F. S. L. Lyons, 'The Irish Question and Liberal Politics, 1886–1894', in *Historical Journal*, XII (1969).

On the Liberal Unionist revolt, see B. Goodman, 'Liberal Unionism: The Revolt of the Whigs', *Victorian Studies*, Dec. 1959; and P. Fraser, 'The Liberal Unionist Alliance: Chamberlain, Hartington and the Conservatives, 1886–1904', *English Historical Review*, LXXVII (1962). Rosebery's career is covered by R. R. James, *Rosebery* (London, 1963). There is much useful material in a recent important study of this period, H. C. G. Matthew, *The Liberal Imperialists* (Oxford, 1973). Morley is well covered by D. A. Hamer, *John Morley: Liberal Intellectual in Politics* (Oxford, 1968). On Morley, see also S. Koss, 'Morley in the Middle', *English Historical Review*, LXXXII (1967). Much the best account of the Newcastle Programme, and the internecine warfare of the party in the 1890s, is to be found in P. Stansky, *Ambitions and Strategies: The Struggle for the Leadership of the Liberal Party in the 1890s* (Oxford, 1964). Two useful regional studies are Kenneth O. Morgan, *Wales in British Politics, 1868–1922* (Oxford, 1963) and J. G. Kellas, 'The Liberal Party in Scotland, 1876–1895', *Scottish Historical Review*, XLIV (1965).

For the whole period after 1895, there is much of use in R. Douglas, *The History of the Liberal Party, 1895–1970*, (London, 1971) – a book sympathetic to the party and even more sympathetic to Free Trade. The most recent life of Campbell-Bannerman is the solid if unexciting account by J. Wilson, *Campbell-Bannerman* (London, 1972). The Liberal Party's involvement in South Africa is well covered by J. Butler. *The Liberal Party and the Jameson Raid* (Oxford, 1968). There is also H. W. McCready, 'Sir Alfred Milner, the Liberal Party and the Boer War', *Canadian Journal of History*, II (1967). See also P. D. Jacobson, 'Rosebery and Liberal Imperialism, 1899–1903', *Journal of British Studies*, XIII (1973).

The revival of Liberal fortunes after 1900 is well detailed in M. Craton, and H. W. McCready, *The Great Liberal Revival, 1903–6* (Hansard Society pamphlet, 1966). The agitation over the 1902 Education Act is very ably discussed by S. E. Koss, *Nonconformity in Modern British Politics* (London, 1975). The Liberal Party's relationship with the Labour Representation Committee is well covered in two articles: F. Bealey, 'The Electoral Arrangement between the L.R.C. and the Liberal Party', *Journal of Modern History*, Dec. 1956 and the same author's 'Negotiations between the Liberals and the L.R.C. before the 1906 election', *Bulletin of the Institute of Historical Research*, XXIX (1956). The 1906 election is ably discussed in A. K. Russell, *Liberal Landslide: The General Election of 1906* (Newton Abbot, 1973).

The period from 1906 to 1914 is extremely well covered by a variety of books and articles. There is much material in P. Rowland, *The Last Liberal Governments: The Promised Land, 1905–10* (London, 1968). The best short study of Campbell-Bannerman's premiership is J. Harris and C. Hazlehurst, 'Campbell-Bannerman as Prime Minister', *History*, XV (1970). The most recent study of Asquith, a model of a concise yet authoritative biography, is S. E.

Koss, *Asquith* (London, 1976). There is also R. Jenkins, *Asquith* (London, 1964) and C. Hazlehurst, 'Asquith as Prime Minister', *English Historical Review*, LXXXV (July 1970). Two specialist articles are J. E. Tyler, 'Campbell-Bannerman and the Liberal Imperialists (1906–8)', *History*, XXIII (1939) and C. C. Weston, 'The Liberal Leadership and the Lords' Veto, 1907–1910', *Historical Journal,* XI, No. 3 (1968).

The definitive biography of Lloyd George is still to be published. There is much of value in P. Rowland, *Lloyd George* (London, 1976), but Kenneth O. Morgan, *Lloyd George* (London, 1974) is a masterly summary. The same author's *Lloyd George Family Letters, 1885–1936* (Cardiff, 1973) is an illuminating source. A highly readable, if now outdated account with some fascinating anecdote, is Frank Owen, *Tempestuous Journey: Lloyd George, his life and times* (London, 1954). Equally entertaining on the struggle with the House of Lords is R. Jenkins, *Mr. Balfour's Poodle* (London, 1954).

Liberal social reform is covered by H. V. Emy, *Liberals, Radicals and Social Politics, 1892–1914* (Cambridge, 1973) and by Bentley B. Gilbert, *The Evolution of National Insurance in Great Britain* (London, 1966). On foreign policy, much useful material can be found in A. J. A. Morris, *Radicalism against War, 1906–1914* (London, 1972). See also the same author's volume of essays, *Edwardian Radicalism, 1900–1914* (London, 1974).

The definitive account of the 1910 elections and the constitutional crisis is in N. Blewett, *The Peers, The Parties and the People: The General Elections of 1910* (London, 1972). For the period from 1910 to 1914 there is also P. Rowland, *The Last Liberal Governments: Unfinished Business, 1911–1914* (London, 1971). The suffragette question is covered by D. Morgan, *Suffragists and Liberals* (London, 1975).

The question of the rise of Labour and the downfall of the Liberal Party has generated one of the major historical debates of our time. G. Dangerfield, *The Strange Death of Liberal England* (London, 1935) can be safely left alone. It is a highly impressionistic account and at times highly misleading. T. Wilson, *The Downfall of the Liberal Party, 1914–1935* (London, 1966) emphasises the importance of the First World War. P. Clarke, *Lancashire and the New Liberalism* (Cambridge, 1971) is an important book whose conclusions need to be tested for other parts of the country. A new approach which hardly fits existing arguments is C. Cook, 'Labour and the Downfall of the Liberal Party', in A. Sked and C. Cook, *Crisis and Controversy: Essays in honour of A. J. P. Taylor* (London, 1976); H. Pelling, *Popular Politics and Society in late Victorian England* (London, 1968) contains useful material. For the mining areas, see R. Gregory, *The Miners in British Politics* (Oxford, 1968). For an older article, see L. Noonan, 'The Decline of the Liberal Party in British Politics', *Journal of Politics*, Feb. 1954.

The period of the First World War is again very well covered. A. J. P. Taylor, *Politics in Wartime* (London, 1964) is stimulating. The studies already cited by Trevor Wilson and Stephen Koss are all useful. C. Hazlehurst, *Politicians at War* (London, 1971) seems as much concerned with rivalries between historians. Specialist articles of importance are B. McGill, 'Asquith's Predicament, 1914–1918', *Journal of Modern History*, XXXIX, No. 3 (1967); S. Koss, 'The

Destruction of Britain's Last Liberal Government', *Journal of Modern History*, XL, No. 2 (1968), C. Hazlehurst, 'The Conspiracy Myth' in M. Gilbert, *Lloyd George* (Englewood Cliffs, N.J., 1968) and E. David, 'The Liberal Party Divided', *English Historical Review* (1972). For the 'Coupon' arrangements, see T. Wilson 'The Coupon and the British General Election of 1918', *Journal of Modern History* (1964).

For the inter-war period, the basic starting point is T. Wilson, *The Downfall of the Liberal Party* (London, 1966). This can be supplemented by C. Cook, *The Age of Alignment: Electoral Politics in Britain, 1922–1929* (London, 1975), which contains much material on party organisation and municipal politics as well as on electoral strength. For a personal view of high politics, see M. Cowling, *The Impact of Labour, 1920–1924* (Cambridge, 1971). The 1922 election is covered in M. Kinnear, *The Fall of Lloyd George: the Political Crisis of 1922* (London, 1973). A succinct discussion of the Coalition Liberal Party can be found in K. Morgan, 'Lloyd George's Stage Army' in A. J. P. Taylor (ed.), *Lloyd George: Twelve Essays* (London, 1971). On the philosophy of the party, see J. Campbell, 'The Renewal of Liberalism: Liberalism without Liberals', in G. Peele and C. Cook (eds) *The Politics of Reappraisal, 1918–1939* (London, 1975) and M. Bentley, 'The Liberal Response to Socialism, 1918–29', in K. D. Brown, (ed.), *Essays in Anti-Labour History* (London, 1974). A very useful source is T. Wilson, (ed.), *The Political Diaries of C. P. Scott* (London, 1970). Two specialist studies are R. Dowse, 'The Entry of the Liberals into the Labour Party, 1910–1930', *Yorkshire Bulletin of Economic and Social Research*, XIII, No. 2 (1961) and K. Morgan, 'The Twilight of Welsh Liberalism: Lloyd George and the Wee Frees, 1918–35', *Bulletin of the Board of Celtic Studies*, XXII, Pt 4 (May 1968). The 1929–31 period lacks a detailed Liberal study. Trevor Wilson's book remains useful, but see also R. Skidelsky, *Politicians and the Slump: The Labour Government of 1929–31* (London, 1967). There is no major study of the Liberal Party in the 1930s. Some material can be found in C. Cook, 'Liberals, Labour and Local Elections', in G. Peele, and C. Cook, *The Politics of Reappraisal 1918–1939* (London, 1975). On the 1935 election, see C. T. Stannage, *Baldwin Thwarts the Opposition* (London, 1980).

For the Second World War, see R. Douglas, *History of the Liberal Party, 1895–1970* and P. Addison, 'By-Elections of the Second World War' in C. Cook, and J. Ramsden (eds), *By-Elections in British Politics* (London, 1973). This book is of use for the post-war period also.

The post-1945 is very short of serious studies of the Liberal Party. There is useful material in J. Rasmussen, *Retrenchment and Revival: A Study of the Contemporary Liberal Party* (London, 1964). Highly readable is A. Watkins, *The Liberal Dilemma* (London, 1966). For the period from 1959 to 1970, see the outline by C. Cook, 'The Liberal and Nationalist Revival' in D. McKie and C. Cook, *The Decade of Disillusion: British Politics in the Sixties* (London, 1972). All the Nuffield election studies (which David Butler has participated in) have relevant material; and there is also material in D. E. Butler and D. Stokes, *Political Change in Britain* (London, 1969). On contemporary developments, see V. Bogdanor (ed.), *Liberal Party Politics* (Oxford, 1983).

Index